TABLE OF CONTENTS

PREACHING IN THE PATRISTIC AGE

Studies in Honor of
Walter J. Burghardt, S.J.

DAVID G. HUNTER
Editor

PAULIST PRESS
New York/Mahwah

BV
4207
.P65
1989

Library of Congress Cataloging-in-Publication Data

Preaching in the patristic age: studies in honor of Walter J. Burghardt, S.J./David G. Hunter editor.
   p.   cm.
   Includes bibliographies.
   ISBN 0-8091-3079-3: $14.95 (est.)
   1. Preaching—History—Early church, ca. 30–600. I. Burghardt, Walter J. II. Hunter, David G.
BV4207.P65   1989
251'.009'015—dc20   8-9210
                                      CIP

Published by Paulist Press
997 Macarthur Boulevard
Mahwah, New Jersey 07430

Printed and bound in the
United States of America

ABBREVIATIONS

AB	Anchor Bible
ACW	Ancient Christian Writers
AnBib	Analecta Biblica
ANF	The Ante-Nicene Fathers
BBB	Bonner biblische Beiträge
BDF	*A Greek Grammar of the New Testament,* ed. F. Blass, A. Debrunner, and R.W. Funk
BJRL	Bulletin of the John Rylands Library
CCSL	Corpus Christianorum, Series Latina
CSEL	Corpus Scriptorum Ecclesiasticorum Latinorum
CSCO	Corpus Scriptorum Christianorum Orientalium
EvT	Evangelische Theologie
EWNT	*Exegetisches Wörterbuch zum Neuen Testament,* ed. H. Balz and G. Schneider
FC	Fathers of the Church
GCS	Griechische christliche Schriftsteller
Greg	Gregorianum
HTR	Harvard Theological Review
JBL	Journal of Biblical Literature
JRS	Journal of Roman Studies
JTS	Journal of Theological Studies
LCL	Loeb Classical Library
LD	Lectio Divina
LQF	Liturgiewissenschaftlichen Quellen und Forschungen
MGH	Monumenta Germaniae Historica
NCE	New Catholic Encyclopedia
NPNF	Nicene and Post-Nicene Fathers
NRT	Nouvelle Revue Théologique
OECT	Oxford Early Christian Texts
OLP	Orientalia Lovaniensia Periodica

PL	Patrologia Latina, ed. J.P. Migne
PG	Patrologia Graeca, ed. J.P. Migne
PS	Patristic Studies
RB	Revue bénédictine
RSR	Recherches de science religieuse
Rech. aug.	Recherches augustiniennes
SBS	Stuttgarter Bibelstudien
SC	Sources chrétiennes
SNTSMS	Society for New Testament Studies Monograph Series
SP	Studia Patristica
ST	Studia Theologica
TDNT	*Theological Dictionary of the New Testament*, ed. G. Kittel and G. Friedrich
TS	Theological Studies
TU	Texte und Untersuchungen zur Geschichte der altchristlichen Literatur
TZ	Theologische Zeitschrift
WMANT	Wissenschaftliche Monographien zum Alten und Neuen Testament
ZNW	Zeitschrift für die neutestamentliche Wissenschaft

EDITOR'S PREFACE
by David G. Hunter

It is a great pleasure to present this volume of essays to the Reverend Walter J. Burghardt, S.J. on the occasion of his seventy-fifth birthday. Fr. Burghardt's many contributions to American theological scholarship, particularly as editor of *Theological Studies,* are well known. His numerous published sermons have gained for him an even wider audience among non-theologians. The biographical appreciation by Gerald Fogarty, S.J. will discuss Fr. Burghardt's personal and professional life in greater detail. Here I wish only to explain the shape and rationale of the other essays in this collection.

The theme of the volume—preaching and patristics—is meant to reflect two of the central concerns of Burghardt's career. Each of the authors has been associated with Walter Burghardt for some years. I am probably the most recent acquaintance in the group, having followed his *Introduction to Patristic Theology* as an undergraduate at the Catholic University of America in the mid-1970s. The list of contributors includes a large contingent of Jesuits, something to be expected in a tome honoring a man who has spent over half a century in the Society of Jesus. Other religious and lay persons are represented, however, and the variety of topics and viewpoints present here attest to Burghardt's diverse contacts and influence.

There are inevitable gaps in a book such as this, but an attempt was made to cover certain essential areas. For example, the essays begin with a discussion of "Preaching in the Apostolic and Subapostolic Age" by the distinguished New Testament scholar Joseph A. Fitzmyer, S.J. Certain classic preachers in the Christian tradition are given individual treatment: Origen of Alexandria, Gregory Na-

1

zianzus, John Chrysostom, Augustine, and Pope Leo the Great are among these. Other papers address more general themes. For example, "Women and Preaching in the Patristic Age" by Agnes Cunningham and "Christian Reaction to the Barbarian Invasions and the Sermons of Quodvultdeus" by Robert B. Eno discuss how early Christian writers addressed issues of pressing concern in their day. An effort also was made to obtain a balance between eastern (Greek) and western (Latin) writers.

Two studies deal with themes indirectly related to preaching. Charles Kannengiesser discusses the yearly Easter letters of St. Athanasius. These letters, as he notes, have a distinctly homiletic tone and reflect the Alexandrian bishop's effort to communicate his incarnational spirituality and exegesis to all the Christians under his jurisdiction. Joseph Kelly's delightful piece, "The Bible in Early Medieval Ireland," offers an illuminating look at the role of biblical exegesis and commentary in early Irish life and culture.

In short, all of the studies here attest to the many diverse modes of communicating God's word utilized in Christian antiquity. This volume, therefore, is offered to Walter J. Burghardt, a scholar whose constant devotion to the word has enabled so many to be better hearers.

1

WALTER J. BURGHARDT, S.J.
AN APPRECIATION
by Gerald P. Fogarty, S.J.

It was over thirty years ago. I had just finished my freshman year at Loyola High School and had come to Woodstock College outside of Baltimore to visit one of my teachers who had just begun his theological studies. At the front door, I was directed to go out to the golf course. On my way, I came upon a man vigorously pacing on one of the greens, saying his breviary, wearing khaki trousers and no shirt— I learned later that he never lost an opportunity to absorb the sun's rays. He greeted me, offered to help me find my friend, and, with twinkling eyes familiar to so many, engaged me in conversation. It was my first meeting with Walter J. Burghardt, priest, theologian, writer, but, most of all, friend. During the next few years, I saw him on television and heard him on radio. I had learned that my shirtless acquaintance was a prominent theologian and writer, so I concluded, mistakenly, that such a busy man hardly had time to talk any further with a high school or college student. We met again as I was leaving Loyola College to enter St. Mary's Seminary in Baltimore. Again, it was at Woodstock and, again, he was saying his breviary, only this time he did have a shirt on—he was in front of the college building. I told him my plans to study for the archdiocese of Baltimore. He looked me in the eye and said, "We will see." Six months later I wrote to him to tell him he was right—I was entering the Society of Jesus that summer, to a great extent because of his intellectual influence on me. Over the years we were to grow yet closer as I was first his student, then his colleague at Woodstock, and, finally, a privileged friend.

As a priest, Walter Burghardt not only has witnessed the changes that took place in theology and the church as a result of Vatican II but has also played a leading role in making them, for his years as a priest almost evenly straddle the exciting years of the council. Patristic theologian and editor, teacher and, above all, preacher, he is equally at home in a lecture hall or television studio, a research library or pulpit—and of course anyplace where there is sun. In his career he has made his own the task of publishing theology by specialists and of publicizing theology for non-specialists. The space of this essay is inadequate fully to disclose who he is and to evaluate his contribution to American Catholic theology. But it is only appropriate to assess Walter J. Burghardt under three points: (1) the man; (2) the theologian; (3) the teacher.

1. THE MAN

Walter Burghardt grew up with his older brother, Edward, on East 55th Street in New York. His immigrant parents, like so many others, inculcated in the boys appreciation for what they themselves did not have—education. The two boys were sent to Xavier High School, and if the Jesuit teachers said the boys were to have three hours of homework each night, then Mr. Burghardt would make sure that the kitchen table was reserved for the boys to study three hours every night. Walter's father was a building superintendent familiar with the tools of a mechanic, but Walter was to be a builder of ideas familiar with the tools of the mind. At the age of six Walter and his father took the train from Grand Central Station to Poughkeepsie, New York. As Walter recalled it, they then "flagged our first cab ever" and soon they were deposited at the front door of the novitiate of St. Andrew-on-Hudson. A depersonalizing "Welcome, Brother Burghardt" and a curt announcement to his father that he had fifteen minutes with his son severed Walter from the usual relationship with his family and introduced him to the new family of the Society of Jesus.[1]

St. Andrew-on-Hudson was one of two novitiates training Jesuits for the Maryland–New York Province in 1931. It had been in place, a stern brick building on a bluff overlooking the Hudson River near the Roosevelt estate of Hyde Park, since 1903. A new novitiate at Wernersville, Pennsylvania had been opened for less than a year; it had amenities unlike its older counterpart, like walls—but not up to the ceiling—surrounding the bed and desk assigned to each novice. St. Andrew's preserved a more rigorous arrangement of dormitories with beds lined up in an open hall and ascetories with rows of desks

—privacy was neither a value nor a luxury frequently found. Despite differences in living conditions, each novitiate maintained a regimen and daily order that transcended time and place and gave young Jesuits the sense of being part of a timeless tradition, which, in turn, was part of a timeless church. Each followed the daily order prescribed in 1805 as reconstructed from memory from the old English province novitiate in Watten, Flanders before the suppression of the Society of Jesus by Pope Clement XIV in 1773. The only concession to change was the shift of the time for rising from 5:00 A.M. to 5:30—the invention of electric lights did not seem to be incompatible with Ignatius Loyola's firm conviction that God could be found in all things.

Ignatian spirituality and exposure to the classics in the "juniorate," the first academic experience for a young Jesuit, shaped Walter's career and his interest. Let him tell it in his own words:

> Two books shaped my future before I was twenty. Each had to do with an individual named Ignatius. At Poughkeepsie, a novice master named Leo Weber put into my heart the *Spiritual Exercises* of Ignatius Loyola, and a classics professor named Philip Walsh put into my hands the seven *Letters* of Ignatius of Antioch. The *Exercises* mapped out my spiritual pilgrimage, the *Letters* my intellectual journey. The sixteenth-century founder of the Jesuits forced me to face myself and the world in the context of Christ, compelled an "election," a basic decision, suggested a spirituality whereby I could know our Lord more clearly, love him more dearly, follow him more nearly. The second-century martyr, with his prayer "God's wheat I am, and by the teeth of wild beasts I am to be ground, that I may prove Christ's pure bread," put me in touch with early Christianity, sparked a love for the Fathers of the Church that has been my life over four decades.[2]

The spirituality of a soldier turned mystic, the writings of a bishop to be martyred—these were not merely utterances of dead heroes of the past but expressions of representatives of a living tradition. They helped shape the young Jesuit scholastic who in later years could feel comfortable in describing the Ignatian election of his youth in terms of the popular song from "Godspell," derived from the prayer of St. Richard of Chicester, the thirteenth century English bishop. His intellectual journey and his spiritual pilgrimage would lead him to find in every age, including the contemporary, the living tradition of the church.

In 1934 Walter exchanged the stern brick of St. Andrew-on-

Hudson for the somber granite of Woodstock College in rural Maryland. It would become his home for thirty-one years. But it was not
yet the locus for the winds of theological change that would blow
through its corridors on the eve of Vatican II. If anything, its intellectual orientation reflected its building material and the nearest village
of Granite, Maryland. John Courtney Murray and Gustave Weigel,
later two of Walter's closest associates and friends, had been studying
theology in the wing opposite where the "philosophers" attempted to
master the intricacies of Plato and Aristotle always passed through
the prism of medieval scholasticism. After three years Walter traveled
north to Manhattan to Regis High School, the only Jesuit high school
that could provide free tuition to all its students. Like most other
Jesuit "regents" of that and later eras, Walter taught Latin and
Greek, the core curriculum of Jesuit secondary education until the
1960s. Reflection on that experience led Walter to produce his first
article, the title of which gave a clue to his later flair for the English
language—"Homer on Park Avenue."[3] Although most Jesuit regents
taught for at least three years, after only one Walter was back at
Woodstock for theological studies and the final preparation for ordination to the priesthood.

But anticipation of ordination was bittersweet. Both Walter's
father and brother Eddie fell sick with cancer. Each in separate hospi-
tals received a daily visit from Walter's mother, who managed on her
own to take over her husband's task of superintending a five-story
apartment house, even to the point of herself shoveling twenty-five
tons of coal during the winter of 1939–1940. Walter's father died
first, at the age of fifty-three. Eddie was too sick to be told. As Walter
himself recalled it: "when we returned from my father's funeral, I
(whose life was, on principle, for others) went to bed; my mother
changed into bright-colored clothes, subwayed to the hospital, and
told my brother how wonderful everything was with my father."[4]
Within three weeks, Eddie too was dead at the age of twenty-seven.

The deaths of father and brother, both young men by twentieth
century standards, seared Walter's memory. Years later he would
resonate with a prominent physician that "death is an insult; the
stupidest, ugliest thing that can happen to a human being." He would
reject with Pauline disdain those theologians who claim that personal
survival is insignificant and state, "If heaven is not for real, I shall be
madder than hell."[5] Death looms large for Walter. And so does fear
—fear "that maybe, like my mother, I will lose my memory, my
arteries will harden, senility will set in."[6] But so does hope—hope
"that the Spirit who never ceases to surprise me—with sorrow and

joy, through events and people—will surprise me singularly at the moment I die."[7] Fear of death tempered by hope of life, a normal human reaction to an abnormal painful experience—this would be the powerful emotion dominating Walter during that year before his ordination. It was a year of sorrow and promise—sorrow because he lost two people so close to him; promise because he had just published the first in what would become a series of scholarly articles on patristics. And then the year ended with that decisive event as, on June 22, 1941, Archbishop Michael J. Curley of Baltimore imposed his hands on Walter ordaining him a priest in the Catholic Church. He was only twenty-six, young for a Jesuit to be ordained, or, as he likes to put it, "one of the youngest Jesuit priests in captivity."

The course of training for a Jesuit included in those days a fourth year of theology after ordination and then a year of tertianship, a year of novitiate-like prayer, study of the *Spiritual Exercises,* preaching novenas and parish missions, and hospital ministry. After that, Walter proceeded to further studies in the field to which Father Walsh had first introduced him back in the juniorate—the fathers of the church. The Second World War precluded the possibility of any study in Europe, but it also brought to the United States several outstanding European scholars. To the Catholic University of America had come Father Johannes Quasten, one of Germany's foremost patristic scholars. Under him Walter began studying in 1943 for a doctorate in theology with a specialization in patristics. His doctoral dissertation on *The Image of God in Man according to Cyril of Alexandria*[8] set the tone for much of his subsequent work in theology, both in the formal setting of the classroom and in the less erudite ambiance of the pulpit and radio studio. For Walter, theology is a "searching for God. Not for a God who dwells only in light inaccessible, outside time and space. Rather for a God who has a history. . . . For a God whose pulsing image is every man. For a God who *became* man."[9] To be made in the image of God meant that human nature is not depraved but deprived, is good not evil, must be taken seriously because it is the special focus not only of God's creation but also of God's redemption. Walter had embarked on a career of making theology not only a quest for God but also a search for the meaning of man.

2. THE THEOLOGIAN

In March 1940 *Theological Studies* published its first issue. The first article was by a second year theological student at Woodstock

College. The title was "Did Saint Ignatius of Antioch Know the Fourth Gospel?" Walter J. Burghardt entered the world of American Catholic scholarship as scholarship began its entry into the American Church. His career that began in that inaugural issue of *TS* coincided with the reawakening, development, and sometimes painful assimilation of theology into American Catholic life.

From the beginning of the twentieth century, intellectual life in the American church had been in a dogmatic slumber. The condemnation of Americanism in 1899 halted reflection on American religious liberty and seemed to assert in the words of John Courtney Murray that the American church with its separation of church and state would "live forever in the shadow of 'hypothesis,' " a situation merely to be tolerated as long as the "thesis" of union of church and state could not be realized.[10] The condemnation of modernism in 1907 cast a pall over scholarship and isolated the church from the modern world. Catholic seminaries, religious houses of studies and the Catholic University of America all slipped away from creative scholarship down the slope to mere mouthing of theological manuals imported from Rome. American Catholic theology was safe, orthodox, always loyal to Rome, but totally lifeless. The late 1930s witnessed a renaissance. In 1936 teachers of scripture in seminaries and religious houses met originally to prepare a new translation of the New Testament. They met again to form the Catholic Biblical Association. In 1939 the American Dominicans began publication of *The Thomist*. A year later the first national liturgical week was held under the auspices of the American Benedictines. The same year the faculties of the American Jesuit theologates introduced *TS* to be published (after 1941) at Woodstock College, the Jesuit house of studies outside of Baltimore, Maryland.

Walter would be more closely associated with *TS* than any other individual. Upon his return from graduate studies in 1946, he was named managing editor under John Courtney Murray as editor-in-chief. In 1967 he would succeed Murray as editor-in-chief—a post he continues to hold. Murray exercised a deep influence on Walter, as would Gustave Weigel who began teaching ecclesiology at Woodstock in 1948.

The 1940s were years of theological transition. In France proponents of the "new theology" had begun their work that would bring them into conflict with a more entrenched mind set. M.-D. Chenu, O.P., Yves Congar, O.P., Henri de Lubac, S.J., and Jean Daniélou, S.J.—all would fall under some type of censure by the early 1950s. Closer to home and Walter Burghardt, Murray had begun in 1943 a series of articles on church-state relations and religious liberty. Murray saw the necessity of cooperation between Catholics, Protestants, and Jews to combat the growing trend of privatization of religion and of secularism in the United States. To do this he had to address the question that had lain dormant since 1899: whether it was official Catholic doctrine that there should be a union between church and state whenever Catholics were in the majority. He aroused opposition first in the United States and later in Rome. In 1955 his Roman superiors informed him that he had aroused serious opposition from the Holy Office. He was then preparing to publish in *TS* an article on Leo XIII's theory of church-state relations, but pulled out the galleys and set them aside. Walter watched as Murray immediately removed every book on church-state relations from his room to return to the library. Years later, Walter remarked that all the time Murray knew he was right, and he would recall Murray's oft-repeated advice: "Courage, Walter! It's far more important than intelligence."[11]

The 1950s were Walter's maturing years as a theologian, and he would witness at first hand the pain and rejection that maturity might bring. His own theological training, he once said, had stressed proof texts rather than historical context; it was the age of manuals like Rouet de Journel's *Enchiridion Patristicum* rather than of careful attention to historical theology and its sources. That was Walter's training before studying with Quasten, and he absorbed it well. But he also outgrew it. In 1951 he delivered a paper to the Catholic Theological Society of America on "The Catholic Concept of Tradition in the Light of Modern Theological Thought." A splendid and erudite survey of various theological reflections on tradition, it concluded that Louis Billot, S.J. had virtually written the last word on the topic.[12] Billot held that tradition was "immutable," a static deposit separate from scripture. Like most other Catholic theologians of the time, Walter accepted this view. Unlike many, however, he researched, listened, read, and was ready willingly to embrace Vatican II's dynamic view of tradition so intimately entwined with scripture, a view that placed Billot aside and picked up the thread of thought developed in the nineteenth century Tübingen school that was so dependent on patristic thought. From Murray's pain Walter learned courage. From his own reflections he learned honesty—that quality so admirable in a scholar that enabled him to reject a former position once new evidence was uncovered or old evidence was seen in a new light.

While Walter grew, he never abandoned his conviction that theology is as much the quest for human nature as for God. Where better to look for this than on the effect of the Christ event on humanity, mere humanity called to be part of the "new creation" in Christ but sharing with him and with us only human nature? Where better to discover this than in that exemplar of the perfect human response to grace, the Virgin Mary? Walter's first scholarly article on Mariology appeared in 1955—"Mary in Western Patristic Thought."[13] Other studies followed over the next two years: "Theotokos: The Mother of God,"[14] "Mary in Eastern Patristic Thought,"[15] and "The Testimony of the Patristic Age concerning Mary's Death."[16] These articles would bring Walter the first of numerous national honors—the Mariological Award in 1958.

Marian studies might seem to the reader of the 1980s a relatively safe topic for a theologian of the tumultuous 1950s, but Walter was to give that field too a new twist. The other major influence on Walter during his maturing years was Gustave Weigel. After almost a decade of work in the theological faculty in Santiago, Chile, Weigel came to the United States for a visit only to be told he was to remain. He was assigned to teach ecclesiology at Woodstock and began, at Murray's suggestion, reviewing books on Protestant theology for TS. Gradually—even hesitantly—Weigel introduced a new note in Woodstock's theology—ecumenism. "Weigel was ever the realist," Walter has written, always ready to tease him about his concern for his health. On one occasion Walter "announced in triumph" that hospital tests revealed some minor problems, but "Gus looked up from his book, looked at me calmly, and said so simply and so truly: 'All right; now you have a peg on which to hang your neurosis.' "[17] As much as being realistic and witty, however, Weigel, conservative though he remained in his theology, was open to Protestant thought. So was Walter. By 1962 he was showing the influence of the nascent American ecumenical movement, a movement, he realized, that had to be integrated into every branch of theology. "The Mariologist as Ecumenist" was the title of Walter's first article consciously trying to articulate Catholic doctrine about the Virgin Mary to a broader non-Catholic audience.[18] In 1962 he was appointed to the Baltimore Archdiocesan Commission for Christian Unity. Three years later he became a member of U.S. Catholic Dialogue Group, Lutheran-Roman Catholic Conversations, sponsored jointly by the American Catholic hierarchy and officials of the Lutheran denominations. From 1968 to 1976 he served on the Faith and Order Commission of the World Council of Churches, and for four years (1971–1975) he served on the Faith and Order Commission of the National Council of Churches. Ecumenism, in which Weigel had been a Catholic pioneer, became part of the heartbeat of Catholic theology and of Walter as a result of dramatic changes brought about in the church by Vatican II.

The council was a heady period for Walter and his two close colleagues at Woodstock, but it opened on a somber note. Murray had been "disinvited," to use his term, at the request of Cardinal Alfredo Ottaviani, secretary of the Holy Office, and Archbishop Egidio Vagnozzi, the apostolic delegate. Invited to the council by the same sources was one of Murray's arch-opponents, Monsignor Joseph C. Fenton of the Catholic University of America.[19] That situation was changed during the second and subsequent sessions as Cardinal Francis Spellman of New York had Murray named a *peritus*, and he played a major role in the drafting of the council's *Declaration on Religious Liberty*. Weigel, too, was in attendance as an interpreter of the Latin proceedings for Protestant observers. Walter remained at Woodstock eagerly reading the accounts of the council that would so alter the face of the church with which he was so familiar.

Little did Walter realize that the period of the shift from a classical to historically conscious theology, from a Latin to a vernacular liturgy, would also mark the end of his relationship with Murray and Weigel. Weigel died in January 1964. Murray died in August 1967. Walter preached at Murray's funeral—"surely the most difficult of my homilies," he later wrote. Let Walter tell of his emotion in his own words:

> It was late on an August afternoon in 1967 when word came to us at Woodstock College in rural Maryland that John Courtney Murray had died in a taxicab on Long Island. The shock on Woodstock's corridors echoed through much of the country: a voice immeasurably effective for human and Christian freedom had been stilled. But for so many who not only admired the mind but loved the man, the grief was far more personal. I, for one, had lost my dearest friend. After the death of Gustave Weigel only three and a half years before, this was a dreadful blow to absorb.[20]

But Walter did absorb the deaths of Weigel and Murray and would absorb more dreadful blows in the years to come. The lessons of courage and openness he had learned from his two close friends he now had to express on his own. With Murray's death, Walter now became editor-in-chief of *TS* at a critical turning point in the history of the American church, as theologians now sought to help implement the council and turned to new directions of thought.

If Murray's years as editor-in-chief were focused principally on the controversy over religious liberty, Walter's would begin with the controversy over birth control. Within a year of his assuming the editorship of *TS*, Paul VI issued *Humanae Vitae*. Not only were theologians who hoped for a change in the church's traditional opposition to artificial contraception disappointed; they also expressed it. Many signed a statement expressing their respectful dissent from the encyclical. Walter was among them. "Dissent" had for the first time entered the vocabulary of American Catholic theology. But, of late, the term has become too sensational. Too little has been made of the way in which Cardinal Lawrence Shehan, archbishop of Baltimore, summoned all the priests in his jurisdiction who had signed the statement and gained from all, including Walter, the assurance that they were not rejecting the authentic magisterium. Too infrequently is notice made that not all the "dissenters" were subject to reprisals and other penalties. In 1969, a year after signing the statement against the encyclical, Walter received word from the Vatican that Pope Paul VI had named him a member of the Pontifical Theological Commission, the international group of theologians advising the pope. The courage he had learned from Murray and the intellectual honesty he gained on his own had won a reward, but he would frequently have to draw upon those qualities during the coming years, as he persisted in providing the English-speaking church with a consistently high quality journal of theology.

On one occasion it appeared that he would have to evoke his courage. In April 1974 he received word that the Vatican secretariat of state did not want him to publish in the current issue of *TS* a note by Archbishop Denis E. Hurley of Durban, South Africa on "Population Control and the Catholic Conscience: Responsibility of the Magisterium."[21] This time, however, courage was not needed. A few phone calls brought the information that that issue was already in the mail. Whether it was providence or luck, Walter would not have to have the galleys of hastily withdrawn articles cluttering up his office. But on another issue, Walter would have to call upon his courage.

In the fall of 1968 Walter and I entered a new phase of our relationship. Fresh back from graduate studies, I had begun my formal training in theology. Not only was he recovering from the loss of his roots in Murray and Weigel, he was about to be uprooted from the place that had been his home for twenty-nine years. In 1966 Yale University had made overtures through Murray, to whom it gave an honorary degree that year, to have Woodstock move to New Haven. This set in motion a series of discussions culminating in the decision to move to New York City. When the school year opened, some of the students were already packing, though the move was still at least a year away. Concern for civil rights, the inner-city poor, and the anti-war movement had taken their place alongside the traditional theology student's wrestling with the Councils of Nicaea and Chalcedon and mastery of moral theology. Not everyone was happy either with the new orientation of the theological students or with the new site for their education. For Walter it was a wrenching away from the familiar rural isolation of the Maryland countryside and the insertion into the bustling, never sleeping, noisy/exciting, chaotic/creative atmosphere of Morningside Heights.

Difficult as it was, Walter packed his bags with the rest of us in 1970—some had already moved in 1969—and moved into 352 Riverside Drive, a lovely old mansion overlooking the Hudson. Walter had come home to the place of his birth—but not to the place that he could really call home or that he could identify with the theological enterprise. In November 1971 he celebrated his twenty-fifth anniversary on the Woodstock faculty. Preaching on that occasion, he poignantly told of the meaning of the "Old Woodstock" for him. It was his "third point."

> . . . Woodstock. There this priest played the theologian. No matter what the travels and where—Oxford or Rome, Geneva or Jerusalem—Woodstock in Maryland has been more home to me than any other place in my life. Seven years of study, twenty-four of teaching. All the openness of 650 acres, all the privacy of a goldfish bowl. And profoundly home.
>
> What I had to learn is that Woodstock is not primarily a place. It takes much learning. For there is something that grabs you in blades of grass that sing in the breeze, and earth that gives beneath your feet day upon day; in a small room that smells of your sweat and imprisons your deepest thoughts; in a chapel underground, carved by a friend for you and your Sacrifice out of that eternal granite; in library shelves that you have learned to read eyes closed; in a recreation room that echoes the cultured tones of a Murray and the wit of a Weigel; in a cemetery that looks back on a century of love and forward to endless life; even a homemade golf green with your consistent par.[22]

On this occasion, however, Walter had little opportunity really "to learn that Woodstock is not primarily a place," whether in rural Maryland or urban New York. On January 8, 1973 the Jesuit provincials of the United States announced that Woodstock, after over a century in Maryland and only three years in New York, was closing.

For some of the younger faculty it was devastating enough, but for Walter it was almost the final insult—the loss of his two close Jesuit brothers, the move from his "home," and now the closing of the institution he loved and served so well. He and his distinguished colleague, Avery Dulles, S.J., even undertook a trip to Rome in an unsuccessful effort to have the decision reversed. "Courage, Walter," Murray would have said, and courage Walter had. In 1974 he made another beginning and another return, this time to the Catholic University of America as professor of patristic theology. Patristics had shaped his approach to theology, and since 1958 he had been a co-editor of *Ancient Christian Writers,* published at the Catholic University. With him from Woodstock also went Avery Dulles.

In 1978, Walter decided to concentrate more on the editing of *TS* and accepted the position of theologian in residence at Georgetown University. It meant another move—this time only across town in Washington—but also another return—to a Jesuit community. More important than either editing or moving, however, it also meant increased productivity in the area he loved most—making theology available to a broader audience, particularly through preaching.

3. THE TEACHER AND PREACHER

Walter's students at Woodstock recall his polished lectures, always consisting of three points, beginning promptly at the bell and ending with a prayer timed precisely to coincide with the bell ending the period. But he was always a teacher not only in the classroom but also in the pulpit. From 1951 to 1959 he had his own bi-weekly radio program in Baltimore. His second major book, *All Lost in Wonder,* was a collection of sermons published in 1960. By that time, he had already achieved national notoriety. In the Easter 1957 issue of *Life,* he was the only Catholic listed in an article on "Best Easter Sermons." He was a guest on the Catholic Hour in 1959 with a series of lectures that explained to a national radio audience the meaning of the fathers of the church. He was again on the program in 1964.

Georgetown University's Dahlgren Chapel and nearby Holy Trinity Church provided the pulpits for Walter's homilies during the last decade. Reflecting on his development as a preacher, he noted:

> The point is, the homily is liturgy. In Jungmann's strong sentence, the homily "should emanate from the consciousness that although it is freely created by the liturgist, it is liturgy itself." And the liturgy is prayer. Conclusion? The homily is prayer.[23]

In shaping his homilies, his communication of theology to the laity, it is not surprising that Walter acknowledges his debt to another Catholic theologian who combined preaching with the study of the fathers of the church—John Henry Newman. Walter's conviction of the importance of preaching was shaped not only by Newman's idea that "the preacher persuades by what he is as well as by what he delivers," but also by Newman's "mastery of language."[24] Then, of course, there were the fathers of the church themselves—those great men who preached their theology and theologized in their preaching, not merely the abstract truths upon which later theologians would reflect, but the truths of a living faith. Walter cites with approval, for instance, Gregory the Great's detailed list of thirty-six "contrasting sets of people that must be distinguished by the preacher and teacher." It is not Gregory's style or allegorical interpretation of scripture that should influence the preacher today, Walter concludes, but "Gregory's concern for the different types of people who have to listen to us calls for our admiration and imitation, however much we may have grown in psychological insight over the past fourteen centuries."[25]

To Newman and the fathers, Walter joins the influence of the ecumenical movement on him. It was an influence missing in his Jesuit training, he admits, but began

> initially and powerfully through involvement in the Lutheran–Roman Catholic dialogue. Close contact for more than a decade with theologians such as Joseph Sittler, Arthur Carl Piepkorn, Warren Quanbeck, and George Lindbeck shattered ingrained prejudices, humbled me. . . . They were deeply devoted to the Lord, had a profound spirituality, loved the liturgy, and were engagingly human. The Reformers could no longer be cavalierly dismissed as hard-nosed, disgruntled rebels bent on destroying God's Church. And on a sheerly human level, I shall never forget the Reverend Edwin Seymour, blind for most of his Presbyterian ministry, but incorrigibly convinced by experience that he sees more in his blindness than he ever saw before his accident. The last quarter century has enlarged and enriched my Christian sensibility immensely.[26]

Gradually Walter discovered and was enthralled by Frederick Buechner and David H. C. Read, both Presbyterians. "Fresh language," "poetic vision," "unexpected twists"—these were but some of the qualities that Walter discovered in Protestant preachers—and that they discovered in him. But most of all, it was their "biblical preaching." "Not that my earlier, pre-Vatican II sermons were unscriptural," says Walter, rather that the biblical heritage in my preaching was transmitted through, all be hidden in, the Church's doctrine. I rarely wrestled with the text myself; that had all been done for me. What was lost in such transmission was a personal experience of the word. It's the difference between seeing a movie, say the Mozart *Amadeus,* and reading a summary of the plot and its meaning; between an experience of the symbols and an explanation thereof.[27]

Walter's own specialization in patristic theology, years of editing *Theological Studies,* including reviews of Protestant theologians, ecumenical contacts, and, perhaps most of all, experience of people, of the human condition, including his own—all these factors have shaped Walter's preaching, especially in the last ten years.

Walter's days at Georgetown University have graced the American Catholic community. Since 1980 he has published five books of homilies, one book on preaching, and another on the rich experience of being human. Their titles reveal how much he has absorbed his quest for "fresh language," "poetic vision," and "unexpected twists"—*Tell the Next Generation: Homilies and Near Homilies* (1980); *Sir, We Would Like to See Jesus: Homilies from a Hilltop* (1982); *Seasons That Laugh or Weep: Musings on the Human Journey* (1983); *Still Proclaiming Your Wonders: Homilies for the Eighties* (1984); *Grace on Crutches: Homilies for Fellow Travelers* (1986); *Preaching: The Art and the Craft* (1987); *Lovely in Eyes Not His: Homilies for an Imaging of Christ* (1988). But it is not only the American Catholic community that has benefited.

What better accolade could come to an American than praise from an Englishman? A reviewer of *Preaching: The Art and the Craft* in the London *Tablet* said it well:

> Though not all good preachers write well, Burghardt, the grand old man of American homilists, does. He has much to say about the art and the craft of preaching in contemporary culture and this lucid, well structured and stimulating book shows why he is not a mere propagandist, but a true artist. Each chapter tells us more about the techniques used by this great preacher. A well-rounded, complete man, with a zest for life, he is at home in the Bible, and his book is full of scriptural quotations and references; at the same time, he also draws inspiration from the arts and sciences.[28]

The reviewer warned parish priests not to be put off by Walter's taking sixty to seventy hours in preparing a fifteen minute homily. Walter's "approach and techniques," the reviewer asserted, "can be used by any preacher, no matter how short a time he has at his disposal." As Walter was shaped by the great John Henry Newman's preaching, now the *Tablet* reviewer suggested that Walter's book "would make a splendid present for any priest whose homilies needed improving or whose efforts deserved a reward."[29]

Walter has made his mark as a preacher on the American church. Future generations of both American and English priests may study Walter's preaching in much the same manner he studied Newman. His homilies express, illustrate, and illuminate his theology. As theologian, he has been courageous mediator and honest critic, sometimes of his own work. To the American scholarly community he has made the contribution not only of his own work, but also of the work of others published in his carefully edited *TS*. More than thirteen institutions of higher education, both Catholic and Protestant, have awarded him honorary degrees, not to mention other academic awards. His wide-ranging interests have led him not only to publish on film in *Variety*, but also to address some of the pressing problems in health care—a concern that won him the Catholic Hospital Administrative Personnel Award in 1987. But for those of us who know him, he is more than the recipient of so many awards. He is more than preacher and teacher, theologian and editor; he is a man, a priest, a sun-worshiping friend, who at seventy-five is younger than most men half his age.

NOTES

1. Walter J. Burghardt, "Why I Am a Jesuit," *The Jesuit* (Autumn 1975).
2. Ibid.
3. Walter J. Burghardt, "Homer on Park Avenue," *Woodstock Letters* 68 (1939) 114–37.
4. Burghardt, "Why I Am a Jesuit."
5. Walter J. Burghardt, *Seasons That Laugh or Weep* (New York: Paulist Press, 1983) 118–19.
6. Ibid., 97.
7. Ibid., 119.
8. Walter J. Burghardt, *The Image of God in Man According to Cyril of Alexandria* (Washington, DC: Catholic University of America Press, 1957).
9. Walter J. Burghardt, "American Church and American Theology: Response to an Identity Crisis," *Catholic Theological Society of America. Proceedings of the Twenty-eighth Annual Convention* (New York, 1973) 2.
10. Archives of Woodstock College, Murray to Vincent McCormick, Woodstock, November 23, 1953 (copy).

11. Burghardt, "Why I Am a Jesuit."
12. Walter J. Burghardt, "The Catholic Concept of Tradition in the Light of Modern Theological Thought," *Catholic Theological Society of America. Proceedings of the Sixth Annual Convention (1951)* (New York, 1952) 42–77.
13. Walter J. Burghardt, "Mary in Western Patristic Thought," in *Mariology* 1 (ed. J.B. Carol; Milwaukee: Bruce Publishing Co., 1955) 109–55.
14. Walter J. Burghardt, "Theotokos: The Mother of God," in *The Mystery of the Woman* (ed. E.D. O'Connor; Notre Dame, IN: University of Notre Dame Press, 1956) 3–33.
15. Walter J. Burghardt, "Mary in Eastern Patristic Thought," in *Mariology* 2 (ed. J.B. Carol; Milwaukee: Bruce Publishing Co., 1957) 88–153.
16. Walter J. Burghardt, "The Testimony of the Patristic Age Concerning Mary's Death," *Marian Studies* 8 (1957) 58–99.
17. Burghardt, "Why I Am a Jesuit."
18. Walter J. Burghardt, "The Mariologist as Ecumenist," *Marian Studies* 13 (1962) 5–12.
19. Donald E. Pelotte, *John Courtney Murray: Theologian in Conflict* (New York: Paulist Press, 1975) 77.
20. Walter J. Burghardt, *Tell the Next Generation: Homilies and Near Homilies* (New York: Paulist Press, 1980) 211.
21. Denis E. Hurley, "Population Control and the Catholic Conscience: Responsibility of the Magisterium," *TS* 34 (1974) 154–63.
22. Burghardt, *Tell the Next Generation*, 97.
23. Walter J. Burghardt, *Preaching: The Art and the Craft* (New York: Paulist Press, 1987) 10.
24. Ibid., 192–93.
25. Ibid., 197–98.
26. Ibid., 200.
27. Ibid., 207–08.
28. Vladimir Felzmann, "Ministry of the Word," *Tablet* (July 2, 1988) 754.
29. Ibid., 755.

2

PREACHING IN THE APOSTOLIC AND SUBAPOSTOLIC AGE
by Joseph A. Fitzmyer, S.J.

"In the beginning was the Word" (Jn 1:1). Though this opening of the Johannine prologue speaks of the Word in an entirely different sense, few readers will fail to perceive its pertinence, in an accommodated sense, to the topic to which this essay is devoted. The essay itself forms part of a tribute being made to a learned Jesuit priest, Walter J. Burghardt, S.J., whose career has been marked by extraordinary preaching. If I now relate his career to primitive Christian preaching, it is with the deliberate intention of associating such ministry to the beginning of Christianity itself, which began with the Word. Walter J. Burghardt has engaged in apostolic preaching in our day.

Christian preaching is a venerable tradition among us despite the ups and downs that have marked that tradition. Like all other Christians, modern preachers have to look to the biblical roots of their ministry, for these ever stand as a norm over such ecclesiastical practice and institution. The biblical roots of Christian preaching are many, and they would include as well the normative character of Old Testament prophetic preaching. In this essay, however, I have limited my discussion to preaching in the apostolic and subapostolic periods of the Christian church. Many of the preachers of those periods were not eyewitnesses of the events that initiated the church, and in this regard a modern preacher like Walter J. Burghardt shares their heritage. In the prologue to his gospel Luke tells of his dependence on "original eyewitnesses and ministers of the word," i.e. eyewitnesses who became ministers of the word.[1] Though dependent on such persons, Luke was not one himself, and he clearly shared that status with many others in the apostolic and subapostolic ages of the Christian church, when the word was being spread abroad in the eastern Mediterranean world of the first century A.D.

In my title I am using the terms "apostolic" and "subapostolic" in the sense that R.E. Brown has proposed for them.[2] He confines the "apostolic age" to the second one-third of the first century and the "subapostolic age" to the last one-third of that century. With the exception of the uncontested letters of Paul (1 Thessalonians, Galatians, Philippians, 1–2 Corinthians, Romans, and Philemon), which would have been composed during the apostolic age, the rest of the New Testament would be products of the subapostolic age—composed for churches that the apostles had left behind. Thus the preaching that they record represents the preaching of those who *did not see,* i.e. did not witness the ministry of Jesus of Nazareth itself. Though Paul writes from the apostolic age, he was conscious of his not having witnessed that ministry (see 2 Cor 5:16).

In a brief essay such as this I must further limit the discussion of preaching in the apostolic and subapostolic ages of the Christian church in two regards. First, among the many Greek terms used in the New Testament to express some form of communicating the Christian message, I shall concentrate chiefly on *kēryssein,* "proclaim, preach," and *euangelizesthai,* "preach, announce good news,"[3] and their cognate substantives. In this regard, it is good to recall that the Johannine literature makes no use of *kēryssein* or *euangelizesthai,* but prefers rather *anangellein,* "declare, announce," or *martyrein,* "bear witness." The difference is probably to be sought in the character of subapostolic preaching which emerged later and was less attuned to the demands of dynamic proclamation of missionary endeavor in the apostolic age itself.[4] Second, I shall examine in some detail preaching in Paul's letters and in Acts, wherein the main terms mostly occur. As I have already intimated, what will emerge from Paul's letters may reveal aspects of apostolic preaching, but what will emerge from the Lucan story may be mixed, for though it narrates the activity of Christian preachers of the apostolic age, it often recounts that activity with the concerns of subapostolic Christianity. The Lucan portrait of Paul may be so affected.

Lastly, by way of an introductory remark, we must recall that any adequate discussion of Christian preaching in the apostolic or subapostolic age must reckon with the clear roots of such activity in the precedents of John the Baptist and Jesus. Their preaching is diversely presented by the evangelists, but the substance of it on which the evangelists agree is at the root of apostolic preaching.

Whereas all three synoptic evangelists present John as a preacher of repentance and baptism, "a voice of someone crying out in the desert, 'Make ready the way of the Lord' " (Is 40:3), only Matthew makes of him a kingdom preacher, putting on his lips (3:2) the very proclamation, "Repent, the kingdom of heaven has drawn near," that Jesus himself will utter as he begins his ministry (4:17). John's preaching is most elaborately presented by Luke, who gives three samples of it (his eschatological preaching, 3:7–9; his ethical preaching, 3:10–14; and his messianic preaching, 3:15–17). Luke concludes, "With these and many other exhortations John preached to the people" (3:18). In the third gospel, however, John never appears as a kingdom preacher.

In the Lucan gospel only Jesus preaches the kingdom (see Lk 16:16a–b), for he is the kingdom preacher par excellence: "I must proclaim the kingdom of God in other towns as well, for that is what I was sent for" (*hoti epi touto apestalēn*, Lk 4:43). Yet even before he first mentions the kingdom (4:43), the Lucan Jesus has already proclaimed himself as the content of his own *kērygma:* He and his preaching are the fulfillment of something mentioned in the scriptures of old, something associated with God's mode of salvation. Jesus and his preaching inaugurate the year of God's favor that was spoken of in Isaiah 61:1–2: "Today this passage of scripture sees its fulfillment, as you sit listening" (Lk 4:21). Here, Luke, writing from the subapostolic period, recasts the content of Jesus' own preaching so that it includes not only the kingdom of God (cf Mk 1:15b[5]), but even Jesus himself. What is above all noteworthy about apostolic and subapostolic preaching is that he who was the kingdom preacher par excellence has become the preached one. This one notes already in Luke 4.

Rudolf Bultmann overstated his case when he maintained that "theological thinking—the theology of the New Testament—begins with the kerygma of the earliest Church and not before."[6] He was wrongly playing down any connection between the kerygma of the primitive church and the preaching of Jesus of Nazareth himself. But Bultmann rightly defined the primitive kerygma as the proclamation of Jesus Christ, crucified and risen, as God's eschatological act of salvation, or as the challenging word occurring in the salvific act of Christ—God's proclamation in the crucifixion and resurrection of Jesus the Christ for our salvation. In that early Christian kerygma Jesus was not only a preacher or prophet announcing that act of salvation, but also the "one who formerly had been the *bearer* of the message [but who] was [now] drawn into it and became its essential content. *The proclaimer became the proclaimed.*"[7]

Thus one may again refer to the accommodated sense of John

1:1 with which these introductory remarks began, "In the beginning was the Word." For Jesus of Nazareth, as the Word of God, was at the root of early apostolic kerygma or preaching. His preaching, as remembered by his followers, was developed and explicated for the needs of subsequent generations in the light of his death and resurrection. Eventually, a form of it was recorded under the guidance of the Spirit in the literary portraits of him that the evangelists have made part of the early Christian heritage.

On the basis of such preliminary remarks I may turn to the two main parts of this essay: (1) Paul's awareness of his apostolic preaching, and (2) the Lucan portrait of apostolic preachers.

PAUL'S AWARENESS OF HIS APOSTOLIC PREACHING

Paul's awareness of his role as a Christian preacher shines through many of the passages in his uncontested writings.[8] Even if his heritage comes to us in the form of letters and he has had great influence on later Christian writers who have imitated his epistolary practice, Paul never boasts of having been called by God to write letters to Christian communities. By and large he insists on three aspects of his mission: he is aware (1) of having been called as an apostle, (2) of having been sent to preach the gospel, especially to Gentiles, and (3) of being a preacher of the gospel of Christ Jesus, crucified and raised, which was meant to elicit faith from human beings.

(1) Though Paul himself was keenly aware of his apostolic commission, his call to such a role seems to have been challenged at times. Some of his utterances, even protestations, reflect situations in which his call to apostolic service was at least queried. "Am I not an apostle? Have I not seen Jesus our Lord? . . . If to others I am not an apostle, to you at least I am" (1 Cor 9:1–2). In the letter to the Galatians he explained how he had "seen" the risen Lord: God himself had accorded him a revelation of "his Son" (1:16). Thus he could insist with the Galatians that his status as an apostle was "not from human beings or through a human being, but through Jesus Christ and God the Father who raised him from the dead" (1:1). That revelation of Jesus as the risen Son of God constituted the basis of Paul's apostolic status. In his eyes it put him on a par with "those who were apostles before me" (Gal 1:17; cf 1 Cor 9:5), even though he was keenly aware that that appearance of the risen Christ was the "last of all, as to one untimely born" (1 Cor 15:8). Because of that revelation he rightly

considered himself as one "called to be an apostle" (Rom 1:1), "an apostle of Jesus Christ" (1 Cor 1:1; 2 Cor 1:1). He recognized this personal status, while insisting that not all Christians had such a status (1 Cor 12:29). And yet Paul himself had to acknowledge that he was "the least of the apostles, unworthy to be called an apostle," because he had "persecuted the church of God"—yet "by God's grace I am what I am, and his grace toward me has not been in vain" (1 Cor 15:9–10). Indeed, that very grace made him "the apostle to the Gentiles" (Rom 11:13); for this purpose was he called.[9]

(2) Paul was well aware of his having been called to preach the gospel, especially to the Gentiles. Indeed, in a somewhat puzzling passage Paul contrasted his commission to preach with the task of baptizing: "I thank God that I baptized none of you except Crispus and Gaius, lest anyone might claim that you were baptized in my name. (I did baptize the household of Stephanas too—but I am not aware of having baptized anyone else.) For Christ did not send me to baptize but to preach the gospel, not with eloquent wisdom, lest the cross of Christ be emptied of its meaning" (1 Cor 1:14–17). In this passage Paul has been rejecting the implications of the Corinthian faction that proclaimed, "I belong to Paul" (1 Cor 1:12): "Paul was not crucified for you, was he? Or were you baptized in Paul's name?" (1:13). What is strange is that Paul has clearly put more importance on preaching the gospel than on baptizing or on subjecting converts to the liturgical rite of Christian initiation. To many modern preachers the latter would seem to be a goal of preaching. Yet Paul has insisted that the commission that he received from the Lord was to preach the gospel.

That commission is further explained by Paul in Galatians 1:15–16, where he says, "When it pleased God, who had set me apart from my mother's womb and had called me with his grace, to reveal his Son to me, that I might preach him among the Gentiles, I did not confer with flesh and blood . . ."—i.e. with other human beings. Thus that revelation on the road near Damascus gave Paul not only the basic insight into the mystery of Christ, but a commission to preach him to the Gentiles. Again, Paul has not expressed his commission in terms of converting or baptizing the Gentiles, either individually or by households, but in terms of "preaching him [Christ] among the Gentiles" (*euangelizōmai auton en tois ethnesin*). Paul compared himself with Peter and noted that even "the pillars" of the Jerusalem church (James, Cephas, and John) recognized that as Peter had been entrusted with "the gospel for the circumcised," he too had been entrusted with "that for the uncircumcised" (Gal 2:7), for God was at work in both of them in this ministry of preaching (2:8).

(3) Paul was also aware of preaching the gospel of Christ Jesus, crucified and raised, as a means of eliciting faith from human beings. He formulated the object of his preaching in diverse ways, but especially in the following three succinct ways: (a) *Christ crucified.* "We preach indeed Christ crucified, to Jews a stumbling block and to Gentiles foolishness, but to those who are called, whether Jews or Greeks, Christ the power of God and the wisdom of God" (1 Cor 1:23–26; cf 2 Cor 1:19; 11:4). (b) *God's gospel.* Paul preached "the gospel of God" (Rom 1:1; 15:16; 2 Cor 11:7) or "the gospel of Jesus Christ" (Gal 1:7; 1 Cor 9:12; 2 Cor 2:12; Rom 15:19). In the latter instance it is sometimes difficult to say whether the genitive is subjective (the gospel stemming from Jesus Christ) or objective (the gospel about Jesus Christ). (c) *The faith.* "He who once persecuted us is now preaching the faith that he once tried to destroy" (Gal 1:23). This last formulation expresses not only the content of Paul's gospel (the *fides quae* of later theologians) but also the purpose of his preaching. For the faith that was once reckoned to Abraham as uprightness (Gen 15:6) was to be reckoned to us too "who believe in him who raised from the dead, Jesus our Lord, who was handed over [to death] for our trespasses and raised for our justification" (Rom 4:24–25).

Elsewhere I have described the characteristics of Paul's gospel.[10] For him *euangelion* denoted the activity of evangelization or the content of his apostolic message, what he preached, proclaimed, announced, or talked about: his personal way of summing up the significance of the Christ-event. For Paul the "gospel" was revelatory or apocalyptic (manifesting God's new way of bringing salvation to humanity, Rom 1:17), dynamic (unleashing a new salvific force into human history, Rom 1:16), kerygmatic (proclaiming how God had done this in the death and resurrection of Christ, 1 Cor 15:1–7), normative (standing critically over Christian conduct, even that of church officials, Gal 1:7; 2:4, 11–14; Phil 1:27), and promissory (bringing to fulfillment promises made by God through the prophets of old, Rom 1:2). This is why Paul could boast that he was not ashamed of the gospel, because it was the power of God for the salvation of everyone who had faith, for the Jew first and also for the Greek (Rom 1:16).

All Paul's preaching was designed to elicit a response from those whom he accosted with this "gospel of God." C.K. Barrett recently devoted a short study to "Proclamation and Response,"[11] which he begins with the statement, "New Testament Christianity was a proclaimed faith. 'Faith comes as a result of hearing, and hearing comes through the word of Christ' (Rom 10:17)." Significantly, Barrett takes his cue from Paul's famous discussion of the role of faith in Romans 10. The root of Paul's proclaimed faith is "the word of Christ," i.e., the word about Christ as well as the word that stems from Christ. The human being accosted by that word must respond with faith: this is "the word of faith that we preach" (10:8). The response of one so accosted is double: "If you confess with your lips that Jesus is Lord and believe in your heart that God raised him from the dead, you will be saved" (10:9). So Paul has formulated what is often regarded as a summary confession of belief in Christ. It begins with an assent of the lordship of the risen Christ: "Jesus is Lord" (see also 1 Cor 12:3). This is actually a minimal interpretation of that early Christian slogan, for it is not merely a credal formula, but undoubtedly is to be understood as well as a kerygmatic formula, especially when one considers the context in which Paul makes use of it, "the word of faith that we preach" (10:8). "Jesus is Lord" is what Paul proclaimed. That is why he could write in 1 Corinthians 8:5–6, "For though there may be many so-called gods in heaven or on earth—indeed many are the 'gods' and many are the 'lords'—yet for us there is one God, the Father, from whom are all things and for whom we exist, and one Lord, Jesus Christ, through whom are all things and through whom we exist." So Paul proclaimed Christ the risen Lord to the Greco-Roman Gentiles of the eastern Mediterranean world of his day.

For Paul the response to that proclamation was not merely faith as the result of hearing (*pistis ex akoēs*) or an assent of lips and heart about the lordship of Christ. It had indeed to begin in this way. But it had to entail eventually *hypakoē pisteōs*, "a commitment of faith,"[12] a dedication of the whole person to God in Christ Jesus. That is why Paul could write to his beloved Philippian community, "Only let your manner of life be worthy of the gospel of Christ, so that whether I come and see you or am absent, I may hear of you that you stand firm in one spirit, with one mind striving side by side for the faith of the gospel . . ." (Phil 1:27).

A few other aspects of "the faith that we preach" mentioned in Romans 10 have to be singled out so that the picture of Paul's awareness of himself as an apostolic preacher may be adequately presented. In that chapter Paul brings himself to propound that "everyone, Jew and Greek alike, who calls upon the name of the Lord will be saved" (10:13, quoting implicitly the LXX of Joel 3:5). By "Lord" he means, of course, the risen Christ. Then he proceeds to take up objections to the thesis so propounded, answering each one with a relevant (or not too relevant) quotation from the Old Testament (10:14–21). The first objection, formulated in three expostulations of an imaginary interlocutor, reveals an aspect of Paul's own awareness of himself as a preacher: "How are they to believe in him about whom they have never heard? How are they to hear [about him] without a preacher (chōris kēryssontos)? And how may they preach unless they have been sent?" (10:14b–15). Clearly, for Paul here the genuine "preached word" is brought to human beings, Jews or Greeks alike, only by commissioned, apostolic preachers.[13]

Still other aspects of Paul's awareness of his role as an apostolic preacher might be considered, but the main aspects of it have been covered in the three foregoing points. With this we may turn to a consideration of the Lucan picture of apostolic preachers.

THE LUCAN PORTRAIT OF APOSTOLIC PREACHERS

In the Acts of the Apostles Luke narrates the activity of several early Christian preachers of the apostolic period: Peter, Stephen, Philip, Barnabas, and Saul/Paul. The speeches that Luke puts on the lips of some of them are, in effect, intended as samples of their preaching: Peter's sermons in 1:16–22; 2:14b–36, 38–39; 3:12b–26; 4:8–12, 19–20; 5:29–32; 10:34–43; 11:5–17; 15:7–11; Stephen's sermon in 7:2–53; the speech of Barnabas and Paul in 14:15–17; Paul's discourses in 13:16b–41; 17:22–31; 20:18–35; 22:1–21; 24:10–21; (25:8, 10–11); 26:2–23; 27:16–21; 28:17–20, 25–28.

The fact that these discourses are often referred to generically as "speeches" reveals some of the problems that one has in interpreting them because Luke also puts on the lips of other characters in his narrative addresses or utterances of various sorts which would scarcely be samples of Christian preaching: thus the address of Gamaliel before the Sanhedrin (5:35–39); of the twelve before the assembled Jerusalem disciples (6:2–4); of the town clerk before the Ephesians (19:35–40); of Festus before King Agrippa (25:14b–21, 24–27)—to which category possibly should be assigned the address of James before the assembly in Jerusalem (15:13–21).

In the case of Peter and Paul one should distinguish their missionary sermons (their preaching proper) from other discourses, apologetic, valedictory, or explanatory. The latter may have, however, some implicit edifying thrust, but they have really been delivered for a different purpose. Hence Peter's missionary sermons would be limited to his preaching to the Jews assembled in Jerusalem on Pentecost (2:14b–36, 38–39), to that in the temple at the cure of the lame man (3:12b–26), to that at his appearance with John before the Sanhedrin (4:8–12, 19–20; 5:29–32), and to that in the house of Cornelius (10:34–43). Similarly, Paul's missionary sermons would be confined to that delivered in the synagogue of Pisidian Antioch (13:16b–41), to that before the Gentiles in Lystra (with Barnabas, 14:15–17), and to that before the Athenians on the Areopagus (17:22–31). Whereas Peter's sermons and the first of Paul's (in Pisidian Antioch) were directed to Jews, those of Paul delivered in Lystra and Athens were samples of apostolic preaching to pagans. Though Paul's discourse before King Agrippa (26:2–23, 25–27) begins as an apologia, it ends with something of a missionary thrust, at least implied. The same thrust may be detected in his speech on board ship (27:21–26), even though it is basically an exhortation of different sort; the same has to be said about his apologia in 28:17–20, 25–28. Lastly, Stephen's discourse is devoid of any kerygmatic or missionary thrust; with its summary of the history of Israel, it turns out to be an indictment of the Jews in Jerusalem. The mixed character of some of the last-mentioned discourses must be respected, but they at times do represent samples of early Christian oratory, if not of preaching proper.

A problem that one encounters in judging the samples of missionary sermons that Luke has incorporated into his narrative in Acts is to decide whether any of them can be regarded as samples of *apostolic* preaching or whether they represent rather *subapostolic* preaching. In the latter case, they would reflect the way preachers in Luke's own day (the penultimate decade of the first Christian century) were constructing their missionary discourses. Indeed, the variety of discourses that emerges in Acts may reflect precisely the kinds of problems that were confronting Christians of that period.

Years ago C.H. Dodd isolated in the early missionary speeches of Acts addressed to Jews elements that he regarded as traces of the Jerusalem kerygma.[14] These he compared with similar elements embedded in various Pauline passages. The Jerusalem kerygma for Dodd made use of the following elements:

(i) the age of fulfillment has dawned (Acts 2:16; 3:18, 24);

(ii) this has occurred in the ministry, death, and resurrection of Jesus, as the scriptures foretold (Acts 2:24–31; 3:13–15, 22);

(iii) by virtue of the resurrection Jesus has been exalted to God's right hand as Israel's messianic head (2:33–36; 3:13; 4:11);

(iv) in the church the Holy Spirit is the sign of Christ's present power and glory (2:33, 17–21; cf Jl 2:28–32);

(v) the messianic age will shortly reach its consummation in the return of Christ (3:21);

(vi) an appeal for repentance with the offer of forgiveness and of the Holy Spirit (2:38–39).

Dodd compared these elements of the Jerusalem kerygma in Acts with what he had called the Pauline kerygma; many of the elements were identical, but he noted that three items in the latter were not found in the Jerusalem kerygma. There (i) Jesus is not called "Son of God" (contrast Rom 1:4); (ii) Christ is not said to have died "for our sins"; forgiveness of sins is not specifically connected with his death (contrast 1 Cor 15:3; Rom 4:25); (iii) it is not asserted that the exalted Christ intercedes for us (contrast Rom 8:34). "For the rest all the points of the Pauline preaching reappear."[15] Thus some indication of genuine apostolic preaching would be recovered not only from Pauline writings, but even from the early missionary sermons of Acts.

However, a later study of the missionary sermons in Acts by U. Wilckens claimed instead that they reflect rather the preaching of Luke's own day—in effect, subapostolic preaching. Wilckens maintained that in their present context the missionary sermons of Acts have to be understood in function of the general theological conception that Luke has of salvation history. Whereas the sermons in chapters 14 (to Gentiles at Lystra, vv. 15–17) and 17 (to Athenians on the Areopagus, vv. 22–31) clearly depend on a traditional form of a missionary sermon addressed to pagans, the existence of such a form for the sermons addressed to Jews in chapters 2–13 cannot be shown. The content of these sermons and their structure as well cannot be dissociated from the peculiarly Lucan interpretation of salvation history. Indeed, the outline and thrust of these sermons addressed to Jews has been fashioned by Luke himself.[16]

Wilckens' thesis, however, did not go without some protest. J. Dupont subjected his book to a thorough analysis and raised many questions about it, pointing out weaknesses in it.[17] The issue is, nevertheless, still hotly debated and involved in many aspects of the interpretation of Acts.[18] It is complicated by the question of the sources of Acts: Can one sort them out or engage oneself in any sort of *Quellenkritik?* Dupont himself once contributed a thorough study of the alleged sources of Acts and showed how unsatisfactory the attempt was to distinguish them or sort them out from Lucan composition.[19] He has more recently restated his position: "*Source Criticism,* which seeks to identify and delimit the extent of the sources used by Luke, is scarcely held in esteem today. This method proved to be very disappointing, not because the text furnished no traces of the use of sources, but because the researcher who seeks to begin from it to trace a path perceives soon enough that it disappears in the sands. The situation stems above all from the mastery with which Luke has stamped with his personal mark all that he writes."[20] For such a reason one has to be careful in assessing the samples of Petrine or Pauline missionary preaching in Acts. Yet it is hardly likely that they are to be taken solely as reflections of subapostolic preaching.[21]

The Lucan narrative in Acts not only includes such samples of early Christian preaching, purporting to be of the apostolic period —missionary, apologetic, valedictory, or explanatory—but it also reports the preaching activity in generic terms. Thus Peter and John, having been released by the Sanhedrin, are reported as "teaching and preaching Jesus as the Messiah every day in the temple and at home" (5:42). Paul and Barnabas are similarly portrayed preaching in Antioch (15:35). No sample is given of the preaching of Philip (the evangelist, 6:5; 21:8), but Luke recounts that he was "preaching (ekēryssen) the Messiah" (8:5), "preaching (euangelizomenos) the kingdom of God and the name of Jesus Christ" (8:12), or "preaching (euēngelisato) Jesus" (8:35). This Philip was among the seven appointed by the twelve or the apostles (8:2, 6) to "serve tables," as was Stephen, so that the apostles could devote themselves to "prayer and the ministry of the word" (6:4). Yet the Lucan narrative immediately depicts these two of the seven "preaching the word" (8:4).[22] The discourse of Stephen, in which he indicts Jews in Jerusalem (7:2–53), forms part of a larger narrative in which Luke recounts how Stephen, one of the Jewish Christian seven, "full of grace and power" (6:8), was finally brought before the Sanhedrin and put to death for so preaching to various Jews of Jerusalem and of the diaspora (6:9–12; 7:54–59).[23]

Luke similarly reports the preaching activity of Paul—apart from the samples that he gives of his sermons. Thus toward the end of the narrative of Paul's conversion Luke records that in Damascus Paul "immediately engaged in preaching Jesus in the synagogues: 'He is the Son of God' " (9:20).[24] What is surprising is the way Luke depicts Paul saying in his valedictory discourse to the elders of Ephesus at Miletus that he has gone about among them "preaching the kingdom" (20:25); the same role is attributed to Paul elsewhere (19:8) and in the concluding verses of Acts: Paul lived at Rome for two years, "preaching the kingdom of God" (28:31; cf 28:23). Though Paul often uses kēryssein or euangelizesthai about his preaching activity, "the kingdom of God" is rarely found as the object of such verbs in the Pauline corpus.[25] The combination of "preaching" and "the kingdom" in such passages in Acts is the Lucan attempt to make the apostle also preach what Jesus preached.

A brief mention must be made of the succinct formula that Luke often uses in Acts to sum up apostolic preaching, "the word" (*ho logos*) or "the word of God/the Lord" (*ho logos tou theou/Kyriou*). Though Luke uses these phrases with many verbs,[26] he is not alone, since both Paul and John also employ them, though less frequently in this formulaic usage.[27] The frequency with which Luke uses them makes appropriate the accommodation of the phrase from John 1:1, with which we began.

The Lucan picture of apostolic preaching would not be complete unless reference were made to a characteristic feature of it that Luke has singled out in Acts, *parrhēsia*, the "frankness of conviction, fearlessness, boldness" with which the early preachers are portrayed carrying on their missionary activity. So Peter preaches on Pentecost to the Jews assembled in Jerusalem for the feast (2:29). With such fearlessness Peter and John appear before and address the Sanhedrin (4:13). The Jerusalem Christians pray that their preachers will "utter the word with all boldness" (4:29; cf. 4:31). So too Luke depicts Paul preaching in Damascus (9:27–28); and again at the end of Acts Paul in Rome preaches and teaches "unhindered with all boldness" (28:31).[28] Cf Acts 13:46; 14:3; 18:26; 19:8; 26:26.

Lastly, the apostolic preaching depicted in Acts has to be related to the great commission of the risen Christ. At the end of the Matthean gospel (28:19–20) that commission is formulated in terms of "making disciples" (*mathēteusate*), "baptizing" (*baptizontes*), and "teaching" (*didaskontes*). In the canonical appendix to the Marcan gospel (16:9–20) the risen Christ appears to the eleven and charges them "to preach the gospel to all of creation" (*kēryxate to euangelion pasē tē ktisei*, 16:15). But in the Lucan gospel Christ appears to the eleven and their companions gathered together (24:33, 47–48) and bids them "to preach in his name repentance for the forgiveness of sins to all the nations—beginning from Jerusalem; you are witnesses of this!" In the Lucan form of the great commission the task of preaching is clearly linked to bearing witness. When one turns from the final chapter of the Lucan gospel to the opening of Acts, one sees the risen Christ charging the *apostles* there: "You shall be my witnesses in Jerusalem, in all Judea and Samaria, and to the end of the earth" (Acts 1:8).[29] In this programmatic verse of Acts the risen Christ thus imposes on his apostles the task of testimony, a task that they "fearlessly" carry out (4:33; 14:3; 23:11).[30] The next to last scene in the Lucan gospel thus makes eyewitnesses of Jesus' own preaching, death, and resurrection into ministers of the word. But, as R.J. Dillon has pointed out, they are eyewitnesses not merely as "uniquely qualified vouchers for the historical *facta salutis*," but rather as those instructed by the risen Lord's revealing *word*. This has made them who were eyewitnesses of "uncomprehended facts" into potential "ministers of the word, for without his word they remained only the "foolish and slow of wit to believe" (Lk 24:25), "the startled and the frightened . . ." (who) "supposed that they were seeing a ghost" (24:37). The eleven and their companions, Cleopas and his companion, may have been witnesses, but now, instructed by the risen Christ, they have become "the ministers of the word" (Lk 1:2), the propagators of apostolic faith.[31]

Why the shift from proclaiming to witnessing in this subapostolic view of preaching? Undoubtedly the missionary task had taken on different shapes with the passage of time. Initially the kerygmatic process was proclamatory, like the activity of a "herald" (*kēryx*)—with an urgency born of an expectation of Christ's imminent parousia. With the passing of those who had *seen*, the proclamation came to be joined with testimony to what had been at the beginning. Thus the process of preaching took on more of the character of bearing witness. What one thus detects in the Lucan association of testimony with preaching is further found in the Johannine emphasis on *martyria*, "bearing witness."

CONCLUSION

The above observations have revealed, I hope, some idea of what preaching was meant to be in the apostolic and subapostolic age of the Christian church. I have reserved for this concluding paragraph a Pauline statement about that activity that may sum it all up: "Since in [the time of] God's wisdom the world came not to know God through wisdom, it pleased God to save those who believe by the foolishness of preaching" (*dia tēs mōrias tou kērygmatos*, 1 Cor 1:23). As in Romans 1:19–21 Paul castigated the pagans for not coming to know God properly "from the things that had been made," so in 1 Corinthians 1:21 he affirmed that they came not to know God. So God made use of what was folly in their sight—preaching—to bring some of them to a knowledge of him and to faith and salvation.

NOTES

1. See further my commentary, *The Gospel according to Luke* (AB 28, 28A; Garden City, NY: Doubleday, 1981, 1985) 294.
2. *The Churches the Apostles Left Behind* (New York/Ramsey, NJ: Paulist, 1984) 13–30, esp. p. 15.
3. The New Testament uses a variety of terms to express the communication of the Christian message of salvation: e.g. various forms of *angellein*, "announce, declare," *gnōrizein*, "make known," *paradidonai*, "pass on" (a tradition), *didaskein*, "teach," *lalein*, "utter, speak," and *parakalein*, "exhort." Such forms of communication may come close to what is often called preaching today. For further discussion of such terms, see C. Brown, "Proclamation, Preach, Kerygma," *The New International Dictionary of New Testament Theology* (3 vols.; Grand Rapids, MI: Zondervan, 1975, 1976, 1978) 3. 44–68. Cf. H.G. Wood, "Didache, Kerygma and Evangelion," *New Testament Essays: Studies in Memory of Thomas Walter Manson* (ed. A.J.B. Higgins; Manchester: Manchester University, 1959) 306–14. C. Burchard, "Formen der Vermittlung christlichen Glaubens im Neuen Testament: Beobachtungen anhand von *kērygma, martyria* und verwandten Wörtern," *EvT* 38 (1978) 313–40. J.I.H. McDonald, *Kerygma and Didache: The Articulation and Structure of the Earliest Christian Message* (SNTSMS 37; London: Cambridge University, 1980). On *kēryssein* itself, see O. Merk, "*Kēryssō* . . . verkünden," *EWNT* 2. 711–20.
4. G. Friedrich (*TDNT* 2. 717) maintains that *euangelizesthai* does not fit the realized eschatology of the [fourth] gospel, which rather reflects "the calm of fulfilment." Perhaps one should also recall in this regard the levels of composition that have controlled the final redaction of this writing, such as have been laid out in R.E. Brown's *The Community of the Beloved Disciple* (New York/Ramsey, NJ: Paulist, 1979). I shall return to the question of *martyrein* below, because it is involved in the Lucan view of preaching.
5. Mark depicts Jesus continuing, "Repent and believe in the gospel" (1:15c; cf 1:14). In the Marcan gospel Jesus preaches "the gospel" (8:35; 10:29; 13:10; 14:9; [16:15]; cf 1:1), and in this he is followed by the Matthean Jesus (4:23; 9:35; 24:14; 26:13). Yet strikingly enough, *euangelion* never appears on the lips of the Lucan or the Johannine Jesus. Though Luke uses of him the cognate verb *euangelizesthai*, it carries its etymological meaning, "preach, announce good news," only in Luke 4:18, where Isaiah 61:1 is being quoted, and probably in 7:22, where allusion is made to the same Isaian passage. Otherwise, it means in the Lucan writings simply "preach, announce" (Lk 1:19; 2:10; 3:18; 4:43; 8:1; 9:6; 16:16; 20:1), often with diverse direct objects (e.g. Acts 5:42, *ton Christon Iēsoun*).
6. *The Theology of the New Testament* (2 vols.; London: SCM, 1952, 1955) 1. 3.

See further B. Reicke, "A Synopsis of Early Christian Preaching," *The Root of the Vine: Essays in Biblical Theology* (ed. A. Fridrichsen et al.; Westminster: Dacre, 1953) 128–60. C.F. Evans, "The Kerygma," *JTS* ns 7 (1956) 25–41. W. Baird, "What Is the Kerygma? A Study of 1 Cor 15, 3–8 and Gal 1, 11–17," *JBL* 76 (1957) 181–91. Cf K. Goldammer, "Der Kerygma-Begriff in der ältesten christlichen Literatur," *ZNW* 48 (1957) 77–101. D. Grasso, "Il kerigma e la predicazione," *Greg* 41 (1960) 424–50. G. Delling, *Wort Gottes und Verkündigung im Neuen Testament* (SBS 53; Stuttgart: Katholisches Bibelwerk, 1971).

7. *Theology,* 1. 33 (Bultmann's italics).

8. See further A. Oepke, *Die Missionspredigt des Apostels Paulus: Eine biblisch-theologische und religionsgeschichtliche Untersuchung* (Leipzig: Hinrichs, 1920). F.W. Grosheide, "The Pauline Epistles as Kerygma," *Studia paulina in honorem Johannis de Zwaan septuagenarii* (ed. J.N. Sevenster and W.C. van Unnik; Haarlem: Bohn, 1953) 139–45. J. Murphy-O'Connor, *Paul on Preaching* (New York: Sheed and Ward, 1963). J. Roloff, *Apostolat—Verkündigung—Kirche: Ursprung, Inhalt und Funktion des kirchlichen Apostelamtes nach Paulus, Lukas und den Pastoralbriefen* (Gütersloh: Mohn, 1965). W. Barclay, "A Comparison of Paul's Missionary Preaching and Preaching to the Church," *Apostolic History and the Gospel: Biblical and Historical Essays Presented to F.F. Bruce on His 60th Birthday* (ed. W.W. Gasque and R.P. Martin; Grand Rapids, MI: Eerdmans, 1970) 165–75. D.J. Harrington, "New Testament Perspectives on the Ministry of the Word," *Chicago Studies* 13 (1974) 65–76.

9. See further C.K. Barrett, *The Signs of an Apostle* (London: Epworth, 1970; Philadelphia: Fortress, 1972) 34–54.

10. "The Gospel in the Theology of Paul," *To Advance the Gospel: New Testament Studies* (New York: Crossroad, 1981) 149–61.

11. *Tradition and Interpretation in the New Testament: Essays in Honor of E. Earle Ellis for His 60th Birthday* (ed. G.F. Hawthorne with O. Betz; Grand Rapids, MI: Eerdmans, 1987) 3–15.

12. *Hypakoē pisteōs* is often translated as "the obedience of faith" (thus *RSV*, *NAB*, Rom 1:5; 16:26). But "obedience" often carries a pejorative connotation today. Greek *hypakoē* is literally "a hearing under," i.e. a listening with submission; it implies rather a personal dedication—what is called in French "engagement."

13. This passage (Rom 10:14b–15) seems to be at the basis of the venerable tradition in the Christian church of ordained ministers of the gospel (deacons, priests, and bishops). It probably also lies behind Paul's own conviction that he had been sent "not to baptize, but to preach the gospel" (1 Cor 1:17 [discussed above]). What bearing Romans 10:14b–15 has on the question of preaching within monastic communities or that by lay persons I leave to systematic colleagues to discuss.

14. *The Apostolic Preaching and Its Developments* (London: Hodder and Stoughton, 1936; reprinted, New York: Harper & Row, 1964) 17–24.

For other attempts to isolate elements of the kerygma in various parts of the New Testament, see A. Oepke, *Die Missionspredigt* (n. 8 above); J. Gewiess, *Die urapostolische Heilsverkündigung nach der Apostelgeschichte* (Breslauer Studien zur historischen Theologie ns 5; Breslau: Müller & Seiffert, 1939).

15. *Apostolic Preaching*, 26.

16. *Die Missionsreden der Apostelgeschichte: Form- und traditionsgeschichtliche Untersuchungen* (WMANT 5; Neukirchen: Neukirchener V., 1961) 100. A third edition, published in 1974, adds further bibliography on the subject and comments on many reviews of the original edition.

17. "Les discours missionnaires des Actes des Apôtres: D'après un ouvrage récent," *RB* 69 (1962) 37–60; reprinted in his *Etudes sur les Actes des Apôtres* (LD 45; Paris: Cerf, 1967) 133–55.

18. See, e.g., F. Bovon, "Tradition and rédaction en Actes 10,1–11,18," *TZ* 26 (1970) 22–45. D.L. Jones, *The Christology of the Missionary Speeches in the Acts of the Apostles* (Ann Arbor, MI; University Microfilms, 1967). L.M. Mundy, *Tradition and Composition in the Speeches of the Early Chapters of Acts* (Ann Arbor, MI: University Microfilms, 1979).

19. *The Sources of Acts: The Present Position* (London: Darton, Longman & Todd, 1964).

20. *Nouvelles études sur les Actes des Apôtres* (LD 118; Paris: Cerf, 1984) 89–90.

21. See further J. Dupont, "Les discours de Pierre," ibid., 58–111. Cf. H.N. Ridderbos, *The Speeches of Peter in the Acts of the Apostles* (London: Tyndale, 1962; reprinted, Leicester: Theological Students Fellowship, 1977).

One example of the problems may be cited. See Acts 10:36–37, where Peter is about to give a summary of Jesus' earthly ministry. Verse 36 begins with an accusative, *ton logon, hon apesteilen tois huiois Israel,* "the word he sent to the children of Israel"; then after a few more words, v. 37 begins repetitiously, *hymeis oidate to genomenon rhēma kath' holēs tēs Ioudaias,* "you know the word proclaimed throughout all Judea." The shift from *ton logon* to *to rhēma,* as well as the introductory accusative (dependent on what?), almost cries out for a source-critical explanation. Something pre-Lucan is being used here, and Lucan redaction has not eliminated the obvious suture.

22. The phrase *euangelizomenoi ton logon* is used in 8:4 of all those who were scattered from Jerusalem at the time of the "great persecution against the church" (8:1). Since "the apostles" were not among those so scattered, the phrase has to be understood to include at least some of the seven, and the ministry of Philip is immediately recounted as an example of such itinerant preachers.

23. See further Acts 11:20.

24. I take *ekēryssen* in 9:20 to be an iterative imperfect; see BDF § 325. Cf Acts 19:13 (iterative present, BDF § 318.3).

25. The phrase "kingdom of God" does occur on occasion in the Pauline corpus, but when it does appear, it usually forms part of ethical exhortations that sound like Paul quoting from contemporary catechetical instructions. See Gal 5:21; 1 Cor 6:9–10; 15:50; cf Rom 14:17; [Eph 5:5]. In a few places it may appear as part of his own preaching (1 Thess 2:12; 1 Cor 4:20; [cf. Col 1:13; 4:11]).

26. Thus *lalein,* "utter, speak" (4:29, 31; 8:25; 11:19; 13:46; 14:25; 16:6, 32), *euangelizesthai,* "preach" (8:4; 15:35), *katangellein,* "announce" (13:5; 15:36; 17:13), *didaskein,* "teach" (18:11), *apostellein,* "send" (10:36), *diakonein,* "serve" (6:2,4), *dechesthai,* "receive" (8:14; 11:1; 17:11), *akouein,* "hear" (4:4; 10:44; 11:22; 13:7, 44; 15:7; 19:10), etc.

27. See further H. Ritt, "*Logos* . . . Wort, Rede, Rechenschaft, Predigt, Logos," *EWNT* 2. 880–87.

28. See further S.B. Marrow, *Speaking the Word Fearlessly: Boldness in the New Testament* (New York/Ramsey, NJ: Paulist, 1982). Cf. W.C. van Unnik, "The Christian's Freedom of Speech in the New Testament," *BJRL* 44 (1961–62) 466–88.

29. "The end of the earth" is probably to be understood as Rome, as it is used in *Ps. Sol.* 8:15, where God brings from "the end of the earth the one who strikes ruthlessly," i.e. Pompey coming from Rome to smite Jerusalem in 63 B.C.

30. See further E. Nellessen, *Zeugnis für Jesus und das Wort: Exegetische Untersuchungen zum lukanischen Zeugnisbegriff* (BBB 43; Bonn: Hanstein, 1976).

31. *From Eye-Witnesses to Ministers of the Word: Tradition and Composition in Luke 24* (AnBib 82; Rome: Biblical Institute, 1978) 291–96.

3

ORIGEN AS HOMILIST
by Joseph T. Lienhard, S.J.

It is a joy to dedicate this essay to Father Walter J. Burghardt, S.J., so well known as a patrologist, a preacher, and a theologian. I knew him first as teacher at Woodstock College in Maryland, more than twenty years ago; then as preacher; then as editor; and always as friend. I hope one can honor a contemporary homilist by reflections on an ancient one—the third century father of the church, Origen.

Origen is generally admired as the first Christian biblical scholar and one of the most significant Christian theologians of all time. He also merits attention as a homilist. Almost two hundred of his homilies survive, and together give us a clear and fascinating picture of biblical preaching in the third century.[1]

THE BEGINNINGS OF THE HOMILY

In Christian usage a homily is a discourse given on a biblical text for a congregation as part of a service of worship. The Greek word *homilia* could mean "instruction" or "lecture," and designated the instruction that a philosopher gave his pupils in familiar conversation. Its distinctive characteristic was its apparent artlessness, which marked the homily off from the studied and stylized speech.

The Christian homily is distinguished by its relation to a sacred text. Christians believed, just as Jews did, that the Bible was God's inspired word and, as such, should speak to each believer. The homilist's task was to explain a passage that had just been read and show how it could teach and profit each of the faithful. In other words the

36

homily had three characteristics: as liturgical, it belonged to the order of Christian worship; as exegetical, it explained a text from the Bible, God's living word for his people; as prophetic, it demonstrated the significance of the text for the hearers.

Following the practices of Jewish worship, the homily was probably part of the Christian liturgy from its earliest days. Luke 4:16–21 describes Jesus preaching in the synagogue at Nazareth on a passage from Isaiah. The New Testament probably contains fragments of more than a few early homilies, for example some of the explanations of Jesus' parables. The eucharistic liturgy of the second century, as Justin Martyr described it, began with a reading taken from the Old Testament or the gospels and then continued with a homily: "When the reader has finished," Justin writes, "the president in a discourse urges and invites us to the imitation of these noble things."[2]

The oldest extant Christian homily is *2 Clement,* once wrongly named the *Second Epistle of Clement.* It is a straightforward exhortation to repentance, wholehearted service of God, and hope in the resurrection. The next oldest homily is Melito of Sardis' paschal homily, a complex, florid poetic sermon on Exodus 12. Clement of Alexandria composed a formal discourse entitled *Who Is the Rich Man Who Is Saved?* on Mark 10:17–31. All three date from the second century. Hippolytus of Rome's homily *On the Antichrist* dates from the early third century. Apart from these works, only fragments and scraps of Christian preaching survive from the time before Origen.

ORIGEN'S LIFE

Origen is the most important theologian of the Church before Nicaea, and one of the most influential Christian writers of all time. Unlike Justin Martyr, Origen did not come to Christianity after a long search through the philosophical schools; he was born into a Christian family. Unlike Irenaeus of Lyons, Origen did not devote his main energies to refuting error. Unlike Clement of Alexandria—who may have been his teacher—Origen saw no point in trying to make Christianity more palatable to the sophisticated and the curious. Origen was, heart and soul, a man of the Bible, a man who devoted his life to explaining God's word. His mind was acute, his memory tenacious, his curiosity inexhaustible, and his patience unbreakable. He was a man who was most content when he could study, analyze, and comment on a written text. Significantly, all but one or two of his works are, in one form or another, commentaries on texts. Origen even helped shape the Bible: five or six of the shorter books of the New Testament are in the canon, finally, because fourth century writers appealed to Origen's authority. In and from his study of the Bible Origen developed a theological system, perhaps the first in the history of Christianity. His system was intellectually rigorous, but it did not stop there. It had a practical goal, for it was a system of mysticism, a system that would lead the believer to union with God.

Theologians after Origen might criticize him, but they could not ignore him. Almost three centuries after Origen's death the fifth ecumenical council, the Second Council of Constantinople, condemned Origen as a heretic. G.L. Prestige has written touchingly: "Origen is the greatest of that happily small company of saints who, having lived and died in grace, suffered sentence of expulsion from the Church on earth after they had already entered into the joy of their Lord."[3] But wariness of Origen, and outright rejection of him as a man who merely adorned Platonic philosophy with a few Christian terms, continued well into the twentieth century, until scholars like Walther Völker, Jean Daniélou, Henri de Lubac, Antoine Guillaumont, Henri Crouzel, and others took a fresh look at Origen and convinced much of the scholarly world to revise its picture of this great scholar and theologian.[4]

Origen was born in 185 or 186 in Alexandria in Egypt.[5] Alexandria was a cosmopolitan city and, at the time, the center of Greek learning. Its library, founded by Alexander the Great, attracted scholars from the whole Mediterranean world. Origen's education was twofold, both Hellenistic and biblical. From Hellenistic rhetoric he learned the careful analysis of texts. The student of rhetoric in the ancient world learned by analyzing a text word by word, discussing each word until every possible allusion and every conceivable relationship was wrung out of it. This sort of education goes far in explaining Origen's approach to the Bible, which differs so markedly from modern exegesis. For modern readers, the unit of understanding is the sentence or the idea. For Origen, the unit of understanding was the word. Again and again, in his homilies and commentaries, Origen puzzles for page after page over the meaning of a single word, a practice he learned as a young boy when he was taught Homer.

When Origen was seventeen his father Leonides was martyred for the faith, and the young Origen became a teacher to support his mother and his six younger brothers and sisters. At the same time, he began to teach catechism—that is, to instruct pagans interested in

Christianity. A few years later, probably when his brothers were able to support the family, Origen gave up teaching secular subjects and devoted himself—for the rest of his life, as it turned out—to studying and teaching the scriptures. He also began to live an intensely ascetical life, and Eusebius gives a moving account of Origen's ascetical regimen.[6]

Origen's career as a writer would have been difficult if he had had to depend on his small income. But when he was still young, he converted a wealthy man named Ambrose from Valentinian gnosticism to orthodox Christianity. Ambrose became Origen's literary patron, and virtually supplied Origen with his own publishing house. Eusebius writes:

> Ambrose . . . not only exerted verbal pressure and every kind of persuasion, but supplied him in abundance with everything needful. Shorthand-writers more than seven in number were available when he dictated, relieving each other regularly, and at least as many copyists, as well as girls trained in penmanship, all of them provided most generously with everything needful at Ambrose's expense. And not only that: in the devoted study of the divine teaching he brought to Origen his own immeasurable enthusiasm.[7]

Origen lived at Alexandria until 233. On a journey he made in 232, he was ordained a priest in Caesarea in Palestine by Theoctistus, the bishop there. It may have been this ordination, done without the consent of Demetrius, the bishop of Alexandria, that turned Demetrius against Origen and caused Origen to leave Alexandria for Caesarea. He took his library and his assistants with him, and spent the last twenty years of his life in Caesarea, greatly respected and free from rancorous controversy. He died in 254 or 255; his death was probably hastened by the torture he suffered in the persecution of the emperor Decius, the first of the three general persecutions of the church.

THE HOMILIES

Origen's extant works on scripture are in two distinct literary forms: commentaries and homilies, and the difference between the two is significant. The commentaries are the product of a library or a study, where a learned author wrote for learned readers, and their form set no extraneous limit to the number of pages Origen might spend on an intriguing point. The homilies, in contrast, were naturally limited in length by the structure of the liturgy and the congregation's span of attention, and in scope by the hearers' ability to comprehend and use what the preacher said.

Date

Most of Origen's homilies on the Old Testament were delivered at Caesarea. In a passage that is often discussed, Eusebius wrote:

> At this period of rapid expansion of the Faith [that is, under the emperor Philip, 244–249], when our message was being boldly proclaimed on every side, it was natural that Origen, now over sixty and with his abilities fully developed by years of practice, should, as we are told, have allowed his lectures to be taken down by short-hand-writers, though he had never before agreed to this.[8]

Henri Crouzel accepts Eusebius' testimony and dates most of Origen's homilies after 245, except for the homilies on the gospel of Luke, which he dates at the beginning of Origen's residence in Caesarea.[9]

Pierre Nautin, in his impressive book on Origen, rejects Eusebius' notice that Origen was sixty before he allowed his homilies to be recorded, considering it a hagiographical gloss meant to glorify Origen's virtue.[10] Nautin has a different chronology: he believes that the homilies on the Old Testament were preached in a cycle of three years, probably from 239 to 242, and that the homilies on Luke were preached at the same time.[11]

Liturgical Setting

Far more significant than the dates, however, is the liturgical setting of the homilies. Nautin is particularly helpful on this topic, and I follow him here.[12]

In Origen's time, Christian communities had three types of liturgical assemblies. The first, and oldest, was the synaxis or assembly on Sunday, at which the eucharist was celebrated. This assembly undoubtedly took place in the morning. Then, on Wednesdays and Fridays, there was an assembly in the afternoon, perhaps about three o'clock, which ended the fast customary on those two days. This assembly also included the celebration of the eucharist. And finally, on every day but Sunday there was an assembly early in the morning, which was not eucharistic.

The eucharistic assembly on Sunday had three readings: one from the Old Testament, one from the apostolic writings, and one from the gospels. Because Origen's homilies on Luke are so much shorter than his homilies on the Old Testament, Nautin concludes that on Sunday a short homily was given after each of the three readings, perhaps by different preachers.

Nautin believes that the gospels were also read at the two other weekly eucharistic assemblies. If the gospels were read three times a week at the rate of about eight verses to each reading (Origen's homilies on Luke treat six to ten verses each), then the four gospels could be read in full in the course of three years.

The synaxis on weekday mornings had only one reading. It was always from the Old Testament, since not only the baptized but also the catechumens attended, and the catechumens had not yet been introduced to the New Testament. A homily followed to explain the reading, and prayers concluded the service. This assembly probably lasted about an hour. The reading would be long, equivalent to two or even three chapters in our Bibles. And the reading was continuous —that is, a book was read from beginning to end, even if the preacher did not comment on the whole of the reading. At the rate of two or three chapters a day, the reading of the Old Testament would last about three years; and this, according to Hippolytus' *Apostolic Tradition*, was the duration of the catechumenate in the third century. If Nautin is correct, then both the Old Testament and the gospels were read in one three-year cycle.

Extant and Lost Homilies

Most of Origen's homilies that are extant survive only in Latin translation. The full list is this: sixteen on Genesis, thirteen on Exodus, sixteen on Leviticus, twenty-eight on Numbers, twenty-six on Joshua, nine on Judges, all in Rufinus' Latin; one in Latin on 1 Samuel 1–2, and one in Greek on 1 Samuel 28, the passage on the witch of Endor; nine on Psalms 36, 37, and 38 in Rufinus' Latin; two on the Song of Songs in Jerome's Latin; nine on Isaiah in Jerome's Latin; twenty in Greek and fourteen in Jerome's Latin on Jeremiah (twelve of the Latin homilies are translations of the extant Greek texts); fourteen on Ezekiel in Jerome's Latin; and, finally, the only homilies on the New Testament, thirty-nine on Luke in Jerome's Latin.[13]

St. Jerome, in his letter 33 addressed to Paula, listed the works of

Origen that he knew and included homilies on Deuteronomy, Job, Proverbs, Ecclesiastes, Matthew, Acts, 2 Corinthians, Thessalonians, Galatians, Titus, and Hebrews, besides homilies on Easter, peace, fasting, and monogamy; all are lost.

There is no suggestion anywhere that Origen ever preached on the historical books after 1 Samuel; and he preached on 1 Samuel in Jerusalem, not in Caesarea. Nautin suggests that Origen may have broken off his course of homilies at Caesarea before he finished the three-year cycle because of objections to his allegorical exegesis, his doctrines, or his use of translations other than the Septuagint; all these complaints can be documented from his writings.[14]

The Preacher

Origen's homilies give us a good picture of a third century preacher.

Origen has no specific word for "preacher"; he calls him simply *didaskalos,* or "teacher"; that is, the preacher was one sort of educator.[15] When Origen preached, he stood before the congregation and had the book of the scripture open before him; it was a corrected version of the Septuagint.[16]

By the third century, the office of preaching was generally, but not exclusively, restricted to presbyters and bishops. Eusebius quotes a letter in which bishops Alexander of Jerusalem and Theoctistus of Caesarea defend themselves against Demetrius of Alexandria's charge that they were wrong to allow Origen, then a layman, to preach. Alexander and Theoctistus answer that it is not unheard of for laymen to preach; but their answer shows that it was, nevertheless, an exception.[17] Origen did not preach regularly until he had been ordained a presbyter.

When Origen was preaching in his own city, Caesarea, the bishop was not present. But when he spoke on 1 Samuel as a guest preacher in Jerusalem, the bishop attended. In his homily on 1 Samuel 1-2, Origen paid the bishop a compliment: "Do not expect to find in us what you have in Pope Alexander, for we acknowledge that he surpasses us all in gracious gentleness. And I am not the only one to commend this graciousness; all of you, who have enjoyed it, know and appreciate it."[18]

Origen readily admitted that learning alone did not make a good preacher. Again and again he asks his congregation to pray for him, and especially for his enlightenment, that he might understand the scriptures and explain them correctly. In one homily he says to his hearers: "If the Lord should see fit to illuminate us by your prayers, we will attempt to make known a few things which pertain to the edification of the Church."[19] In another passage, he urges the congregation to pray for insight during each reading of the scriptures:

> We should pray the Father of the Word during each individual reading "when Moses is read," that he might fulfill even in us that which is written in the Psalms: "Open my eyes and I will consider the wondrous things of your Law (Ps 118:18)." For unless he himself opens our eyes, how shall we be able to see these great mysteries which are fashioned in the patriarchs, which are pictured now in terms of wells, now in marriages, now in births, now even in barrenness?[20]

Elsewhere he says: "Lord Jesus, come again; explain these words to me and to those who have come to seek spiritual food."[21]

The Congregation

Origen's congregation included catechumens, simple believers, and others who were more educated or spiritually advanced. Origen writes:

> To "dismember the calf" (Lev 1:6) means to examine the reasons for each of the degrees [of union with Christ] and to apply them: some are for the beginners, others for those who are already making progress in the faith of Christ, and still others for those who are already perfect in their knowledge and love of him.[22]

But a distinction must be made: Origen did not preach catechetical homilies as such, like those that Cyril of Jerusalem delivered during Lent in the fourth century to those preparing for baptism. In Origen's time, apparently, candidates for baptism were expected to attend a morning service six times a week for three years, and in the course of that service to hear an explanation of the whole Old Testament—certainly a rigorous initiation.

Although all the faithful and the catechumens were expected to attend the morning assembly each day, many were apparently lax in their attendance, and others were inattentive or even left after the reading of the scripture. In a petulant mood, Origen once complained about those who did not come to the synaxis:

Does it not cause [the Church] sadness and sorrow when you do not gather to hear the word of God? And scarcely on feast days do you proceed to the Church, and you do this not so much from a desire for the word as from a fondness for the festival and to obtain, in a certain manner, common relaxation.[23]

Tell me, you who come to church only on festal days, are the other days not festal days? . . . Christians eat the flesh of the lamb every day, that is, they consume daily the flesh of the word.[24]

In another homily, he complains that some do not stay for the homily:

Some of you leave immediately as soon as you have heard the texts which are selected read. . . . Some do not even patiently wait while the texts are being read in church. Others do not even know if they are read, but are occupied with mundane stories in the furthest corners of the Lord's house.[25]

Origen's annoyance grew as his congregation became even more impatient with his explanations of details from the book of Exodus:

But what would it profit should [other things] be discussed by our vast toil indeed, but be despised by hearers who are preoccupied and can scarcely stand in the presence of the word of God a fraction of an hour, and come to nothing? . . . There are some who understand in heart what is read; there are others who do not at all understand what is said, but their mind and heart are on business dealings or on acts of the world or on counting their profit. And especially, how do you think women understand in heart, who chatter so much, who disturb with their stories so much that they do not allow any silence? Now what shall I say about their mind, what shall I say about their heart, if they are thinking about their infants or wool or the needs of their household?[26]

In other places, Origen suggests that it was not only lack of attention that annoyed him. Some members of the congregation objected to his method of interpreting the scriptures, in particular to his discovery of a spiritual sense there; biblical literalism is not only a modern temptation. In one homily Origen said:

If I shall wish to dig deeply and open the hidden veins "of living water," immediately the Philistines will be present and will strive with me. They will stir up disputes and malicious charges against me and will begin to refill my wells with their earth and mud.[27]

Origen is even clearer on the topic of his opponents as he sets out on one of his most challenging and difficult tasks, preaching on the book of Leviticus:

> For if, according to some people, who are even among our own, I should follow the plain sense [of Scripture] and understand the voice of the lawgiver without any verbal trick or clouded allegory— thus they usually ridicule us—then I, a man of the Church who live under faith in Christ and stand in the midst of the Church, am compelled by the authority of God's law to sacrifice calves and lambs and to offer flour, along with incense and oil. For they who force us to spend our time on the narrative and to keep the letter of the law do this. But it is time for us to use the words of the blessed Susanna against the unprincipled presbyters, words that they themselves indeed repudiate when they lop the story of Susanna off from the catalogue of inspired books. But we accept this story [as Scripture] and conveniently bring its words against them and say: "Straits are round about me." For if I agree with you and follow the letter of the law, "death is my lot"; if I do not agree, "I shall not escape your hands. But it is better for me to fall into your hands without any act than to sin in the sight of the Lord" (Dan 13:22–23).[28]

There can be little doubt that by "presbyters" Origen meant not only the two elders who accused Susanna in the biblical story but also some presbyters of the church of Caesarea who were jealous of him and criticized his explanations of the Bible.

Origen's Preaching and Exegesis

Origen's homilies were preached spontaneously, not prepared in writing. Their subject matter, always the scriptures, was dictated by the serial reading of the books of the Bible. They were utterly lacking in rhetorical polish, and showed the simplicity that led the church to choose to call discourses on the scriptures *homiliai*. After the reading, and with little or no introduction, Origen would begin to explain the scripture, verse by verse. He dealt first with the literal sense, then with any spiritual senses he discovered. He always tried to find a way for his hearers to apply the passage to their lives. He ended his homilies, sometimes quite abruptly, with a doxology.[29]

The most spectacular example of Origen's spontaneity is in the homily on the witch of Endor. On the day Origen preached this homily—in Jerusalem, before bishop Alexander—chapters 25 to 28 of 1 Samuel were read. Origen began by saying that the reading contained four pericopes or narratives, and that it would take several hours to explain the whole passage. He then turned to the bishop and asked him which passage he would like to hear explained. The bishop answered: the one about the witch. And Origen explained it.[30]

Another incident is equally interesting. While Origen was preaching on the story of Hannah in 1 Samuel 2, a member of the congregation suffered an attack of epilepsy or the like and began to shout out. Others rushed to aid the person. Origen, who was commenting on Hannah's words "My heart rejoiced in the Lord" (1 Sam 2:1), worked the incident into his homily, explaining it as the work of an unclean spirit that could not bear the congregation's rejoicing in the Lord and tried to change their joy into sorrow.[31]

When Origen begins to consider a text, he first looks carefully at its literal meaning. It is too often forgotten that spiritual exegesis, Origen's and others', is based on an utterly literal reading of the text. In Henri Crouzel's felicitous expression, the literal sense is for Origen "the brute materiality of the word,"[32] or the text read without assuming any literary figures or figurative language. Hence to speak of a "literal interpretation" would be, in Origen's mind, a contradiction in terms.

The continuous reading of the scriptures, without omissions, demanded courage—or, better, confidence in the power of God's word. Anyone who reads Origen's homilies on Leviticus, for example, may not find all of them inspiring or even credible, but one has to ask how many Christian preachers since Origen have offered a course of sermons on this difficult book. Origen's convictions gave him courage, and inspired him: the Holy Spirit was speaking in every word of scripture, and the Holy Spirit could never be trite or irrelevant. Origen was convinced that the Holy Spirit was the author of the scriptures, and that the Holy Spirit could never compose carelessly or awkwardly; every word had to have a profound meaning—or, rather, a meaning that would profit the reader and the hearer. Genesis 18:8, for example, must mean more than it appears to say, namely, that Abraham stood under a tree:

> We ought not to believe that it was of greatest concern to the Holy Spirit to write in the books of the Law where Abraham was standing. For what does it help me who have come to hear what the Holy Spirit teaches the human race, if I hear that "Abraham was standing under a tree"?[33]

Or an odd expression at Genesis 12:10 cannot be a mere slip of the pen:

And certainly if, as some think, the text of the divine Scripture was composed carelessly and awkwardly, it could have been said that Abraham went down to Egypt to dwell there because the famine prevailed over him.[34]

No detail is glossed over; no word is neglected. For example, when he is preaching on Leviticus 8:7–9, Origen notices that this passage mentions seven insignia of the high priest, whereas Exodus 28:4 mentions eight. "Will we concede forgetfulness in the words of the Holy Spirit," he writes, "so that, when he narrated everything else for the second time, one kind that was previously mentioned escaped his notice?"[35] The Holy Spirit, of course, could not have been forgetful; so the omission must have an intended meaning. Or, to cite only one other example, Origen's speculations in the second homily on Genesis on the construction of Noah's ark are a fascinating witness to his concern with the letter of scripture.

But Origen's real interest is the spiritual interpretation of scripture. "The priest," Origen said explaining Leviticus 1:6 (which mentions skinning the carcass of a sacrificial animal), "is the one who removes the veil of the letter from God's word and bares the members within, which are the elements of a spiritual understanding."[36]

If someone knows only one passage from Origen's writings, it is probably *On First Principles* 4.2.4, where Origen says that "Just as man consists of body, soul, and spirit, so in the same way does the Scripture."[37] The flesh of the scripture, he writes, is "the obvious interpretation." The soul of the scripture may edify "the man who has made some progress"—not, one notices, a definition. The spirit is for "the man who is perfect." Scripture may have three senses, but their perception is conditioned by the reader's spiritual progress. In practice Origen prefers other terms for the senses of scripture—for example, historical, mystical, and allegorical; literal, mystical, and moral; the letter, the spirit, and the moral point.[38] More often, though, Origen writes of only two senses of scripture, and calls them the letter and the spirit, the literal meaning and the spiritual meaning, the flesh and the spirit, or the carnal meaning and the spiritual meaning.

Origen's consistent principle of interpretation was: explain the Bible by the Bible—that is, obscure or difficult passages should be explained by other passages, from anywhere else in the Bible, in which the same word or phrase or idea or situation occurs.[39] In his *Commentary on the Psalms* Origen related an intriguing comparison that he heard from his Hebrew master: the scripture is like one great house that has many, many rooms. All the rooms are locked. At each locked door there is a key, but not the key to that door. The scholar's task is to match the keys to their doors; and this is a great labor.[40]

The accusation most often made against Origen's exegesis—and for these purposes it is usually called "allegorical exegesis"—is that of utter arbitrariness. Origen, his critics contend, made a text mean whatever he wanted it to mean; allegorical exegesis meant the absence of any control over the interpretation of the text. But such assertions are most often made by those who have read only *On First Principles*, if that. For many years this work (or even the anathemas of 553) were judged to contain the "real" Origen; the Origen of the homilies, especially, was considered a pious deceiver.

Henri de Lubac, in his brilliant book on Origen's exegesis, showed how wrong this is. De Lubac enunciated the principle "Observe Origen at work"[41]—that is, the principle that to understand Origen's method of exegesis one has to observe what he does. It will not do to write about his methods only from the fourth book of *On First Principles*. Instead, we need many detailed studies of the commentaries and the homilies. De Lubac successfully, and fruitfully, shifted attention away from Origen's dogmatic work to his exegetical work. The task is formidable, but the results are rewarding.

In particular, de Lubac was able to show that Origen's exegesis is anything but arbitrary. He discovered two schemas in Origen's exegesis.[42] The first is echoed in the terms Origen uses in *On First Principles* 4.2.4. According to this scheme, the *historical* sense is found in an account of the events narrated in the scriptures, or the text of the law. The *moral* sense refers to the soul, without any necessarily Christian dimension. The *mystical* sense refers to Christ, the church, and all the other objects of faith. The other scheme, which Origen did not explain anywhere theoretically but often used in practice, is this: the *historical* sense is found in the events of Israel's history. The *mystical* sense refers to the mystery to be fulfilled in future ages, that is, Christ and the church. The *spiritual* sense is found in applying the text to each single soul (person). This last, or "spiritual," sense differs from the "moral" of the first schema because it refers to the soul of the believer, "the soul in the Church," de Lubac says. In the believing soul, the mysteries of Christ are present and effective for the individual. Seen as a unity, the second schema means that "Once signified by the narratives of the Old Testament (historical), the mystery of Christ (mystical) attains its full effect in the Christian believer (spiritual)."[43]

This, too, is more typical of the mature Origen. In his surviving works, which span three decades, one can easily see a shift from cosmological interests, in his earlier works, to mystical and even pastoral interests (if he would have distinguished the two) in his later works. The homilies, in particular, show a clear and ever-present concern for the spiritual progress of his hearers.

CONCLUSION

Does Origen still speak to us? Can the preacher of the twentieth century learn from the preacher of the third? Adalbert Hamman remarked that the fathers of the church preached and wrote to instruct their congregations, not to provide universities with topics for doctoral dissertations.[44] Of course, even the most enthused reader of Origen would admit that one cannot repeat the details of his exegesis. A modern congregation would have little patience with some of his interpretations; there is evidence that the congregations in Caesarea in the 240s also had some difficulties with it. But one cannot help but admire Origen's persistence. He passionately believed that the scripture, the whole scripture, every word of the scripture, was God's inspired word, and that the whole scripture should speak to God's people. What would he have thought of lectionaries, one wonders, which select the "good" parts of the Bible and leave out the difficult ones? He would, I imagine, have been surprised at us: he would have thought we were a little cowardly, and a little impoverished, too. How, he might wonder, can we judge some parts of God's word not worth hearing in church?

Origen struggled with the whole Bible. He also struggled with the Bible as a whole. For all the difficulties involved, the Christian church cannot, or rather may not, ignore the fact that it accepts the Old Testament as its scripture precisely because it interprets that work christologically. The Old Testament is the church's book because it is related to Christ. How it is related may be a problem; but the problem is no reason to sever the relation.

Origen struggled with the whole Bible. He struggled with the Bible as a whole. And he struggled with the Bible in the church. He never pursued exegesis for its own sake, but only to instruct and guide his readers and hearers; he offered an ecclesial and pastoral exegesis. Origen cared passionately for each individual in the congregation, from the simple catechumen to the scholar. Much of what this great father said belongs to the past, but the spirit of his preaching belongs to every Christian age.

NOTES

1. The following works proved especially helpful on Origen as homilist: Y. Brilioth, *A Brief History of Preaching* (tr. Karl E. Mattson; Philadelphia: Fortress, 1965); H. Crouzel, *Origène* (Paris: Lethielleux, 1985); Thomas K. Carroll, *Preaching the Word* (Message of the Fathers of the Church 11; Wilmington: Michael Glazier, 1984), although some of Carroll's translations are misleading; Henri de Lubac, *Histoire et Esprit. L'intelligence de l'Ecriture d'après Origène* (Théologie 16; Paris: Aubier, 1950); Pierre Nautin, *Origène. Sa vie et son oeuvre* (Paris: Beauchesne, 1977); and idem, "Origène predicateur," in *Origène. Homélies sur Jérémie* 1 (SC 232; Paris: Cerf, 1976), 100–191. This last is the best treatment available on the topic.
2. Justin, *Apology* 1.67, tr. E.R. Hardy, *Early Christian Fathers* (ed. C.C. Richardson; Philadelphia: Westminster, 1953) 287.
3. G.L. Prestige, *Fathers and Heretics: Six Studies in Dogmatic Faith with Prologue and Epilogue* (first published in 1940; reprinted London: SPCK, 1968) 43.
4. Walther Völker, *Das Vollkommenheitsideal des Origenes* (Tübingen: Mohr-Siebeck, 1931), showed the singular importance of Origen's mysticism. Jean Daniélou, *Origen* (tr. Walter Mitchell; New York: Sheed and Ward, 1955; French original published in 1948), began to reinterpret Origen as orthodox. De Lubac, *Histoire et Esprit*, cast a new light on Origen's exegesis: far from being arbitrary, it is guided by clear, and rather orthodox, doctrinal principles. Antoine Guillaumont, *Les "Kephalaia Gnostica" d'Evagre le Pontique et l'histoire de l'origénisme chez les Grecs et chez les Syriens* (Paris: Editions de Seuil, 1962), showed that the fifth ecumenical council condemned the teachings of Evagrius of Pontus more than those of Origen. H. Crouzel published two masterful annotated bibliographies on Origen, and several important monographs. They are: *Bibliographie critique d'Origène* (Steenbrugge: Abbatia Sancti Petri, 1971); idem, *Supplément I* (ibid., 1982); *Théologie de l'image de Dieu chez Origène* (Paris: Aubier, 1956); *Origène et la "conaissance mystique"* (Paris and Bruges: Desclee de Brouwer, 1961); *Origène et la philosophie* (Paris: Aubier, 1962); and *Origène* (note 1 above).
5. Many of the details of Origen's biography here follow Crouzel, *Origène*. The principal ancient source for Origen's biography is the sixth book of Eusebius' *Ecclesiastical History*.
6. Eusebius, *Ecclesiastical History* 6.3.

7. Ibid., 6.23, tr. G.A. Williamson, *Eusebius. The History of the Church from Christ to Constantine* (Minneapolis: Augsburg, 1975) 262–63.
8. Ibid., 6.36 (Williamson, 271).
9. Crouzel, *Origène*, 53.
10. Nautin, *Origène*, 93.
11. Ibid., 407–08.
12. Ibid., 389–409.
13. English translations of some of the homilies are available: *Homilies on Genesis and Exodus*, tr. Ronald Heine (FC 71; Washington, DC: Catholic University of America Press, 1982); homily 6 on Leviticus in Joseph T. Lienhard, *Ministry* (Message of the Fathers of the Church 8; Wilmington: Michael Glazier, 1984); homily 27 on Numbers in *Origen: An Exhortation to Martyrdom*, etc., tr. Rowan A. Greer (Classics of Western Spirituality; New York: Paulist Press, 1979); the two homilies on the Song of Songs in *Origen: The Song of Songs: Commentary and Homilies*, tr. R.P. Larson (ACW 26; New York: Newman Press [1957]); and *Selections from the Commentaries and Homilies of Origen*, tr. R.B. Tollinton (London: SPCK, 1929).
14. Nautin, *Origène*, 405.
15. Idem, "Origène prédicateur," 152.
16. Ibid., 114, 116.
17. Eusebius, *Ecclesiastical History* 6.19.
18. *Homily on Samuel 1–2*, 1. This and other unmarked translations are my own.
19. *Homily on Exodus* 9.2 (Heine, 337).
20. *Homily on Genesis* 12.1 (Heine, 176).
21. *Homily on Jeremiah* 19.14.
22. *Homily on Leviticus* 1.4.
23. *Homily on Genesis* 10.1 (Heine, 157).
24. Ibid., 10.3 (Heine, 162–63).
25. *Homily on Exodus* 12.2 (Heine, 369).
26. Ibid., 13.3 (Heine, 378).
27. *Homily on Genesis* 12.4 (Heine, 180–81).
28. *Homily on Leviticus* 1.1.
29. On the structure of Origen's homilies, see Nautin, "Origène prédicateur," 123–31.
30. *Homily on 1 Samuel 28*, 1.
31. *Homily on 1 Samuel 1–2*, 10.
32. Crouzel, *Origène*, 93.
33. *Homilies on Genesis* 4.3 and 16.3 (Heine, 106 and 217).
34. Ibid., 16.3 (Heine, 217).
35. *Homily on Leviticus* 6.6.
36. Ibid., 1.4.
37. Tr. G.W. Butterworth, *Origen. On First Principles* (London: SPCK, 1936; reprinted Glouster, MA: Peter Smith, 1973) 276.

38. *Homilies on Genesis* 2.1, 2.6, 11.3 respectively.

39. On this important point see Rolf Gögler, *Zur Theologie des biblischen Wortes bei Origenes* (Düsseldorf: Patmos, 1963) esp. 45–47.

40. On Ps 1, in *Philocalia* 2.3, ed. Marguérite Harl (SC 302; Paris: Cerf, 1983) 245.

41. De Lubac, *Histoire et Esprit,* 34.

42. Ibid., 139–50.

43. Ibid., 144.

44. Adalbert Hamman, "Dogmatik und Verkündigung in der Väterzeit," *Theologie und Glaube* 61 (1971) 109.

4

WOMEN AND PREACHING
IN THE PATRISTIC AGE
by Agnes Cunningham, S.S.C.M.

The title of this essay is dangerous because it can be misleading. At first glance a reader might be tempted to think that some newly-found documentation provides proof that women were allowed to preach in the age of the fathers of the church. A second—suspicious —thought might suggest the discovery of texts that contain legislation prohibiting preaching by women who attempted to "usurp" that privilege illicitly. A more sober, realistic insight would conclude that the well-known exclusion of women from the ministry of preaching will, once again, be set forth as a *fait accompli;* a fact not to be discussed; a closed question.

In fact, none of the above interpretations reflects the purpose to be pursued in the following pages. Rather, I propose to address the subject of women and preaching in early Christianity by way of three questions: (1) What evidence exists to indicate that women were recognized as full members of the community in the patristic era? (2) What signs of attention to the concerns and interests of women do we find in the preaching of the early church fathers? (3) How are we to interpret what the fathers say to and about women in a mode of preaching that seems discriminatory and chauvinistic today? I shall consider these questions in light of what we know about the practice of preaching in Christian antiquity.

PREACHING IN THE EARLY CHURCH[1]

Jesus sent his disciples to proclaim the good news of the kingdom to all of creation until the end of this world (Mt 10:6ff; 28:16ff; Mk

16:15; Lk 9:1–6). This "proclamation" rapidly assumed multiple forms: teaching, prophecy, evangelization, catechesis, preaching. Preaching, too, found diverse expression in the homily, the instruction, the admonition, the sermon. In Jerusalem and Caesarea, an individual gifted by the Spirit was welcome to address the congregation, following the practice known in the synagogue. In Alexandria this practice was looked upon as a violation of church order.[2]

During the first three centuries of Christian antiquity, preaching was understood as the prerogative and duty of a specific group of Christians.[3] The bishop was the ordinary preacher in a community. Presbyters could be delegated or granted permission to preach. Neither presbyters nor laity were authorized to preach in the presence of a bishop. However, there is evidence from the life of Origen that a male lay person, recognized as a qualified teacher, could not only preach, but could do so in the presence of a bishop.[4]

The exclusion of women from preaching in early Christianity is attested to by more than one author. Taking St. Paul as his authority (cf. 1 Cor 14:34–35), Tertullian exclaims, ". . . how credible would it seem, that he who has not permitted a *woman* even to *learn* with overboldness, should give a *female* the power of *teaching* and of *baptizing!*"[5] Again, he states, "It is not permitted to a *woman* to speak in the church. . . ."[6] Epiphanius claimed that the "Word of God does not permit women to teach in church."[7] St. John Chrysostom upheld this discipline which he finds first of all in scripture: "The Blessed Paul does not permit [women] even to speak in the church" (cf. 1 Tim 2:12).

The prohibition against the preaching of women does not seem to have lessened what has been called an "important participation" of women in the mission, the worship and, indeed, the entire life of the church. Although extensive study on women in early Christianity has been pursued in the last twenty years,[8] the exact status of women's ministry seems not to have been clearly defined. Nevertheless, the presence of women in the Christian community emerges as a significant factor in the development of preaching in the early church. *What evidence is there to indicate that women were recognized as full members of the Christian community?*

WOMEN: HEARERS OF THE WORD

Women constituted an essential part of the Christian community in the patristic age. As Quasten has pointed out in reference to their participation in the singing of the congregation, the exclusion of women would have stood in sharp contrast to the idea of the communion of souls which Ignatius of Antioch had emphasized so strongly and which was so important to the Fathers of the first centuries.[9]

The final chapters of the earliest extant Christian homily[10] are addressed to "my brothers and sisters." St. Ambrose affirms that the singing of psalms "is fitting for every age and for both sexes." Ephraem, the deacon, founded choirs of consecrated virgins so that by their singing of hymns the teaching of heretics might be opposed.[11]

Women as well as men are educated by Christ, according to Clement of Alexandria.[12] He insists that the word *mankind* refers to both women and men, as does the word *sheep* when we say, "the Lord is our shepherd." St. Augustine's instructions to the deacon Deogratias include suggestions for catechizing candidates of either sex.[13] So, too, St. Gregory the Great insists on the need to distinguish between men and women when one is preaching.[14]

One of the more colorful preachers of the patristic era is St. Caesarius of Arles (470–543). Contrary to the common practice of the age, this sixth century bishop ordinarily limited his sermons to a quarter of an hour, out of consideration for his hearers. However, when he did choose to preach for a longer period of time, he frequently ordered the doors shut to keep people in the church! In keeping with a generally accepted custom in early Christianity, Caesarius, like Gregory the Great and other fathers, did not hesitate to read a homily from someone recognized as an outstanding teacher of the church.[15] One of his favorites was St. Augustine, although he also frequently quoted Origen, St. Ambrose and St. Jerome.

There is ample evidence that women were regularly among those who were present to the preaching of the bishop of Arles. He addressed them as sisters, as daughters. He mandated them to report faithfully what he had said in his sermon to the women who had not come "to the vigils" that day. St. Caesarius is usually considered a "defender" of women. One mark of this was his foundation of a monastery for the virgins of the city, constructed at Arles in an age when the establishment of monasteries for women was known to be a difficult and perilous undertaking. This was one of the first monasteries for women known in Gaul. Some of the bishop's sermons were addressed to the women religious of that place.

WOMEN: CO-WORKERS IN SERVICE TO THE WORD

In addition to their membership in the Christian community through the sacraments of initiation, women were recipients of instruction given by the early fathers, by reason of their share in the ministry of the church. It has already been pointed out above that the ministry of women in early Christianity seems not to have been clearly defined. There are exceptions to this lack of clarity, of course. Such was the case with the order of virgins and the order of widows.[16]

If we understand "preaching" in the sense of instruction, admonition and exhortation,[17] we find the fathers addressing in treatises and epistles those women who shared in the mission of the church in a unique manner by their choice of an ecclesial way of life. Virginity as an "order" in the church began in the third century. Virgins were the "contemplatives" in the Christian community. They lived a life in which study of the scriptures and prayer for the church were regarded as their particular ministry.

Concern for the integrity of the consecrated virgin resulted in forceful and, at times, harsh language on the part of the church fathers. For example, Cyprian of Carthage (200/210–258) writes:

[I]f you adorn yourself too elaborately and appear conspicuous in public, if you attract to yourself the eyes of the youth, draw after you the sighs of young men, foster the desire of concupiscence, enkindle the fire of hope, so that, without perhaps losing your own soul, you nevertheless ruin others and offer yourself a sword and poison, as it were, to those who behold you, you cannot be excused on the ground that your mind is chaste and pure. Your shameless apparel and your immodest attire belie you, and you can no longer be numbered among maidens and Virgins of Christ, you who so live as to become the object of sensual love.[18]

Of course, it can be said that Cyprian learned his lessons well from the one he called "the master." Tertullian (+ c.220) is notorious for his criticism—often biting and cruel—of women:

You are the one who opened the door to the Devil, you are the one who first plucked the fruit of the forbidden tree, you are the first who deserted the divine law; you are the one who persuaded him whom the Devil was not strong enough to attack. All too easily you destroyed the image of God, man.[19]

St. Jerome does not spare the virgins "who have prostituted the members of Christ" by their infidelity and hypocrisy:

> It becomes wearisome to tell how many virgins fall daily; what important personages Mother Church loses from her bosom; over how many stars the proud enemy sets his throne; how many rocks the serpent makes hollow and then enters through their openings. You may see many who were widowed before they were wed, shielding a guilty conscience by a lying garb. Did not a swelling womb or the crying of their infant children betray them, they would go about with head erect and on skipping feet.[20]

Examples such as these, along with the eloquent praise of virginity penned by Gregory of Nyssa and John Chrysostom in the east, and by Ambrose and Augustine in the west, bear witness to the recognition accorded to the spiritual ministry of the consecrated virgin in early Christianity.[21] A similar esteem was extended to the women who served the church as widows.

Widows, like virgins, served the church through a ministry of prayer. In addition, they took part in the worship of the community and were associated with the clergy in bringing sinners to repentance and in comforting the distressed.[22] Polycarp tells us that widows can be called "the altar of God," on condition that they recognize their own dignity:

> Teach the widows to be prudent in the faith of the Lord, and to pray without ceasing for all, to keep far from all calumny, slander, false witness, love of money and every evil. . . .[23]

Widows were frequently supported financially by the church. Care for them seems to have been founded on the understanding that they were an image of the church in her poverty and humility.[24] Only "good widows," however, could symbolize the church,

> not voluptuous, loquacious, inquisitive, envious, haughty ones. . . .[25]

The widow who lived a life of pleasure was considered to be "dead," even when she was living. Widows who were "angry, haughty, or covetous" were to be assigned to the left hand of the Lord at the final judgment.[26] Widows "falsely so called"

. . . esteem gain their business . . . they ask without shame, and receive without being satisfied. . . . [T]hey run from one of their neighbours' houses to another, and disturb them, heaping up to themselves plenty of money, and lend at bitter usury, and are only solicitous about mammon, whose bag is their god; who prefer eating and drinking before all virtue, saying, "Let us eat and drink, for to-morrow we die". . . .[27]

The solicitude of the early fathers for widows in the Christian community is reflected in the instructions addressed to them. For example, St. John Chrysostom wrote two such documents: one (*Ad viduam iuniorem*)[28] to console a young widow whose husband had just died, another (*De non iterando coniugio*)[29] to encourage widows to persevere in that state. St. Ambrose addressed widows in a work that is thought to have been, originally, a homily (*De viduis*).[30] Augustine, also, in one of his letters (*De bono viduitatis liber seu epistola*),[31] seeks to give instructions on the advantages of widowhood.

Virgins and widows, as co-workers with other ministers in the early Christian community, were committed in service to the word of God through their presence, their prayer and the witness of a life inspired by the gospel. Certainly the church treasured and esteemed them, expressing concern for them in admonition and commendation. These expressions of concern seem to have been motivated by a recognition and appreciation of the service of love (*caritas*) and prayer (*oratio*) assured to the Christian community by those women who had dedicated their lives to the Lord. *Can we find signs of attention to the concerns and interests of women themselves in the preaching of the early church fathers?* What were these concerns and interests? How were they expressed?

CONCERNS OF WOMEN IN EARLY CHRISTIANITY

The patterns and practices associated with the status of women in the Roman empire necessarily had an impact on the life of Christian women. The emergence of an "order" of widows early in the history of Christianity attests to this fact. How was a woman whose livelihood had been assured by marriage to adjust to widowhood— particularly if she had been cut off from family ties by conversion to the Christian religion? What was a widow to do with her time and her energy if a husband's death deprived her of the dignity and the responsibilities that rightfully belonged to the woman as *matrona* in a

Roman household? The means of an honorable livelihood and integration into the life of the community were primary concerns for a Christian widow.

A Christian woman who found herself in the state of widowhood was the first one to be aware of and concerned about her situation. She was not above making it known. The first persons indicated to receive her appeal were her own children, especially, her sons. Were not the followers of Jesus Christ held to the admonitions of scripture?

> Honor your father and your mother, that you may have a long life in the land which the Lord, your God, is giving you (Ex 20:12). If a widow has any children or grandchildren, let these learn that piety begins at home and that they should fittingly support their parents and grandparents; this is the way God wants it to be (1 Tim 5:4).

St. John Chrysostom, the greatest preacher of the early church, has recorded at length the pleas of his mother when she realized her son was considering the monastic life: "Do not make me once more a widow, nor awaken a grief that has been stilled."[32] The presence of a faithful child assured the widowed mother's livelihood. In the absence of that support, the church assumed the responsibility.[33]

The church that cared for the widows' livelihood looked to these women for a particular presence and service within the community of the faithful. "Good widows" were to serve God by "fasting, almsgiving and prayers."[34] Their patroness and spiritual companion was to be "blessed Anne." From her the Christian widow was to learn those virtues which enabled her to inspire and teach younger women, to be an example of faith and devotion to children and young girls. Caesarius of Arles returns repeatedly in his homilies to the theme of the widow as an image, a type or a figure of the church. In the widow of Sarephta who assisted Elias (1 Kgs 17) and the widow who "bought the kingdom of heaven for . . . two coins" (Mk 12:43–44; Lk 21:3–4), Caesarius found a seemingly endless source of homiletic material.

In the widow's desolation and loneliness, the fathers saw an image of the soul estranged from God. "The widow," St. Jerome taught in his homily on Psalm 93 (94), "is the soul of the sinner who has lost God as his spouse." The widow's chastity, like that of the virgin's, "is a sacrificial offering to Christ."[35] Widows who live in fidelity to the Lord through continence were to be a sign to the community of fidelity to a promise made freely in their choice of a way of life. Their persevering witness is a necessary gift to the church.

In the themes and images woven into their homilies and sermons, the fathers of the church revealed their awareness of the situation of the Christian widow in the Roman empire. Along with the poor and needy of every kind, with orphans and the homeless, widows were embraced by the love and care of the community of believers. Within that community, the widow enjoyed a position of respect and honor, as she devoted herself to prayer and to works of compassion for those in suffering and want. Her own livelihood was assured. She was an integral member of the Christian community.

Consecrated virgins in early Christianity experienced concerns not unlike those known by Christian widows. There was the matter of the living conditions available to them, with problems that attended their presence in both Christian and pagan households. There was the question of their participation in the life and worship of the community. In their homilies, the fathers of the church reflected a greater or lesser awareness of what it meant for a young woman to live in virginity, as "a holocaust to Christ."[36]

The situation of the virgin in the church derived from her identification as one who attends the Lord personally.[37] The virgin's solitude is relieved by the presence of "One whom [she] may wed without defilement." The virgin's sterility leads to "fertility of the soul."[38] The spiritual advantages attached to the virgin's solitary, "sterile" way of life were not sufficient to solve the problems to which these factors contributed.

As Jean LaPorte has pointed out,[39] the supervision of virgins was a difficult task because of the situations in which these women found themselves. Virgins lived in private houses: alone, if they were wealthy; in a specified section of a family residence, if they were able to live at home. In any case, they lived "in the world," among other Christians or pagans. Fidelity to their commitment was threatened by the worldliness they saw all around them.

Virgins who were exposed to the temptations and spiritual dangers of a large, pagan city were frequently entrusted to a priest appointed by the bishop. St. John Chrysostom called attention to the "alarm . . . the danger and distress" known by the person who has the "superintendence" of virgins.[40] The virgin was admonished to avoid "unnecessary journeys," the marketplace and those social gatherings that might place her in a compromising situation.

The practice of the *virgines subintroductae* developed as a solution to the virgin's concern for an appropriate way of life. This custom was sometimes referred to as a "spiritual marriage," since it provided for female and male ascetics to live together under the same roof. Thus, a virgin might live with a deacon, as Cyprian notes, for mutual help, protection and spiritual benefit.[41] The potential danger of this living arrangement led to a rejection of the custom and its prohibition by the Council of Ancyra (314). By the fourth century, monasteries and convents appeared to provide a life in which virgins were able to pray, worship, study and work in total dedication to God.

The fathers, in their admonitions and instructions, called attention to the concerns of women who desired to lead a life of virginity. They found in the virgin's life, as they had in the widow's, a source of inspiration for the church:

> Christ, intending to establish virginity in the heart of the Church, preserved it first in the body of Mary. . . . [T]he Church could not be a virgin unless she had first found the Son of the Virgin as a spouse to whom she might be given.[42]

> [T]he Church is . . . virgin by the integrity of faith and piety. . . . [S]he bears the likeness of the Virgin because in the midst of many she is the mother of unity.[43]

The ideal of virginity in the church was to be maintained by the prayers of the poor who interceded for the virgins who supported them with alms.[44] Virgins were to find strength for perseverance in the midst of temptation by watchfulness and fervent virtue:

> [B]odily virginity is of no value if charity and humility have departed from the heart. . . . [A] humble wedded life is much better than haughty virginity; those who with God's help protect themselves in the midst of the sea are more praiseworthy than those who sink in port because of too much carelessness and a false security.[45]

Not all women in the early Christian community were widows or virgins. The married woman who sought to live a gospel life found herself in a situation that challenged her faith and her baptismal commitment to the Lord. In society she was to be an example of values that set her apart from her pagan companions. In her household she was to be a model of virtue. In her relationship with her husband she was to be a source of inspiration.

In praising his sister, St. Gorgonia, St. Gregory Nazianzen paints a picture of the Christian woman who chooses to resist the demands of vanity:

She was never adorned with gold fashioned by art into surpassing beauty, or with fair tresses fully or partly exposed, or with spiral curls, or with the ingenious arrangements of those who disgracefully turn the noble head into a show piece. Hers were no costly, flowing, diaphanous robes, hers no brilliant and beautiful gems, flashing color round about and causing the figure to glow with light. . . . But while she was familiar with the many and various external ornaments of women, she recognized none as more precious than her own character and the splendor which lies within.[46]

In the same vein, St. John Chrysostom describes woman's true adornment, the beauty that "comes from almsgiving and modesty." Nothing, Chrysostom tells us, is "more disgusting than a suspiciously beautiful face."

Do you wish to adorn your face? Do not do so with gems but with piety and modesty. . . . For that other kind of adornment generally arouses suspicions which give rise to jealousy, enmity, strife and quarrels.[47]

There is a more fundamental reason for avoiding the artificial adornment of one's face:

I wish you women to abstain . . . from the habit of painting your faces and adding to them, as if the workmanship were defective. By doing so you insult the Workman. . . . By using rouge and eye shadow you cannot add to your natural beauty nor change your natural ugliness, can you? These add nothing to your beauty of face, but they will destroy the beauty of your soul.[48]

Another area in which the Christian woman was to differ from her pagan associates was that of responsible motherhood.

If women attempt to kill the children within them by evil medicines, and themselves die in the act, they become guilty of three crimes on their own: suicide, spiritual adultery, and murder of the unborn child. Therefore, women do wrong when they seek to have children by means of evil drugs. They sin still more grievously when they kill the children who are already conceived or born, and when by taking impious drugs to prevent conception, they condemn in themselves the nature which God wanted to be fruitful.[49]

The homilies and sermons of the church fathers reflect an awareness of and a sensitivity to the demands placed on Christian women by the ideal of marriage in Christ. In the first place, there was the matter of a fitting preparation. St. Caesarius of Arles counsels a man and a woman who want to marry to observe virginity until they are united in marriage.[50] This admonition applies equally to men and to women, although pagan society would grant a wider berth here to men. Caesarius sets the record straight: "In the Catholic faith, whatever is not lawful for women is equally not lawful for men."[51] Lest anyone think this expectation unreasonable, Caesarius points to the tyranny of the evil one which prevails over those who would seek to live a chaste life, after having practiced fornication or adultery. The fact that preparation for Christian marriage did not demand more of a woman than of a man was the first step toward a transformation of the *mores* of a pagan society.

The Christian wife, no less than a pagan woman, had a duty to seek to please her husband, as Paul had already noted (1 Cor 7:34). St. John Chrysostom suggests the way in which this is to be done:

> Adorn your face, therefore, with modesty, piety, almsgiving, benevolence, love, kindliness toward your husband, reasonableness, mildness and forbearance. . . . When God shall approve of you, He will win over your husband to you in every way; for if wisdom illumines the face of a man, much more does virtue make the face of a woman shine forth.[52]

There was one particular area of married life concerning which the fathers of the church wanted clear understanding: Christian women were to have nothing to do with practices that led to abortion or the abandonment of children after birth.

> No woman should take potions for purposes of abortion. . . . Is anyone unable to warn that no woman should accept a potion to prevent conception or to condemn within herself the nature which God wanted to be fruitful?[53]

> No woman should . . . kill her children that have been conceived or are already born.[54]

Caesarius adds, however:

> If a woman does not want to bear children, she should enter upon a pious agreement with her husband, for only the abstinence of a Christian woman is chastity.[55]

Indeed, chastity is one of the characteristics of a marriage blessed by God. The man who is unfaithful to his wife, when he is far from her, will incur eternal punishment from God.[56] Those who "use marriage rightfully," according to Cyril of Jerusalem, may rejoice. They "recognize times of abstinence, that they may give themselves to prayer." They "order their marriage according to law, not making it wanton by uncontrolled license."[57]

Under the guidance of the fathers, Christian wives came to understand their responsibility to bear witness in their marriage to gospel values, to fidelity in love, to commitment to Jesus Christ. They knew how "to provoke" their children by word and example "to what is commanded." The "ministry of Christian love" exercised by a faithful wife and mother reached "from spouse to children, from children to relations, from kindred to strangers, from strangers to enemies."[58] In the preaching of the fathers, the instruction and encouragement to live the ideal of Christian marriage was provided for women. In the light of the recognition of, the attention to and the concern for women which are reflected in the homilies, sermons, instructions and admonitions of the fathers, one question must be asked: *How are we to interpret what the fathers say to and about women in a mode of preaching that seems discriminatory and chauvinistic, today?*

THE FATHERS AND WOMEN

It is too easy to dismiss the hard sayings against women which we find in the preaching of the church fathers by accusations of misogynism. Christianity does not exist in a vacuum. Religious practice is always, to some extent, historically conditioned and sociologically enculturated. Like any other "special institution," preaching responds to the general influence of the society in which it immersed. In early Christianity, no less than at any other time, it shared in the character and movement of the age.[59] There are at least two considerations that cannot be overlooked in trying to understand the way in which the fathers spoke to and about women. One of these has to do with the status of women in the Roman empire. The other refers to the perceived function of preaching itself.

The fathers of the church were not alone in their condemnation of certain aspects of the lifestyle of women in the Roman empire. We are told that poets and critics looked upon the "unprecedented freedom" enjoyed by Roman women in the century after Augustus as a sign of the lamentable breakdown in Roman morality. Efforts to control women by legislation directed at their ownership of property and money seem not to have been particularly successful. A woman's conversion to Christianity was frequently a rejection of both Roman religion and Roman social values.[60]

Women converts to Christianity were expected to break with their former patterns of living. Association with former companions and attendance at certain public gatherings were discouraged. The bathhouses frequented by both men and women were perceived as especially dangerous to moral virtue.[61] Under pressure from prevailing customs, a Christian woman might find occasion and opportunity to return to a way of life incompatible with the gospel.

Actually, the fathers fell heir to a twofold tradition concerning women in the Graeco-Roman world.[62] At one level, a strain of anti-feminism can be traced through the writings of the Jewish rabbis, on the one hand, and through the works of pagan poets and philosophers, on the other. The Jewish attitude seems to have been founded on a perception of woman as a creature inferior to man, because she was taken from him. Rabbi Eliezar is known to have taught that it would be better to burn the books of the law than to entrust them to women!

Among the pagans, myths like Pandora's box were a reminder of the evils visited on all human beings because of a woman's curiosity. Plato considered the female sex a punishment inflicted by Zeus on men who had somehow been a failure in a previous existence. Aristotle defined woman by what she lacked in comparison with man. Philosophers who upheld the principle of a dualistic cosmology understood that order, light and man stood in contrast and opposition to chaos, darkness and woman.

At a second, though not a lesser, level, it is possible to find evidence of a pro-feminist mentality. Plato, in his *Republic*, suggests that women ought to undertake the same tasks as those engaged in by men. He also admitted two women into his Academy. The brilliant reputation of Sappho is well known. Aristotle and Plutarch wrote, respectively, of the possibility of friendship and enduring love between man and woman. We find women studying philosophy, as Stoics and Cynics admitted the equality of the sexes.

Looking to both the scriptures and the texts of classical antiquity, the fathers were faced with ambiguity and ambivalence: for every unfaithful, scheming, stubborn woman, there was a noble, generous, upright one. Two creation accounts pointed to two different understandings of what woman was meant to be, in relation to man.

More than that, there were Eve and Mary, Rahab the prostitute and chaste Susanna, the widow of Sarephta or Judith and the treacherous women described in the book of Proverbs. Poetry and legend maintained the dilemma: Helen of Troy and Athena, the virgin goddess; Medea and Penelope.

The homilies and sermons of the church fathers reflect these two conflicting traditions. In addressing women as *naturally* weak, inconstant, emotional, incapable of assuming responsibility in the public domain, the fathers unwittingly affirmed the prevailing moral and social inferiority of women. In heralding the courage of women martyrs, the intelligence of women scholars, the virtue of holy women, the fathers frequently did so in the vocabulary and categories of a pre-Christian era. In other words, they failed to develop an adequate anthropology on which to base a truly Christian idea of woman and a fully Christian ideal of human love.

The complexity of the situation in which the fathers found themselves becomes more apparent when we remember that any attention given to women in early Christianity was part of a wider pastoral concern for the whole church: for its survival under persecution; for the integrity of its faith, in the midst of heterodox teachings; for the growing awareness of a sense of mission beyond its own boundaries. Faced with the aberrations in matters of sexuality which prevailed in a pagan society that was increasingly amoral and dissolute, the fathers promoted virginity and monasticism as ideals to which Christians could aspire. Faced with the exaggerated asceticism of some of the gnostic sects which condemned marriage as a "diabolical invention," the fathers affirmed the value of Christian marriage and its place in the creator's plan.

Nonetheless, it is not impossible to uncover in the teachings of the fathers a certain attitude of suspicion regarding sexuality and what spiritual writers have referred to as "the flesh." The *mores* of the age and the practices of a pagan society certainly contributed to this underlying mistrust of what was still affirmed as one of the "goods" of creation.

Another influence, as many scholars have pointed out, was the discussion of marital sexuality found in St. Paul's first letter to the Corinthians. In chapter seven of that epistle, marriage is presented as a remedy against fornication and unchastity.[63] Contemporary exegetes read Paul in ways other than that known to the fathers. In their perception, conjugal love and sexuality were not necessarily partners.

The disassociation of love and sexuality led fathers like Jerome,

Augustine and John Chrysostom to look on marriage more as a "so-cial obligation" and a "natural necessity" than as the experience of a love that was a mutual gift between the spouses. While this attitude may seem completely foreign to us, it was not at all strange or inap-propriate in a culture where the choice of a marriage partner was not an option. The fathers accepted the institution of the pre-arranged marriage as they accepted other institutions in their society. The "difference" was to be found in the way Christians lived as disciples of a Lord who had overcome all forms of evil through a sinless, holy life.

Finally, we cannot discount the impact on early Christian spiri-tuality, and, consequently, on the thoughts and attitudes of the fa-thers, of a prevailing stoicism and neo-Platonism. More precisely, their teachings bear the marks of a morality that was strongly stoic, developed within the framework of a dualistic, Platonic anthropol-ogy. With such a worldview, how could the unity of spirit and flesh be maintained?

Despite this pessimism, we find that the fathers did, in fact, avoid the extremes of groups that eventually separated themselves from the values and teachings of Catholic Christianity. We find in the homilies of Gregory of Nazianzus[64] and John Chrysostom,[65] for example, in-spiring passages on the mutual love and partnership of women and men who have understood the meaning of marriage *in Christo.*

If we are going to "absolve" the fathers of the church for having failed to establish a clearly pro-feminist posture in early Christianity, we have to be willing to admit the reality and validity of their experi-ence. Some elements of that experience, as we have seen, were socie-tal and cultural. At least two other factors were operative in the themes proclaimed by the fathers as they preached to and about women in homilies and sermons. One of these factors was ecclesial in nature; the other was rhetorical.

The exhortations and admonitions addressed to women by the church fathers reflect a passionate love for the church. The beauty and integrity of the church were to be expressed in the lives of her members and in the effectiveness of their ministry. The participation of women in the mission of the church was uncontested. The blame-less character of their lives and the quality of their service were essential as a witness to Christian faith and love.

As the fathers looked at women in the Christian community and women in pagan society, they could not disregard or deny the differ-ences in lifestyle between the two. As we seek to assess their teachings, we find ourselves considering two images. One of them is the "ideal" Christian woman: virgin or married. The fathers seem to be saying: "This is what you can be as a faithful Christian, as a true disciple of Jesus Christ." The conditions are presented in detail; practices are made explicit; prohibitions are clearly declared. The beauty and charm of woman at her best are envisioned by the fathers. The radiance of holiness enhances every gift and trait of nature, appearance and personality. In these texts, we catch a glimpse of the "divine feminine."

The other image is repulsive and negative in every way. In its contrast to the first, we are impelled to think of the separation of the sheep and the goats described in the gospel according to Matthew (25:31ff). Here, woman is presented at her worst: she is cruel, calculating, seductive, crafty, lascivious, self-seeking, possessive; determined to have her own way, she will not hesitate to destroy man in the achievement of her goals. "See," the fathers seem to be saying, "if you do not forsake your former ways, if you do not pursue virtue, if you forsake modesty, humility, chastity, obedience, love—this will be your end. You will be of no use to yourselves or to anyone else. You will have betrayed the Lord and his church!" To those women who seemed to find the demands of a Christian ideal too difficult or to give signs of a too-easy reconciliation with certain modes of fashion in dress or adornment, there was an added reprimand: "This is what you will become if you fail to return to the way of light, the path of virtuous living!"

Closely related to this ecclesial factor which prevailed in the preaching of the fathers of the church, we can discern another element, the rhetorical. Almost without exception, the great fathers and preachers of the patristic age had been students of rhetoric in the classical tradition. They had studied the pagan philosophers and poets. They knew how to use to advantage the subtleties of the Greek language as well as the force, the clarity and the logic of Latin. Many of the fathers had been rhetoricians.

A careful analysis of the homilies and sermons of the church fathers has led scholars to recognize the influence of rhetoric on early Christian preaching. Indeed, it is not an exaggeration to state that "preaching inherited the legacy of ancient rhetoric."[66] The rhetorical traditions of both non-Christian and secular culture have been kept alive throughout the history of preaching. At a time when the lines between the homily and biblical commentary were not clearly designated, preaching included exposition, instruction, admonition and exhortation. One rhetorical device, in particular, seemed to serve the aims of the Christian preacher. That device was the *diatribe*. Brilioth claims that

> [t]he Stoic diatribe was given a continued existence in early Chris-
> tian preaching as soon as the sermon assumed a literary form on
> Hellenistic soil, the first time that Christian preaching became de-
> pendent on a nonbiblical tradition.[67]

St. John Chrysostom seems to have considered the diatribe as the natural form of the homily. It was the diatribe which shaped the pattern of "less sophisticated preaching" in early Christianity. In fact, a recent study suggests the "controversial and persuasive hypothesis that the origin of the Christian concept of faith can be traced to Greek classical rhetoric."[68]

In practice, the diatribe was employed to compare two opposing values: for example, virginity and marriage, or Christian marriage and sexual liaisons between pagans. The value to be affirmed and promoted (e.g. virginity) was presented in its most favorable light, with an elaboration of the spiritual and human advantages that were to result from it. The opposing value (e.g. marriage), which was, presumably, to be rejected, was presented in its most unfavorable aspects, with graphic descriptions of every human woe and misery that would descend on anyone who subscribed to it. When virginity and marriage were placed in opposition, virginity was the value to be affirmed. When Christian marriage was compared to alternate sexual liaisons pursued in pagan society, Christian marriage was set forth as the value to be affirmed and chosen.

A recognition of the function of the diatribe in the preaching of the fathers of the church helps us to understand why they seem, at times, to express negative views on women, marriage and sexuality. It is only by reading widely and inclusively in the texts that come to us from the age of Christian antiquity that we can begin to appreciate the real contribution of the patristic tradition of preaching and the quality of their preaching to and about women.

WOMEN AND PREACHING IN EARLY CHRISTIANITY

As far as we can tell, women were never authorized to preach in the early Christian church. However, the author of 2 Clement seems to prefer that men not be assigned as preacher to communities made up exclusively of women.[69] This preference, of course, would have been in keeping with the expectations of Roman society.

The question arises, then: Who would have preached to these women? No clear answer comes to us from the past. Still, the emergence of the woman deacon with her ministry to other women suggests that some accommodation must have taken place in the early church. There is some evidence that women were, originally, included among the teachers of the faith.[70] We know that they were encouraged to share their faith with other women who had not yet embraced Christianity. The writings of Jerome to Paula and Eustochium, along with the instructions of Augustine addressed to Proba, tell us that women leaders in ecclesial and monastic communities were able to communicate what they learned to other women. Indeed, they were encouraged to do so.

Perhaps, in the last analysis, the fathers who preached to and about women came to recognize "mothers of the church" whom they were able to love and admire. In these women, they saw exemplified the simple truth that "the most effective and sublime speech" is the life of the preacher.[71] The greatest sermon is the proclamation of the earliest Christian kerygma: God became human so that human beings—women as well as men—might become divine.[72]

NOTES

1. References for further reading include: Y. Brilioth, *A Brief History of Preaching* (Philadelphia: Fortress Press, 1965); Edwin C. Dargan, *A History of Preaching*, 1 (Baker, 1968); Edward P. Echlin, *The Priest as Preacher Past and Future* (Mercier, 1973); John Ker, *Lectures on the History of Preaching* (Armstrong, 1901); Hugo Rahner, *A Theology of Preaching* (Herder & Herder, 1968).
2. Cf. Brilioth, *Brief History*, 23.
3. Cf. Dargan, *History*, 37.
4. Cf. Echlin, *Priest as Preacher*, 25 and 38. While the "lay-doctor" was allowed to preach in Palestine, it seems this practice was not accepted in Alexandria. Cf. Thomas K. Carroll, *Preaching the Word* (Wilmington: Michael Glazier, 1984) 50.
5. *De baptismo* 17.4.
6. *De virginibus velandis* 9.
7. *Panarion* 79.2–3.
8. See Jean Laporte, *The Role of Women in Early Christianity* (New York and Toronto: The Edwin Mellen Press, 1983) 173, n. 172, for an interesting bibliography on the ministry of women.
9. J. Quasten, *Music and Worship in Pagan and Christian Antiquity* (tr. B. Ramsey; Washington, DC: National Association of Pastoral Musicians, 1973) 77.

10. The reference is to the so-called *Second Letter of Clement*. See J.B. Lightfoot, *The Apostolic Fathers* (London, 1890).
11. Cf. Quasten, *Music and Worship*, 78–79.
12. Cf. *Paidagogos* 4.
13. Cf. *De catechizandis rudibus* 15.
14. Cf. *Liber regulae pastoralis* 3.1.
15. Cf. Brilioth, *Brief History*, 67.
16. These "orders" have been treated fully by many authors. For bibliographic references, see Laporte, *The Role of Women*, 166, n. 100 and 167–68, n. 113.
17. Cf. Brilioth, *Brief History*, 8ff,17.
18. *De habitu virginum* 9, tr. A.E. Keenan in R.J. Deferrari, ed., *Saint Cyprian. Treatises* (FC 36; New York: Fathers of the Church, 1958) 39.
19. *De cultu feminarum* 1, tr. E.A. Quain, *Tertullian. Disciplinary, Moral, and Ascetical Works* (FC 40; New York: Fathers of the Church, 1959) 118.
20. Ep. 22, "To Eustochium," tr. C.C. Mierow, *The Letters of Saint Jerome* (ACW 33; New York/Ramsey, NJ: Newman Press, 1963) 145.
21. Classic texts on virginity in the early church include: Gregory of Nyssa, *On Virginity;* John Chrysostom, *De virginitate;* Ambrose of Milan, *De virginibus, De virginitate, De institutione virginis,* and *Exhortatio virginitatis;* Augustine of Hippo, *De sancta virginitate.*
22. Cf. Laporte, *Role of Women*, 59.
23. *Letter to the Philippians* 4, tr. F.X. Glimm in *The Apostolic Fathers* (FC 1; Washington, DC: Catholic University of America Press, 1962) 137.
24. The works of Caesarius will be cited according to the English translation of Sr. M.M. Mueller, *St. Caesarius. Sermons,* 3 vols. (FC 31, 47, 66; Washington, DC: Catholic University of America Press, 1956, 1964, 1973). Cf. sermon 49 (Mueller [FC 31], 250–51).
25. Caesarius, sermon 7 (Mueller [FC 31], 44).
26. Caesarius, sermons 134 and 157 (Mueller [FC 47], 253 and 357).
27. *Constitutions of the Holy Apostles* 3.7 (ANF 7.428).
28. PG 48.399–410.
29. Ibid.
30. PL 16.247–276.
31. PL 40.429–430.
32. *De sacerdotio* 5.
33. Cf. 1 Tim 5:1–16; *Didascalia Apostolorum* 14.
34. Caesarius, sermon 6 (Mueller [FC 31], 44).
35. Jerome, sermon 23, On Psalm 95 (96), tr. M.L. Ewald (FC 48; Washington, DC: Catholic University of America Press, 1964) 187.
36. Ibid.
37. Jerome, homily 46, On Psalm 133 (134) (Ewald, 343).
38. Augustine, sermon 184, On the Birthday of Our Lord Jesus Christ, tr. M.S. Muldowney, *Saint Augustine. Sermons on the Liturgical Seasons* (FC 38; New York: Fathers of the Church, 1959) 5.

39. Laporte, *Role of Women,* 71–77.
40. Cf. *De sacerdotio* 17.
41. Cf. ep. 4.
42. Augustine, sermon 188 (Muldowney, 20).
43. Augustine, sermon 192 (Muldowney, 33).
44. Cf. Cyprian, ep. 4.
45. Caesarius, sermon 237 (Mueller [FC 66], 218).
46. "On His Sister, St. Gorgonia," tr. L.P. McCauley, *Funeral Orations by St. Gregory Nazianzen and St. Ambrose* (FC 22; Washington, DC: Catholic University of America Press, 1953) 107.
47. Twelfth Baptismal Instruction, tr. Paul W. Harkins, *St. John Chrysostom: Baptismal Instructions* (ACW 31; Westminster, MD: Newman Press, 1963) 185–86.
48. First Baptismal Instruction (Harkins, 38).
49. Caesarius, sermon 51 (Mueller [FC 31], 258–59).
50. Sermon 14 (Mueller [FC 31], 81).
51. Sermon 43 (Mueller [FC 31], 214).
52. Twelfth Baptismal Instruction (Harkins, 186).
53. Caesarius, sermon 1 (Mueller [FC 31], 13).
54. Caesarius, sermon 44 (Mueller [FC 31], 221).
55. Sermon 1 (Mueller [FC 31], 13).
56. Caesarius, sermon 43 (Mueller [FC 31], 218).
57. Catechesis IV, tr. L.P. McCauley, *The Works of Saint Cyril of Jerusalem* (FC 61; Washington, DC: Catholic University of America Press, 1969) 131.
58. Caesarius, sermon 21 (Mueller [FC 31], 107).
59. Dargan, *History,* 33.
60. JoAnn McNamara, *A New Song: Celibate Women in the First Three Christian Centuries* (New York: The Haworth Press/Institute for Research in History, 1983) 43–47.
61. Cf. Caesarius, sermons, passim.
62. Two major sources for the material in this section are J.C. Guy and F. Refoulé, eds., *Chrétiennes des Premiers Temps* (Paris: Cerf, 1965) and France Quéré-Jaulmes, ed., *La Femme* (Paris: Centurion, 1968).
63. Cf. Guy and Refoulé, *Chrétiennes,* 42–45.
64. Cf. homily 61.3.
65. Cf. homily 20 on Ephesians.
66. Cf. Brilioth, *Brief History,* 26.
67. Ibid., 17.
68. James L. Kinneavy, *Greek Rhetorical Origins of Christian Faith* (New York: Oxford University Press, 1987).
69. 2 Clement 12.17.
70. Cf. Rosemary Ruether and Eleanor McLaughlin, eds., *Women of Spirit* (New York: Simon and Schuster, 1979) 17.
71. Cf. Brilioth, *Brief History,* 51.
72. Cf. Hugo Rahner, *A Theology of Proclamation* (n. 1, above).

5

THE HOMILETIC FESTAL LETTERS
OF ATHANASIUS
by Charles Kannengiesser, S.J.

Each year, when not prevented by adverse circumstances, Athanasius, bishop of Alexandria from 328 to 373, wrote a special letter to all the churches placed under his ruling in order to let them know the dates of Lent, Easter, and Pentecost. Festal Letters[1] seemed to have become somehow traditional for the Alexandrian bishops. A few remnants of them survive at least from the time of Dionysius, who died in the mid-60s of the third century.[2] After Athanasius, the tradition of the FL was duly continued by his successors, such as Theophilus (385–412) and Cyril (412–444). The latter's collection of as many as twenty-nine so-called *Paschal Homilies* occupies almost half of a volume in Migne's *Patrologia graeca*. The editorial title of the Cyrillian FL is quite unfortunate, for they offer impersonal and abstract dissertations on Christian virtues. Some are filled with heavy polemical outbursts, in particular against the Jews. Others inculcate the dogmatic teaching of their author's intolerant christology. One would hardly praise them for a proper homiletic flavor. Their massive prose stands in striking contrast, in this regard, with the Athanasian FL.

We possess, in their full text or only in fragments, thirty-one of the FL composed by Athanasius during his forty-five years in office.[3] Seven or eight times during his career, Athanasius had to abstain from such a public act of ecclesiastical government. It happened in the years 336–337, when he was exiled by the emperor Constantine to Trier in northern Gaul, as well as a few years later, during his second exile in the west, and again when he was silenced by Constantius and hidden in the desert of Egypt during his third exile, from 356 to 361. Athanasius himself seems to refer to one or another of a few letters now completely lost, at least for the time being. In addition, we also possess the old Syriac version of an *Index* established in Alexandria shortly after Athanasius' death in early May 373.[4] The *Index* gives for each year complete information concerning the paschal chronology, as well as the reason why occasionally a FL could not be written, or why it was sent out from abroad. In other words, we have an excellent material witness to examine precisely how the Alexandrian bishop was able to communicate, year after year, in an epistolary form, with the same communities of believers spread over his canonical territory.

This opportunity to study Athanasius' pastoral communication in the form of continuous, repeated letters is the more welcome if one considers the dramatic circumstances of his career, which imposed their bias on most of his other writings. Here in the FL, the Alexandrian pope addresses exclusively his own parishioners, for the sole purpose of preparing them for a proper celebration of Easter, the feast par excellence of the Christian calendar. Therefore, despite the many obscurities and uncertainties still unavoidable in studying the FL,[5] it is more than tempting to investigate them, and to listen to their message.

There is a clear message in these FL, a message delivered insistently, with their author's unique tone. Athanasius was first of all a pastor, close to his people, and eager to remain always as close as possible to them.[6] The reader accustomed to the Alexandrian bishop's less attractive fame as a stubborn and aggressive church politician may be puzzled by the author of the FL, who not only speaks the language of a pastor, but also expresses his thoughts and emotions with the serene poetry of a contemplative person. His style is plain and imaginative simultaneously, such that one hardly notices its written artistry. The spoken directness of the bishop's vibrant exhortations produces an overwhelming effect. Even the cautious editor and first English translator of the FL would observe: "Perhaps we should not be wrong in supposing that some of the Epistles were, in the first instance, delivered as homilies, at the places where they were written, and afterwards, with slight alterations, and the addition of the concluding parts, sent as Paschal Letters to the various dioceses."[7]

It seems probable that the homiletic shape of the FL had more to do with their author's frame of mind than with any oral delivery of their content. For it is precisely when he shows an awareness of writing to his addressees from some distance that the author of the FL becomes the most familiar and spontaneous. In fact Athanasius shows up in the FL with a sort of candid sincerity and with an appealing enthusiasm, giving the effect of echoing a direct speech, even in circular epistles. The Easter epistles, communicating their author's intentions in a homiletic format, represent a literary exercise by which Athanasius intended to share with his countrymen the common values of their faith in the common language of their native culture. It is precisely thanks to their local, Alexandrian, and popular style that the FL are able to introduce the modern reader into the deeper Athanasian mind.

SEVEN FL BEFORE THE FIRST EXILE IN 335

> Come, my beloved: the season calls us to keep the feast. Again, the Sun of Righteousness (Mal 4:3), causing his divine beams to rise upon us, proclaims beforehand the time of the feast, in which, obeying him, we ought to celebrate it; so that when the time has passed away, gladness likewise may not leave us.[8]

These are the very first known words of Athanasius, written only a few months after he had been installed as the successor of bishop Alexander on June 8, 328. The FL used to be sent months in advance, in order to reach in due time the limits of Upper Egypt and the oasis of the Libyan desert. Some of the Letters would be written about a year in advance, just after the celebration of Easter in the preceding year. In the first two sentences of the first FL, the call is direct, and the solar analogy found in scripture leads to a mentioning of the proper joy of the feast. Over forty quotations from scripture will be written out and paraphrased in the same manner throughout the FL for the year 329. The young bishop for the first time addresses the whole of Alexandrian and Egyptian Christianity, and he does it in the style of Origenian allegorism, but with a new focus, which announces his doctrinal stance for the years to come. I quote:

> Thus, likewise, for instance, not out of season, but in season, the *Wisdom of God* (1 Cor 1:24), but our Lord and Saviour Jesus Christ, passed among holy souls, fashioning the friends of God and the prophets (Wis 7:27); so that, although very many were praying for him, and saying, *O that the salvation of God were come out of Sion!* (Ps 14:7), the spouse also, as it is written in the Canticles, praying and saying, *O that Thou wert my sister's son, that sucked the breasts of my mother* (Cant 8:1), that thou wert like to the children of men, and wouldst take upon thee human passions for our sake! Nevertheless, the God of all, the framer of times and seasons, and who knows our

affairs better than we do, while, as a good physician, he exhorts to obedience in due season—the only one in which we may be healed —so also does he send him not unseasonably, but seasonably, saying, *In an acceptable time have I heard Thee, and in the day of salvation I have helped Thee* (Is 49:8), and on this account, the blessed Paul, urging us to note this season, wrote, saying, *Behold, now is the accepted time; behold, now is the day of salvation* (2 Cor 6:2).[9]

Here, a remarkable memory for the biblical text serves a doctrine of salvation centered on the mystery of God's incarnation. Following a pattern which will be repeated several times in other FL, the incarnational focus calls for a series of analogies and models identified with the Old Testament (here below, Moses and his silver trumpets, or the psalmist and the prophets), before expanding itself in a central theme, which applies the gospel narratives to the actual reality of the church:

Be it that these things were then typical, and done as in a shadow. Let us, having recourse to our understanding, and henceforth leaving the figures at a distance, come to the truth, and look upon the priestly trumpets of our Saviour, which cry and call us, at one time to war, as the blessed Paul saith: *We wrestle not with flesh and blood, but with principalities, with powers, with the rulers of this dark world, with wicked spirits in heaven* (Eph 6:12). At another time the call is made to virginity, and lowliness, and conjugal unanimity, saying, to virgins, the things of virgins; and to those bound by a course of abstinence, the things of abstinence; and to those who are married, the things of an honorable marriage; thus assigning to each domestic virtues and honorable recompense.[10]

After having thus set the stage for the believers of all conditions in the church, the newly-elected bishop invites them all to "listen to a trumpet much greater than all these," namely to John 7:37: *Jesus stood and cried, saying, If anyone thirst . . . .* The Pharisees would not listen. They ignored the true fast, whereas

our Lord and Saviour Jesus Christ, being heavenly bread, is the food of the saints, according to this, *Except ye eat My flesh, and drink My blood* (John 6:53) . . . . Now this (the food of virtue) is humbleness of mind, lowliness to endure humiliation, the acknowledgement of God.[11]

Such motifs of moral exhortation, doctrinal allegory, and symbolic exegesis in the pure style of the Alexandrian and Origenian tradition are intertwined throughout the whole letter. One of these motifs seems to be more apparent, and it is certainly more recurrent than all the others, insisting on the actualizing of all the scriptures in the Christian experience of faith:

> Since then we have passed the time of the shadow, and no longer perform rites under it, but have turned, as it were, unto the Lord: *for the Lord is a Spirit, and where the Spirit of the Lord is, there is liberty* (2 Cor 3:17): as we hear from the priestly trumpet; no longer slaying a material lamb, but that true lamb that was slain, even our Lord Jesus Christ, *Who was led as a sheep to the slaughter, and was dumb, as a lamb before his shearers* (Is 53:7); being justified by his precious blood, which speaketh better things than that of Abel; having our feet shod with the preparation of the gospel; holding in our hands the rod and staff of the Lord, by which that saint was comforted, who said, *Thy rod and Thy staff they comfort me* (Ps 23:4); and to speak collectively, being in all respects prepared and careful for nothing, because as the blessed Paul saith, *The Lord is at hand* (Phil 4:5); and as our Saviour saith, In an hour when we think not, the Lord cometh (Lk 12:40)—*Let us keep the Feast, not with old leaven, neither with the leaven of malice and wickedness, but with the unleavened bread of sincerity and truth* (1 Cor 5:8). Putting off the old man and his *deeds, let us put on the new man* (Eph 4:22–24), which is created in God, in humbleness of mind, and a pure conscience; in meditation of the law by night and by day.[12]

In writing his first FL during the winter of 328–329, the new Alexandrian bishop had not a single word left for Arianism, nor even for the Meletian schism which, at that very moment, impinged on his daily administrative duties. So much for the common opinion dating Athanasius' famous *On the Incarnation* before the start of the Arian crisis for the sole reason that its author maintains the very same kind of silence about Arianism as one notes in the FL. The real enigma of this letter for Easter 329, as well as of the FL published in the next two or three years, would rather be, in my view, the striking fact of that mystic language spoken by Athanasius when he addresses Alexandrian and Egyptian Christianity at large.

In the second FL, for Easter of 320,[13] the Old Testament models exhorting Christians to silence, peace, and prayer serve as an introduction to the apologetic commentary on Exodus 12 required by the liturgical circumstances. The author denounces the failure of the Jews to catch the real meaning of the events related in Exodus 12, which laid down the historic foundations of their own religious tradition. He shares such a negative evaluation with the unanimous judgment of the Christian church since its earliest beginnings. He does not add any antisemitic emphases of his own to the traditional theme, but finds his own way of repeating in a narrative style the common Christian opinion. His real interest lies in the celebration of "the spiritual nourishment of the true lamb, our Lord Jesus Christ," who is "the Image of the Father," the "Logos healing the sick," etc. He then concludes,

> Enough for now of the Mosaic types; before this day they were shining in the dark; but now, as the sun shines, darkness must vanish, the light eliminating all darkness.[14]

The third FL, misplaced by an ancient editor as no. 14 for the year 342, offers in 331 the same pattern, style, and concept as the former letter. Again, Old Testament models open the way to Christ proclaimed in Origenian terms and to his divine incarnation seen as actualized in the church:

> Who then will thus be our guide, as we hasten to this festival? None can do this, my beloved, but him whom ye will name with me, even our Lord Jesus Christ, who said, *I am the Way* (Jn 14:6). For it is he who according to the blessed John, *taketh away the sin of the world* (Jn 1:29). He also purifies our souls, as Jeremiah the prophet says . . . (Jer 6:16).[15]

> These things took place before, as it were, in shadows and were typical. But now the truth is nigh unto us, *the Image of the invisible God* (Col 1:15), our Lord Jesus Christ, the true light, who instead of a staff, is our scepter; instead of unleavened bread, is the bread which came down from heaven; who instead of sandals, has furnished us with the preparation of the gospel; and who, to speak briefly, by all these has guided us to the Father.[16]

Athanasius notes that he is recalling his readers to one of his familiar teachings: "But respecting these matters, I have confidence in your wisdom, and your doctrinal care. Such points as these have been touched upon by us often and in various letters."[17] It is also worth observing how candidly he uses the "we"–form in referring to homiletic addresses and to colloquial exchanges inside the church community. He regularly calls his addressees "beloved," "my beloved," "brethren," and "my beloved brethren," as did his predecessor Dionysius in his letters. In fact, such allusions increase and become more insistent throughout the epistolary career of Athanasius.

The fourth FL, for 332, about five years after Athanasius' installment, shows the first evidence of political interferences in his episcopal ministry:

> I send unto you, my beloved, late and beyond the accustomed time; yet I trust you will forgive the delay, on account of my far travelling, and because I have been tried with protracted illness. Being then hindered by these two causes, and unusually severe storms having occurred, I have deferred writing to you. But notwithstanding my far travelling, and my grievous sickness, I have not forgotten to give you the festal notification, and, in discharge of my duties, I now announce to you the feast. For although the letter has been delayed beyond the accustomed period of the proclamation, yet it should not be considered as ill-timed, inasmuch as, since the enemies have been put to shame and reproved by the church, because they persecuted us without a cause, we may now sing a festal song of praise, uttering the triumphant hymn against Pharaoh (Ex 15:1).[18]

This hymn of triumph will resound a few more times in Athanasius' FL. In early 332, it expresses the bishop's relief at the imperial court of Nicomedia, where he had been cleared of grave accusations brought against him before Constantine. The whole letter, except the quoted preamble and a short postscript, keeps silent about the dramatic circumstances of its composition. But it reveals a typical Athanasian reaction: scripture itself starts telling the story of the bishop's ordeal, in being directly appropriated to Athanasius' actual experience. The Old Testament exempla are now in line with the latter's personal trial:

> Judith . . . overcame the enemies . . . Esther . . . defeated the fury of the tyrant. . . . Moses of old time ordained the great feast of the Passover and the people were delivered from bondage.[19]

The fulfillment of salvation in Christ means "that the devil is slain." Therefore,

> . . . we do not approach the feast, my beloved, as a temporal one, but as being eternal and heavenly. For we proclaim it not as it were in shadows, but we come to it in the truth. . . . Now we, eating of the Word of the Father, and having the lintels of our hearts sealed with the blood of the New Testament, acknowledge the grace given us from the saviour. . . . Let us go beyond the types, and sing the new song of praise.[20]

The unusual distance from which this FL for 332 was written obviously did not distract its author from his homiletic mysticism in addressing his people. The next FL, for 333, opens in the exhortative "we"–form: "We duly proceed, my brethren, from feasts to feasts, duly from prayers to prayers."[21] This initial statement echoes directly FL 4: "For we proceed duly, my beloved, from feast to feast; again festal meetings, again holy watchings stir up our minds. . . ."[22] Easter captures at once the whole attention of the author, and the Athanasian notion of salvation actualized in the church in view of the incarnation of the divine Logos occupies the whole FL. A closer analysis of the letter would reveal its striking closeness to the treatise *On the Incarnation.* One of the main arguments of this treatise states that human beings were no longer capable of reaching up to God in the divine mystery itself; they needed an incarnate Logos who would attract their senses and unify them in a new way.[23] The sacramental unity of the church would result from that revelatory and divinizing process. In FL 5, "it is indeed impossible to make an adequate return to God," but,

> . . . God produces even now from (the cross) the joy of glorious salvation, bringing us to the same assembly, and in every place uniting all of us in spirit. . . . For this is the marvel of his loving kindness, that he should gather together in the same place those who are at a distance; and make those who appear to be far off in the body, to be near together in unity of spirit.[24]

The doctrinal conclusion which Athanasius will articulate only a few months later in *On the Incarnation* emerges here from its liturgical premises. The metaphors and the logic shared by both writings are the same. They may signal that FL 5 and *On the Incarnation* are more or less contemporaneous.[25] Only a short quotation from FL 6, for Easter 334, appears to have survived, and the letters of the two following years are lost, if ever they were even written.

The letters of 334 and 335, FL 6 and FL 7, are lost. The Alexandrian pope left his hometown on July 11, 335 with a delegation of subordinate bishops and monks from the Nile valley. They headed for Tyre, on the Phoenician coast, south of Sidon, where a synod of oriental church authorities, supported by the imperial administration, nullified Athanasius' election to the see of Alexandria in 328. On November 6 of the same year, a bewildered Athanasius was sent by the emperor Constantine himself into exile. Only after the latter's death in the week of Pentecost 337 could the bishop return to Alexandria, where he arrived on November 23. After that unexpected experience of two years spent in Trier, the northern capital of the empire in the west, a new stage opened in Athanasius' career.

TEN FL FROM THE END OF THE FIRST EXILE (337) TO THE START OF THE THIRD EXILE (356)

The first seven letters from before the first exile were all written by Athanasius in the style of Origenian homilies, as far as allegorical exegesis and applications to spiritual experience are concerned. Nonetheless, they showed some distinctive Athanasian features, such as the persistent "we–talk" by which their author never failed to actualize scripture in line with the common practice of faith among Christians. The mystery of the divine incarnation is, at once, the focus of Athanasius' actualizing hermeneutic. The same focus will be at work in the next series of FL. It will help their author to introduce into his written homilies a growing number of scriptural references. It will also radiate through his recommendations a particular warmth, each time Athanasius calls the faithful to the celestial joy of the feast. From FL 10 on, a new dimension opens in this kind of pastoral literature. The author meditates on his personal fate with a pedagogical purpose, using his experience of exiles and church affairs as an illustration of basic Christian virtues. As long as he had felt secure enough in his office during the first years after his election, he enjoyed allegorical mysticism in the FL. After that, when ecclesiastical battles started, he became rather down-to-earth in his pastoral writing.

Thus he reaches a new awareness when carefully preparing the homily which he sends out to the churches in the popular style of the FL. The bishop witnesses a political engagement enriched by his mystic perception of how the incarnate God acts in the present church. He refers more and more to the heretics, as he calls them, Arians or Meletians alike, who perturb the life of the community and oppose his own pastoral action. But, at a closer look, it becomes obvious that his anti-heretical theme serves a prophetic purpose, much less motivated by polemics than by spirituality. Athanasius would not write one line of his Easter epistles that did not, in a way or another, call the addressees to a communitarian celebration of their faith. The same is true of his anti-Judaic stance. The Jews serve in these letters as a type of the religious enemies of the Christian church. They offer the best analogy for understanding the malice of heresy. But the polemical overtones remain strictly within the boundaries of a conventional literary procedure, used in order to emphasize in a contrasting way the Christian values of Easter.

Thus the annual festal letters provide an opportunity for a consistent teaching, visually linked with recent events, and strongly opposed to possible attacks against the orthodoxy of the bishop's community. But, in any circumstances, Athanasius' circular letters for Lent and Easter would engage the faithful, year after year, into their actual participation in the salvific process by which an incarnate Logos conformed to act in the church and in the present world.

FL 10, from the summer of 337, is the longest Easter epistle Athanasius ever made public.[26] It is filled with a thoughtful meditation on the two-year-long exile, just come to an end. It reveals the author's most personal and deeply religious reaction after his enforced stay in western Europe. Still in his late thirties, bishop Athanasius speaks to his people the language of a leader, matured and resolved by his experiences. His eagerness to share with all those under his pastoral responsibility the lesson of his recent exile is only one part of his charisma. He infuses the opportunity of such an intimate report with a pedagogical intent of his own in showing how scripture is capable of helping Christians to reach a more essential self-understanding through the many hazards of their lives. The freedom of speech, which he seems obviously glad to recover, is not used as an occasion for loud utterances of protest against his ecclesiastical adversaries, nor does he exploit opportunistically the favorable circumstance of Constantine's unexpected death on May 22 of that same year 337.

On the contrary, with a characteristic intense spirituality, the bishop focuses in FL 10 on his incarnational doctrine of salvation. His purpose is to introduce the listener and reader of his written homily into the *mystic* value of his unwanted round-trip to "the end of the earth" including his exile in Trier. The abundance of Origenian reminiscences, noticed in the former FL, fades away under the pressure of Athanasius' stronger self-involvement in his hermeneutic and in his doctrinal statements. Bluntly appropriating scripture to himself and to the church, much more decidedly than in FL 4, the author of FL 10 describes Easter as a unique opportunity, given to his people and himself, to experience the actual reality of God's incarnation, as he understands it. It is characteristic of the young bishop's genuine notion of salvation that such a mystic reality be taught in that fiery homily, through doctrine remaining as directly linked as possible with the day's event. Indeed, the doctrine that God became man was already in Athanasius' past, as it would always be in his future, a basic evidence of his faith. For several decades the purpose of his communication with all the people within the church would be to celebrate and verify in a shared experience of the church's community at large a theory of salvation he would never introduce in scholastic terms.

At first, the author of FL 10 insists on the fact that, despite the obstructive surveillance of a hostile administration, he had succeeded in informing his church in advance about "the time of the annual holy feast." For

> the Lord, strengthening and comforting us in our afflictions, we have not feared, even when kept in the midst of such machinations and conspiracies, to indicate and make known to you our saving Easter-feast, even from the ends of the earth.

This short notice is important for us, because it witnesses, as in FL 4, a procedure which will be applied by Athanasius again during his second exile. When no FL could be issued, he would nevertheless succeed in informing his clergy, in Alexandria and elsewhere, about the correct dates of Lent and Easter:

> Thus, keeping the feast myself, I was desirous that you also, my beloved, should keep it; and being conscious that an announcement like this is incumbent on me, I have not kept back from discharging the duty.[27]

In other words, the "announcement" itself, imposed on the Alexandrian bishops as a special duty by a Nicaean decree, could be detached from the regular FL and secured independently. The letters themselves had not been imposed by the imperial synod. Thus they constituted a privileged and amazingly personalized mode of communication between the head of Alexandrian Christianity and the broad body of its culturally diversified faithful. At least during the Athanasian rule, the Festal Letters became the bishop's best vehicle for circulating a distinctive mysticism among the highly differentiated communities of his vast territories.

Still remembering the celebration of Easter 337 in Trier, the bishop touches on a theme inaugurated before his exile, as we noticed it above in FL 5. He stresses the transcendent unity of the Christians celebrating Easter at the same date:

> While I then committed all my affairs to God, I considered it as a duty to celebrate the feast with you, not taking into account the distance between us. For although place divide us, yet the Lord, the giver of the feast, and who is himself our feast, who is also the bestower of the spirit, brings us together in mind, in harmony, and in the bond of peace.[28]

The stress lies here on the divine titles, carefully chosen by Athanasius, as in his more or less contemporary treatise *On the Incarnation*.[29] He himself would highlight their distinctiveness in using again the title "Bestower of the Spirit" further on in this tenth epistle,[30] as well as in the first *Oration against the Arians* which he probably started conceiving around 337.

The author then shifts into considering his present situation, "when more at ease," when "those things which could not be accomplished by man, God hath shewn to be easy of accomplishment, by bringing us to you."[31] The danger is over. He is released from the imperial decree of banishment. He can again exchange letters with his "brethren." That does not necessarily mean that he is already back in Alexandria. No allusion to such a return is made in the long FL 10, whose prevailing theme expands in the form of a rather tense and grave meditation on the trial just overcome. In any case, Athanasius' thought concentrates, at once, on the divine Logos, with the very phrases of a soteriological vision most characteristic of *On the Incarnation* and of his first *Oration against the Arians*:

> For the might of man and of all creatures is weak and poor, but the might which is above man, and uncreated, is rich and incomprehensible, and hath no beginning, but is eternal. It does not, then, possess one method only of healing; but, being rich, it works in divers manners for our salvation by means of His Logos, who is not restricted or hindered in his dealings towards us; but since he is rich and manifold, he varies himself according to the individual capacity of each soul. For he is the word, and the power, and the wisdom of God. . . .[32]

The saving Logos is then quickly shown as the paschal nourishment, sown in such a way, according to Matthew 13:8, that "it does not yield a uniform produce of fruit in this human life, but one various and rich . . . as the Saviour teaches, that Sower of grace, and Bestower of the Spirit."[33] The parable means, in fact, that Christians of all conditions have the same open access to the divine Logos in the church:

> For in sowing, he did not compel the will beyond the power, nor is the grace confined to the perfect alone; but it is sent down also among those who occupy the middle and the third ranks, so that he might rescue all men generally to salvation. Therefore also he hath prepared many mansions with the Father, so that although the dwelling-place is various in proportion to the advance of moral attainment, yet all of us are within the wall, and all of us enter within the same fence, the devil being cast out, and all his host expelled thence.[34]

There are no second-class believers for Athanasius, as Origen admitted them in distinguishing between the few enlightened faithful and the many "simple" people in the church. For Athanasius "all of us," according to this strikingly homiletic "we–speech," undergo one and the same experience of incarnational salvation. The Pharisees mentioned in the gospel narratives excluded themselves from such an experience, whereas "we" should no more be distressed by anything, having all been once and forever included in it:

> Oh! My dearly beloved, if we shall gain comfort from afflictions; if rest from labours; if health after sickness; if after death there is immortality; it does not become us to be much distressed by the temporal ills that afflict mankind. It is not right to be greatly moved because of the trials which befall us.[35]

In forms spoken out of a still awesome experience, the bishop continues in referring to the present salvific institution of the author's church-community, as based on the incarnation of the healing Logos. At the same time, he involves his addressees in the personal ordeal, out of which he has deepened his notion of salvation. It becomes hardly possible to separate what this bishop expresses in his familiar style when referring to the incarnate Logos, or describing the present church, or again when referring to himself.

The contemplation on his return from exile leads the young bishop to glorify the figure of the suffering

> Lord and saviour Jesus Christ . . . who, when he was smitten, bore
> it patiently; being reviled, he reviled not again; when he suffered,
> He threatened not; but he gave his back to the smiters, and his
> cheeks to buffetings, and turned not his face from spitting; and, at
> last, was willingly led to death, that we might behold in him the
> image of all that is virtuous and immortal. . . .[36]

In a typically Athanasian way, the terse narrative replaces any other
form of argument, and it does so with a powerful persuasiveness
proper to the Alexandrian bishop's accustomed style. This central
meditation ends with a few lines which could again be quoted almost
literally from *On the Incarnation:*[37]

> For he suffered to procure freedom from suffering for those who
> suffer in him; and he descended that he might raise us up; he took
> on him the trial of being born, that we might love him who is
> unbegotten; he went down to corruption, that corruption might put
> on immortality; he became weak for us, that we might rise with
> power; he descended to death, that he might bestow on us immor-
> tality, and give life to the dead. Lastly, he became man, that we who
> die as men might live again, and that death should no more reign
> over us; for the apostolic word proclaims, *Death shall not have the
> dominion over us* (Rom 6:9).[38]

The isolated mention of "the Ario-maniacs, being opposers of
Christ, and heretics,"[39] in the final section of FL 10, serves for dra-
matizing a summary of gospel narratives. In fact, the attention of the
author is riveted to the figure of the suffering savior. The polemical
turn, now given to his message, intends only to enhance his actualizing exegesis, and so does also his allusion to the Meletians. As if he
tries to excuse himself at this point he adds:

> I know these are hard sayings, not truly to those who oppose Christ,
> but also to the Schismatics; for they are united together, as men of
> kindred feelings. For they have learned to rend the seamless coat of
> God: they think it not strange to divide the indivisible Son from the
> Father.[40]

Interestingly enough, the Johannine "seamless coat," which had
been used in FL 5 and in *On the Incarnation* 24 before the exile, as an
image of the unity in the incarnate Logos, refers now to the Trinitarian dimension of the Logos, as "the indivisible Son" of the Father.

Thus the author of FL 10 shows up as having already a good grasp of the issues which will soon become central in his first *Oration against the Arians.*

As a matter of fact, his next circular letter, FL 11 for Easter 339, must have been written when he was immersed in the demanding task of composing what has been handed down to us as the first and the second of these *Orations,* but what constituted probably in its original shape only one such treatise.[41] FL 11 is almost as long as FL 10. Its opening offers a carefully summarized praise of the apostle Paul. The one who "was carried up even to heavenly places, and was born in paradise" (2 Cor 12), benefits here from an almost didactic praise. All his epistles are enumerated, as "to the Romans, and the Ephesians, and Philemon . . . the Corinthians and the Galatians . . . to the Colossians and Thessalonians . . . the Hebrews . . . to his elect sons, Timothy and Titus."[42]

> For he was all things to all men; and being himself a perfect man, he adapted his teaching to the need of every one, so that by all means he might rescue some of them. Therefore his word was not without fruit; but, in every place, it is planted and productive even to this day.

The author of FL 11 inaugurates the literary tradition of praising the person of the apostle Paul, according to the ancient models of classical rhetoric, a tradition perpetuated after him by John Chrysostom, Cyril of Alexandria, Augustine, and many others. But, being Athanasius, he directs the laudatory remarks immediately to a pointed commentary which links the Pauline teaching with today's life, and with himself in his service of the church:

> It is planted and productive even to this day. And wherefore, my beloved? For it is necessary that we should search into the apostolic mind. Not only in the beginning of the Epistles, but also at their close, and in the middle of them, he used persuasions and admonitions. I hope, therefore, that by your prayers, I shall, in no respect, give a false representation of the plan of that holy man. As he was well skilled in these divine matters, and knew the power of the divine teaching, he deemed it necessary, in the first place, to make known the word concerning Christ, and the mystery regarding Him; and then afterwards to point to the correction of habit, so that when they had learned to know the Lord, they might readily acquiesce in the observance of those things which he commanded.[43]

The Athanasian pope, eager to restore his hierarchical position after the setback of the forced exile in Trier, finds nothing more urgent than to introduce his many known and unknown fellow Christians into a comprehensive reading of the Pauline letters. It is only the second time since that exile that he has an opportunity to communicate with all the people in his church; but the tensions and the conflicts of the day seem to be forgotten, the heretics are hardly mentioned, not one word is squandered on matters of clerical administration.

Already the horizon of church politics was darkening again for Athanasius. His oriental opponents, in their search for episcopal primacy under the ruling of Constantine's son in the east, Constantius II, not only refused to admit his return from Trier, but they chose a replacement for him in anticipating his next exile. In his own church, Athanasius was under pressure, being requested by his friends, the leaders of the monastic movement, to assert in a public statement what he really thought about Arianism and Nicaean orthodoxy. It is more remarkable that in this Easter letter for 339 the bishop's main concern deals with a pastoral introduction into Pauline exegesis. In fact, his lesson, distributed in a cheerful homiletic address, expands to a consideration of the whole collection of New Testament writings, with, in addition, a heavy quoting of Isaiah and the Psalms. Obviously the author wants to put into the minds of his addressees as many phrases from scripture as possible. He adds a passionate call to "fight the good fight of faith" (1 Tim 3). When he finally alludes to the heretics, he denounces them in the terms of the *Orations against the Arians:* "He from whom the Jews, with the Arians, turn away their faces, but whom we acknowledge and worship."[44]

> For this cause, the Ario-maniacs, who now have gone out of the church, being opposers of Christ, have dug a pit of unbelief, into which they themselves have been thrust; and, since they have advanced in ungodliness, they *overthrow the faith of the simple* (Rom 6[?]:18); blaspheming the Son of God, and saying that he is a creature, and has his being from things which are not.[45]

The polemic reference, as in the *Orations* themselves on a broader scale, turns quickly into a celebration of Christ's paschal mystery:

> For we do not introduce days of mourning and sorrow, as a man may consider those of the Passover to be; but we keep the feast, being filled with joy and gladness. We keep it then, not regarding it

after the deceitful error of the Jews; nor according to the teaching of the Arians, which takes away the Son from the Godhead, and numbers him among creatures; but as viewing it according to the correct doctrine we derive from the Lord. . . . For if he were a creature, he would have been held by death; but if he was not held by death, as the scriptures aver, he is not a creature, but the Lord of the creatures, and the substance of this immortal feast. For the Lord of death would abolish death; and being Lord, what he would was accomplished; for we have all passed from death unto life.[46]

The proximity of *On the Incarnation* and of the *Orations against the Arians* is striking, in particular if one notes how the Athanasian logic always imposes a presentation of the Son's divinity through a series of narrative reminders of the salvation operated by the Incarnate One according to the gospels.

No Festal Letters could be issued by the bishop's chancellery during the second exile of Athanasius (339–346). In FL 19, for Easter 347, the author starts and ends with a grateful sigh of relief, and that was all his devoted listeners could hear about the many unexpected circumstances of over six years spent by him in the west, at the reading of his circular epistle in their liturgical gatherings:

Blessed is God, the Father of our Lord Jesus Christ (Eph 1:3), for such an introduction is fitting for an Epistle; and now more especially, when accompanied with thanksgiving to the Lord, in the Apostle's words, because he has brought us from a distance and granted us again to send openly to you, as usual, the Festal Letters.[47]

I also give thanks to God, as well for those other wonders he has done, as for the various helps that have now been afforded us, in that though he has chastened us sore, he did not deliver us over to death, but brought us from a distance, even as from the ends of the earth, and has united us again with you.[48]

The body of the letter constitutes a vigorous chapter of biblical theology on the mystery of Easter. Athanasius takes over the Christian symbolic of the Passah prescription in Deuteronomy 16, as interpreted by Origen and popularized in the Alexandrian allegorical tradition. He gives a new life to old motifs, and he abounds in original quotations from scripture. The Jews are severely condemned as "faithless," because they did not accept the messianic value of their one religious tradition, which should have culminated in Christ.

"Like these, too, are the heretics, who, having fallen from a true conscience, dare to imagine to themselves atheism."[49] In a discreet but determined way, the author turns the usual preaching on the liturgical symbolism of Easter into a call for a correct trinitarian doctrine. From Moses, the trumpets, and the bitter herbs, his thought shifts incessantly to mentioning the Father and the Son, "Him who is truly God and also his Word," "the Word, which is the pilot of souls," and "the grace of the Spirit was given." The very notion of God as such is at stake, the author insists, in the split between his own church and the heretics, as well as in the reciprocal rejection of Jews and Christians. The theological issues of the Arian debate built up the background of FL 19, despite the complete lack in it of any scholastic controversy.

Only a few general observations may be added on the sequence FL 20 to 28. In FL 20, for Easter 348, Athanasius, once more, holds to a vibrant "we–talk." From the first line on, he conceives his letter as a homily delivered in the name of the whole church community. The church finds in it a voice for celebrating its willingness to get ready for the feast. Gospel narratives pervade each paragraph. Before sentences are written, it looks as if the author's phrasing was born in his mind out of an inexhaustible stock of memorized quotations from scripture. The whole delivery, if there was one, resounded with phrases from the Bible. It is hardly certain that the auditors clearly distinguished between what was God's word and what was Athanasius' when they attended the service in which such Festal Letters were read.

FL 24, for Easter 352, spends much time presenting the patriarchs and the old prophets of Israel as paradigms for a life in complete retreat, and for a deliberate confinement in silence and in solitude. The monastic ideal seems, then, recommended to the church at large. The Passah, misunderstood by the Jews, finds its actual and perfect realization now in the Christian liturgy:

> We, we have close to us that reality which the shadows and types had announced, namely the Image of the Father, our Lord Jesus Christ. If we nourish ourselves with it all the time, and if we anoint the doors of our souls with his blood, we shall be freed from the labors imposed by Pharaoh and his supervisors. I do not mean the labors described in the narrative (cf Ex 3:7; 5:6ff), because they are over; but I mean labors prefigured by them. For through them we have learned what the real labors are.

The serene biblical teaching continues as far as we can read the long fragment preserved. The bishop's purpose in FL 24 was obviously to write on Mosaic types and on their actual fulfillment in the Christian community.

The substantial quotations transmitted in Coptic from FL 25, for the year 353, confirm the same peaceful, symbolic teaching, focusing on the traditional Easter theme. The final part of FL 26, for the next year, shows an engaging and joyful "we–talk." More scattered extracts from FL 27, for 355, start in the same way, before discussing the Jewish failure to grasp the correct, "Christian"(!), meaning of the feast. Only two pages of the Coptic version of FL 28, for 356, seem to survive, partly complemented by a citation of the Greek original. The author invites his folks to enjoy the true happiness of Easter.

Thus he touches on a theme which could easily be studied for itself in these letters of our second sequence. Only a few notations may be collected here on this line of thought. In FL 10, just after having received the needed permit for a safe return from his exile in Trier, the young bishop was all joy and gratitude:

> Thus, anciently, the people of the Jews, when they came out of affliction into a state of ease, kept the feast, singing a song of praise for their victory. So also the people in the time of Easter, because they were delivered from a deadly decree, kept a feast to the Lord; reckoning it a feast, returning thanks to the Lord, and praising him for having changed their condition. Therefore, let us also, performing our vows to the Lord, and confessing our sins, keep the feast to the Lord, in conversation, moral conduct, and manner of life; praising our Lord, who has chastened us a little, but has not utterly failed and forsaken us, nor altogether kept silence from us. For it, having also brought us out of the crafty and famous Egypt of the opposers of Christ, he has caused us to pass through many trials and afflictions, as it were in the wilderness, to his holy church. . . .[50]

In FL 11 Athanasius added more typological examples of happiness after surmounted trails:

> But after this affliction, and sorrow, and sighing, when they depart from this world, a certain divine gladness, and pleasure, and exultation receives them, from which pain, and sorrow, and sighing, flee away.[51]

The types were soon actualized in regard to the author's own tribulation:

> Since then these things are so, let us make a joyful noise with the
> saints, and let no one of us fail of his duty in these things; thinking
> nothing of the affliction or the trials which, especially at this time,
> have been enviously directed against us by the party of Eusebius.
> . . . Let us therefore keep the feast, my brethren, celebrating it not
> as worthy of grief and mourning; neither let us be confounded with
> heretics through temporal troubles brought upon us by godliness.
> But if any thing that would promote joy and gladness should offer,
> let us attend to it. . . .[52]

Again, coming back from his second exile, Athanasius used the same thoroughly typological vein in order to express his joy:

> The saints, having their senses exercised by reason of practice, and
> being strong in faith, and understanding the word, do not become
> faint in trials; but, although, from time to time, circumstances of
> greater trial arise against them, yet they continue faithful; and,
> awaking the Lord, who is with them, they are delivered. So, passing
> through water and fire, to a place where they can breathe freely,
> they duly keep the feast, offering up prayers, with thanksgiving, to
> God who has redeemed them.[53]

It may be quite a commonplace in Easter letters to call the congregation to share joy and gratitude. But Athanasius' distinctive mark in his annually repeated invitations of that sort is to express them always in fresh and vivid terms by linking them closely with his own pastoral experience.

FINAL SEQUENCE OF FL

The most exhilarating moment in a proper study of the Athanasian Easter letters might well happen when the reader realizes that their final sequence leads her or him to follow, year after year, the aging bishop, true to his pastoral homiletic, as far as to his deathbed. In these twelve letters, from 356 to 373, despite the fragmentary state of their transmission, one perceives again the authentic voice of Athanasius. After the abrupt end of Constantius' reign, in 361, a more stable peace of mind would soon pervade the festal letters of the Alexandrian bishop. In the preserved extract of FL 28, for Easter

356, the mood was still tense and oppressed. The author was not really complaining, but was emphasizing in a grave speech the "long road" of suffering in the service of the Lord:

> In fact, it should never happen that we neglect to take on us the yoke because of the long road. . . . Therefore, my brethren, let us not miss receiving such a grace. Let us be submitted to him with ardor, and let us run to him, in order to be, in our turn, firmly positioned in the line of our fathers. For they had not abstained from such a way of life, and the whole inhabited world would benefit from the loving care of the Logos.

In FL 29, written about a year in advance for 357, the bishop, once more exposed to political violence, could only remind his people of the trials endured by all the patriarchs and the old prophets, by Abraham, Isaac, Jacob, Joseph, Moses, as well as by Job in particular. His recurrent image was the burning fire of the moral ordeal through which faith is purified. There was only one hope left: "God's love differs from human love. What men are doing always ends sooner or later, but God's kindness has no end."

After five years in the monastic hiding places of the desert, and again after the awkward months of his fourth exile under the short-lived rule of the emperor Julian, Athanasius succeeded finally in issuing a new Easter letter in 363. He was then at the imperial court in Antioch, where he had just submitted the Nicaean Creed to the newly elected emperor Jovian, himself a pro-Nicaean Christian. There the Alexandrian bishop wrote FL 36 for Easter of the following year. Amazingly enough, the letter itself echoes creedal concerns, as if the pastor wanted to share his political mission in the oriental metropolis with his people left behind him, in Egypt:

> As we always try to become more sons of the church, we know the Monarchy, namely the Unique, the Father of Christ, the sole Ungenerated, the single One without a principle, God of the Law, the Prophets, and the New Testament; and also his unique Son, whom he begot before ages and times, through whom he created the universe, and will come to judge the living and the dead. Thus we know the Three:[54] God, the Son, and the Holy Spirit Who is the crown. As they are not separated from each other, there is one God, one Holy Spirit, one faith, one baptism, one resurrection from the dead. About all these matters, you have learned the testimonies and arguments in books and in the holy scripture which you have all read. Greetings in Christ.

The final section of FL 36 recommends serene behavior in avoiding further disputes with Arians:

> I am begging you, should they publish written statements, do not laugh at anybody, nor laugh at those who spoke against us in the past. For such blame does not come out of you, nor out of any human agency, but only from God. What comes from God, should return to God, so that in sharing a noble attitude God's grace may descend upon you and upon the church in abundance.

Obscure as they are, these lines illustrate nevertheless Athanasius' constant and easy mixture of doctrinal purpose and circumstantial motives in the FL.

The next letter, FL 37 for 365, marked by the hostile attitude of the pro-Arian emperor Valens, deals precisely with the current situation more than with general considerations of a theological nature. In order to give it homiletic shape, the author uses once more the analogy between Jews, Meletians, and Arians, whom he accuses altogether of rejecting Christ's paschal mystery. If correctly identified in the Coptic version, the fragment of FL 38 may well have been written during the fifth and last exile of the Alexandrian bishop. It betrays the latter's nostalgia, before he returned to his community in Alexandria on February 1, 366:

> I, too, I really like such an assembly (the assembly of the apostles in Jerusalem, at Pentecost, according to Acts 2), and I would almost start praying: "Who shall give me the wings of a dove to fly away and find rest with you?" (cf Ps 54:7 LXX); but another thought cheers me up: there must be another way of overcoming the separation between us when we stay under our different tents. For, that same Lamb, we shall eat it as in one and the same embrace, namely in the Lord immolated for us.

Thus, through the decades of his eventful ministry, Athanasius reveals himself as deeply linked with his local church, more than with any other Christian or political institution in the empire of the day. He also articulates his pastoral attachment in the only canonical language recognized by him, a language made out of metaphors and phrases quoted from scripture.

FL 39, for Easter 367, is probably the only one known by a larger body of students, because it contains the oldest complete list transmitted to us of the Old and New Testament writings, as well as a collection of deutero-canonical writings. Again, this dry topic is framed homiletically, in particular with a thoughtful introduction: "As life He went to the dead, and as God He came to the human race,"[55] in order to institute a revelatory process, which goes over from Christ to the apostles and other disciples, from Paul to the doctors and teachers established in Pauline churches. "Let us celebrate Easter according to the tradition of our fathers. We possess the holy scriptures which suffice for our perfect instruction."[56] Because of the literature distributed by heretics and schismatics, a canon of scriptures needs to be established. FL 40, 41, and 42, for 368, 369, and 370, discuss unusual matters belonging to the local administration, such as clerical ordinations and patrimonies, as well as cultic practices at the tombs of martyrs, or translations of the latter's bones. A major part of FL 43, for 371, has been handed down to us, Greek quotations complementing the Coptic version. Its content could hardly be more typical of Athanasius' style. Each sentence, from beginning to end, follows the warmest "we–talk" pattern, and includes a scriptural quotation or a clear reference to scripture. Even when the author feels the need for excusing himself about some repetitions, he cannot help calling on Paul:

> I have written it, as I know well, on several occasions, and there are people who may point it out, as they are for now saturated, and wish to hear me talking about something new. But Paul does not reject such a procedure, neither he nor his predecessor, Moses, that great servant of God. . . .[57]

Almost as if he returned to the writing of his youth in the first years of his episcopal ministry, he expands, in 371, a vision of God's salvation entirely centered on the mystery of the Incarnate. As in one of his later dogmatic letters, *To Adelphius*, which may be dated from around that time, Athanasius comes close, in FL 43, to images and themes proper to the treatise *On the Incarnation*.

In FL 44, transmitted in a fragment of the Syriac version, the aging bishop condenses a lifelong teaching in a few sentences. Divine titles and references to the economy of salvation, with its incarnational focus, build up a biblical paraphrase, animated by the discreet but enthusiastic mysticism of its author:

> For he was truly, as it were, the splendor of the light (cf Heb 1:3), and the Word of God; thus too he was the river from the fountain which gives drink (cf Jn 7:37). And then to Paradise, and now to all men, he gives the same gift of the Spirit. . . .[58]

Athanasius' last Easter letter, FL 45, dates from a few months before his death, in 373. In his accustomed scriptural "we–talk," he delivers a sort of premonition of his own passing away. There would be no better conclusion for the present survey of Athanasian FL than to appreciate the homiletic value of this final circular communication of the Alexandrian bishop with his church in Egypt, Libya, and the Pentapolis:

> Let us all take up our sacrifices, acknowledging our option for the poor, and we enter the holy place, as it is written, *whither also Jesus as a forerunner is entered for us, having obtained eternal redemption* (Heb 9:12). . . . For this is a great proof that, being strangers, we were called friends, and once being aliens, we have become fellow-citizens with the saints, and made children of the Jerusalem from above, whose type was the one built by Solomon. For if Moses executed everything according to the model which he had received on the mount, the cult under the tent was obviously a type of the mysteries in heaven. In order to give us access to them the Lord managed for us a way new and permanent. Namely, if all the realities from old were types of the new ones, in the same fashion the present celebration is a type of the joy in heaven, to which we go with the songs of psalms, and with spiritual hymns as we start to fast.[59]

Many other suggestions are probably contained in the FL for a possible biographer of Athanasius. Their redundant biblical content would need a more analytical treatment in order to reveal the author's closeness to the inspiration or the letter of scripture. It will be enough to summarize briefly the homiletic value of the Athanasian FL.

First, the genre of the homily seems to have served as the most appropriate one in Athanasius' regular communication with his people. In a popular form of preaching, the bishop undertook, year after year, the difficult task of calling the attention of the faithful to the ideals of Easter celebrated in the liturgy. The real task, as Athanasius understood it, was not just to distribute a few lessons of theology or of Christian ethics. He had in mind a more challenging endeavor when he conceived his annual FL. He did not wish only to exhort the communities in their readiness for the paschal fast, in giving them doctrinal and ascetic advice. He was more willing to have them constantly focused on the central mystery of their religious identity, thanks to a critical discernment by which they would constantly interpret their own history, and their history as a church, in the light of the incarnate God's presence among them. Salvation happens now, in the very experience of a political and liturgical body of believers, as the church in Alexandria and Egypt was one. Such an incarnational focus seems to be at work in all the Athanasian FL. It helps to understand their conception and their relevance for a broader study of the Christian traditions. In a more direct way, it introduces us into the deeper soul of Athanasius himself.

NOTES

1. Hereafter abbreviated FL.
2. C.L. Feltoe, *The Letters and Other Remains of Dionysius of Alexandria* (Cambridge, 1904).
3. W. Cureton, *The Festal Letters of Athanasius* (London, 1848), Syriac letters first edited; J. P. Migne, PG 26.1360–1444, includes a Latin translation of Cureton; H. Burgess, *The Festal Epistles of S. Athanasius* (Oxford, 1845), English translation with additional fragments in Syriac for FL 10 and 11; A. Mai, *S. Athanasii epistulae festales* (Nova Patrum Bibliotheca 6; Rome: 1853), Syriac; F. Larsow, *Die Fest-Briefe des heiligen Athanasius* (Leipzig/Göttingen, 1852); A. Robertson, ed., *Select Writings and Letters of Athanasius* (NPNF 2/4; Oxford, 1891; Grand Rapids, 1975) 503–53, translation of Burgess; L.-Th. Lefort, *S. Athanase. Lettres festales et pastorales en Copte* (CSCO 150–51, Scriptores coptici tomus 19–20; Louvain, 1955); P. Merendino, *Osterfestbriefe des Apa Athanasius* (Düsseldorf, 1965), German translation of Coptic letters; M. Alpert, "La 10° lettre festale d'Athanase d'Alexandrie. Traduction et interprétation," *Parole de l'Orient* 6–7 (1975–6) 69–90; R.-G. Coquin and E. Lucchesi, "Un complément au corpus copte des *Lettres Festales* d'Athanase (Paris, B. N., Copte 176) (Pl III)," *OLP* 13 (1982) 137–42, Coptic text with French translation of FL 6; R.-G. Coquin, "Les lettres Festales d'Athanase (CPG 2102). Un nouveau complément: le manuscrit IFAO, Copte 25 (Planche X)," *OLP* 15 (1984) 133–58, Coptic text of FL 39, 40, and 41, with French translation; R. Lorenz, *Der zehnte Osterbrief des Athanasius von Alexandrien. Text. Übersetzung. Erläuterungen* (Berlin and New York, 1986), facsimile Syriac and German translation. A new edition of the FL is being prepared by a student of Prof. Tito Orlandi in Rome. An English translation is also planned by a student of Prof. Birger Pearson, University of California at Santa Barbara.
4. A. Martin, with M. Albert, *Histoire "acéphale" et Index syriaque des Lettres Festales d'Athanase d'Alexandrie* (SC 317; Paris, 1985); R. Lorenz, *Der zehnte Osterbrief* (note 3 above).
5. Problems related to the chronology of the FL were first addressed by E. Schwartz, *Zur Geschichte des Athanasius* I (NGNG, 1904) 337–56; *Gesam-*

melte Schriften 3 (Berlin, 1959) 1–28; "Zur Kirchengeschichte des 4. Jahrhunderts," *ZNW* 24 (1935) 129–37; *Gesammelte Schriften* 4 (Berlin, 1960) 1–11. Responses were given by V. Peri, "La cronologia delle lettere festali di Sant' Atanasio e la Quaresima," *Aevum* 34 (1961) 28–86; L.-Th. Lefort, "Les lettres festales de saint Athanase," *Bulletin de l'Academie royale des sciences, des lettres et des beaux-arts de Belgique* 39 (1953) 641–56. R. Lorenz, *Der zehnte Osterbrief*, has convincingly restated the Schartzian chronology. Problems related to the Index are stressed by T.D. Barnes reviewing A. Martin, *Histoire "acéphale"*, in *JTS* ns 31 (1986) 576–89.

6. C. Kannengiesser, "Athanasius of Alexandria. A Paradigm for the Church Today," *Pacifica* 1 (1988) 85–99; "St. Athanasius of Alexandria Rediscovered: His Political and Pastoral Achievement," *Coptic Church Review* 9 (1988) 68–74.

7. Burgess, *Festal Epistles*, 118a.

8. Translated in Burgess, *Festal Epistles*, 3. All translations, unless otherwise noted, have been taken from this edition (see note 3 above).

9. Burgess, *Festal Epistles*, 4.

10. Ibid., 6.

11. Ibid., 9.

12. Ibid., 11–12.

13. FL 24 in L.-Th. Lefort's citation; see R. Lorenz, *Der zehnte Osterbrief*, 14.

14. Text in L.-Th. Lefort, *Lettres Festales*, 13 (see note 3 above).

15. Burgess, *Festal Epistles*, 112.

16. Ibid., 113–14.

17. Ibid., 113.

18. Ibid., 31–32.

19. Ibid., 33.

20. Ibid., 33–34.

21. Ibid., 37.

22. Ibid., 32.

23. *On the Incarnation* 13–15: "What else could He possibly do, being God, but renew His image in mankind, so that through it men might once more come to know Him? . . . He, the image of the Father, came and dwelt in our midst, in order that He might renew mankind made after Himself. . . . He became Himself an object for the senses, so that those who were seeking God in sensible things might apprehend the Father through the works which He, the Word of God, did in the body." Translated in *St. Athanasius. On the Incarnation* (Crestwood, NY: St. Vladimir's Seminary Press, 1953) 41–43. See P. Merendino, *Paschale Sacramentum. Eine Untersuchungen über die Osterkatechese des hl. Athanasius von Alexandrien in ihrer Beziehung zu den frühchristlichen Überlieferungen* (LQF 42; Münster, 1965) 67–73.

24. Burgess, *Festal Epistles*, 38.

25. See my remarks in "Le témoignage des lettres festales de s. Athanase sur le date de l'apologie *Contre les païens—Sur l'incarnation du Verbe*," *RSR* 52 (1964) 91–100; "Le date de l'apologie d'Athanase *Contre le païens* et *Sur l'incarnation du Verbe*," *RSR* 58 (1970) 383–428.

26. Masterfully discussed in R. Lorenz, *Der zehnte Osterbrief.*

27. Burgess, *Festal Epistles*, 67.

28. Ibid., 67–68.

29. See my introduction to the edition of *On the Incarnation* in SC 199 (Paris, 1973) 86–93.

30. Burgess, *Festal Epistles*, 71.

31. Ibid., 69.

32. Ibid., 70.

33. Ibid., 71.

34. Ibid.

35. Ibid., 75.

36. Ibid., 75–76.

37. For instance, in paragraph eight: "He took to himself a body, a human body even as our own. . . . Thus, taking a body like our own, because all our bodies were liable to the corruption of death, he surrendered his body to death in place of all, and offered it to the Father. This he did out of sheer love for us, so that in his death all might turn again to incorruption men who had turned back to corruption, and make them alive through death by the appropriation of his body and by the grace of his resurrection" (*St. Athanasius. On the Incarnation*, 34).

38. Burgess, *Festal Epistles*, 70.

39. Ibid., 77.

40. Ibid., 79.

41. More on Athanasius' original treatise *Against the Arians* can be found in my Oxford lecture of 1979: "Athanasius of Alexandria. *Three Orations Against the Arians*, a Reappraisal," *SP* 18 (1982) 981–95, and in my book, *Athanase d'Alexandrie évêque et écrivain. Une lecture des Traités Contre les Ariens* (Théologie Historique 70; Paris: Beauchesne, 1983).

42. Burgess, *Festal Epistles*, 84.

43. Ibid., 84.

44. Ibid., 86.

45. Ibid., 93.

46. Ibid., 95–96.

47. Ibid., 121.

48. Ibid., 129.

49. Ibid., 126.

50. Ibid., 80.

51. Ibid., 83.

52. Ibid., 95.

53. Ibid., 128.

54. Text interpolated in the Coptic version: *hypostaseis* is added here.
55. Lefort, *Lettres Festales*, 31.
56. Lefort, ibid., 34. The Greek fragment in PG 26.1436–1440 starts after the next sentence. On FL 39 see S. N. Sakkos, "The 39th Festal Letter of Athanasius the Great," *Tomos heortios* (Thessaloniki, 1974) 131–91 (in modern Greek).
57. Lefort, *Lettres Festales*, 49–50.
58. Burgess, *Festal Epistles*, 140.
59. PG 26.1441–1444.

6

THE ORATIONS OF GREGORY OF NAZIANZUS: A STUDY IN RHETORIC AND PERSONALITY
by Gerard H. Ettlinger, S.J.

A study of the orations of Gregory of Nazianzus is appropriate for a *Festschrift* dedicated to Walter Burghardt, S.J., patrologist and preacher, whose homilies reflect his substantial rhetorical talent, but touch his audience in a direct and personal way.

The forty-five extant orations of Gregory were delivered on various special occasions or feast days, often in memory of, or to honor, someone whom Gregory loved or respected, and they were, therefore, composed in accordance with a prescribed plan and structure. No one who knows Gregory's work could deny that he was a major figure in the church of his time and a learned, skilled practitioner of classical rhetoric; the rhetorical elements in his writings and their influence on his life and work have, therefore, been the object of serious study.[1]

The use of rhetorical technique does not, however, exclude the possibility that the author is expressing his true feelings. One of Gregory's major contributions to ancient literature, both religious and secular, lies in the realm of autobiography, for his poems about himself and his life are the most significant pieces of self-revelation in the ancient world prior to Augustine's *Confessions*.[2] And just as these very personal works are finely crafted examples of classical poetry, so too, there are many passages in his orations, especially in the panegyrics, where Gregory gives voice to obviously sincere feelings in language so rhetorically sophisticated that the whole composition could easily be dismissed as artificial.

Gregory's theological significance is evident from the nickname, "the Theologian," by which he is traditionally known. He and his friends, the brothers Basil of Caesarea and Gregory of Nyssa, made Cappadocia famous through their development of the language and concepts of trinitarian theology; he was also cited by fifth century anthologists such as Theodoret of Cyrus in the christological controversies that resulted in the condemnation of Nestorius and Eutyches.[3]

But due to the nature of this publication, as indicated in the opening paragraph, this paper will not consider Gregory's orations from the viewpoint of rhetoric, theology, or even content as such, although encroachment into these areas will at times be unavoidable. The focus here will be, rather, on the revelation, whether actually intended by Gregory or not, in a few relatively brief and obscure passages, of certain aspects of his personality and character.

The content of the passages selected is varied: interpretation of scriptural texts; remarks, sometimes negative, about ecclesiastical life or practice; discussion of theological issues and statements of his understanding of the truth; praise of a relative or friend, combined, in the midst of praise, with criticism, in a manner that contrasts sharply with the primary thrust of the work. His tone too changes, and is, in turn, serious, light, somber, cheerful, ironical, affectionate, critical, laudatory, or a combination of any number of these and similar qualities. Most of these passages display an ability to penetrate and grasp what can be called the human or humane core of a particular topic.

The personality that emerges belongs, in the first place, to a human being, who happens also to be an ecclesiastical leader and a poet; it is generally, but not always, a pleasant and appealing one. Frankness in speech, for example, can be refreshing and a sign of integrity; but it can also stem from a self-centered disregard for other people and their feelings. Final judgment on Gregory, if possible at all, should be reserved until the texts have been studied; but from the outset it seems reasonable to suggest that his personal appeal stems, not from his theology or rhetoric, but from the fact that he was a complex character and strikingly unique for his time.

Gregory wished, first of all, to be a good Christian and strove to serve God and to be united with God. But he was, although against his will, a public figure, a bishop, who had to teach about God and assist the people who looked to him for guidance or help. And yet Gregory was always acutely aware of his own humanity and limitations, and was deeply disturbed and unhappy with the personal and political consequences of having been placed in a position that he never desired or sought. He loved his family and friends and was able to express his feelings in a way that few other early Christian writers could or did. He was a person of great sensitivity, especially with respect to problems in human relationships, both in the lives of other people, and, to an extent rarely found in ancient writers, in matters that directly affected him and his own life; ironically, this very quality, positive in itself, appears at times to have blunted his sensitivity toward others and occasioned surprisingly negative attitudes.

Few homilists of the early church reveal such a perception of their own humanity and of that of their audience. Some, such as John Chrysostom, were equally if not more frank in expressing their opinions. But Chrysostom's tone, although it was personal, is always that of John the preacher, the minister of God and God's church, exhorting his audience to higher things. Gregory's motivation and purpose are basically the same as Chrysostom's, but his work is transformed by a personal element that circumvents, or perhaps transcends, his official *persona*, and results in self-revelation.

It should be noted at the start that some of the texts to be examined are not particularly well adapted to the twentieth century; they do, however, reflect the religious, cultural, and sociological structures of Gregory's time, so that even as they display patterns of thought and action that are no longer in favor, they reveal a complex person struggling, not unlike people today, with conflicting forces that alternately call for allegiance and demand repudiation.

An example, not from his orations, but from two letters (144–145)[4] dealing with a divorce case, should help to clarify the point at issue:

> *Letter 144:* To a government official about divorce proceedings brought by a young woman under pressure from her father.
>
> Haste does not always deserve to be praised; I have, therefore, put off my answer in the case of the honorable Verianus's daughter, in order to leave some time for correction, and also because I assume that your honor does not approve of the divorce, since you have entrusted the inquiry to me, who you knew would act neither rashly nor thoughtlessly in such a matter. That is why I have, not unreasonably in my opinion, restrained myself until now. But since we are nearing the time limit set to disclose the results of the examination, we shall now make a report. The young woman seems to be divided, as it were, for she is torn between reverence for her parents and affection for her husband. Her words are with her parents, but her thoughts, I feel, are with her husband, as her tears show. You will, therefore, obviously do whatever comes into your mind be-

cause of your justice and because of God, who directs you in everything. I would have been most happy to tell my son Verianus that I
am of the opinion that he should let most of these issues drop, so as
not to confirm the divorce, which is absolutely contrary to our laws,
even if Roman laws decide differently. For justice must always be
preserved, and I pray that you always say and do this.

Letter 145: To the father mentioned in letter 144.

Public executioners do nothing bad since they are serving the
laws, nor is the sword with which we punish criminals an unlawful
one. And yet the public executioner receives no praise, and his
deadly sword is not greeted with joy. In the same way, I cannot bear
to become an object of hatred because I confirm the divorce by my
hand and tongue. It is much better for me to be a source of union
and affection than of division of life and divorce. I think that the
reason why our governor entrusted the inquiry about your daughter
to me is that I could not approach a divorce without care and
consideration. For he obviously proposed me as bishop, not as a
judge, and he appointed me to mediate your problem. I ask you,
therefore, to pardon my timidity. If the better course of action wins
out, use me to serve your wishes; commands like that please me. But
if you follow the worse and more cruel approach, something we
have never done right up to this day, look for someone else better
suited to this purpose. For even though I regard you most highly in
every way, I do not have the time, in order to indulge your friendship, to offend God, to whom I owe an accounting for every action
and thought. I shall believe your daughter, for the truth will come
out, at that moment when she can be free of her fear of you and can
speak the truth openly. At this moment her condition is pitiful, for
she is divided, assigning her words to you and her tears to her
husband.

The first and most important point to note in these letters is the
fact that, for Gregory, the young woman is the central figure in the
case; he sees the difficulty of her position and sympathizes with the
confusion and pain she experiences; he understands the real issue
behind the legal situation, and his major concern is her happiness. He
obviously believes that divorce is contrary to Christian law, which he,
as a bishop, is bound to defend; this is an issue, therefore, but it is not
his primary consideration. He focuses on the young woman and on
the pressures to which she is (unfairly) subjected. To solve her problem, then, he advises and admonishes a government official and implicitly criticizes Roman law; he tells the woman's father (who is a

friend and a person of importance) that his good will and friendship mean nothing to him if he insists on pursuing a course that is both wrong and cruel.

Gregory's comments on the public executioner are also of interest, for they show that he is aware of a possible tension between behavior that is technically correct and human reaction against it. His own actions here reflect a sensitivity to other people's problems and an attitude of directness and fearlessness when striving to deal with them; these texts, in other words, reveal a person who relates to others on the level of human feeling and understanding, not simply as an official administrator or a functionary. It is the self-revelation that flows from this type of material that will be highlighted in Gregory's orations, where it can easily be overlooked in the midst of long, rhetorical discourses.

The letters just discussed concern marriage, an area of life in which Gregory generally displays an approach that is traditional to the core. When he talks about Christian marriage and consecrated virginity, or celibacy, as ways of life leading to union with God, he compares them in the usual way and says that marriage is good, but celibacy is better;[5] in discussing marriage, he follows the conventional theory, based on chapter 5 of the letter to the Ephesians, which makes the husband the head of the household, whom the wife must obey. His comments on the sin of the first man and woman normally attribute to Eve ultimate responsibility for the sin, for the corruption of Adam, and for expulsion from paradise. He refers to the female as the weaker sex and describes female virtue in terms of overcoming the weakness of her sex and acting like a man.[6] In short, Gregory is not, by any stretch of the imagination, a feminist; most of these ideas would be described today as those of a celibate male expressed in the language of a patriarchal religion that originated and flourished in a society dominated by males.

And yet it is precisely when speaking of marriage and the relationship of female and male that Gregory, just before reaffirming the superiority of celibacy over marriage, makes a striking, and, in terms of length, extended, statement that reveals another, different dimension of his thought and personality. In Oration 37 (on Mt 19:1ff, a text which deals with the question of divorce), after commenting on the context of the scriptural passage and referring to the divine and human natures of Christ, Gregory turns to the question the Pharisees put to Jesus about the possibility of divorce. He places the first words of his commentary in the mouth of Jesus and then goes on with further reflections of his own:[7]

> 6. [Jesus says:] It appears to me that this question which you have asked pays honor to chastity and demands a kind reply.
>
> Chastity is a topic about which I see that most people have wrong opinions and the law itself is unfair and inconsistent. For why did they punish the woman, but indulge the man? Why is a woman who sins against her husband's bed guilty of adultery and subject to the law's harsh penalties for this, while the husband who is unfaithful to his wife goes unpunished? I do not accept this legislation. I do not approve the custom. The lawmakers were males,[8] and this is why their legislation is anti-female; for they placed children under their fathers' authority, but left the weaker sex unprotected.
>
> This is not God's way. God says: "Honor your father and your mother, which is the first commandment, with promises, that it may go well with you."[9] God also says, "Let anyone who curses father or mother die the death";[10] in this way God praised good and punished evil. God says too, "A father's blessing strengthens children's houses, but a mother's curse uproots foundations."[11] Look at the equality of the legislation. There is one creator of male and female; both of them share one dust, one image, one law, one death, one resurrection. Children owe one debt to those who begot them.
>
> 7. How then do you dare to demand chastity, when you do not offer it in return? How dare you demand what you do not give? How can you, as a body of equal value, make laws that are not equal? If you consider the lower realities, the woman sinned; but so did Adam. The serpent deceived them both. One was not found stronger and the other weaker. Now think about higher things: Christ saves them both by his sufferings. Did he become flesh for the man? He also became flesh for the woman. Did he die for the man? The woman too is saved by his death. He is said to be "of the seed of David,"[12] and so perhaps you think the man is honored; but he is born of a virgin, and this is in favor of the woman. It says, "The two, therefore, shall become one flesh";[13] let the one flesh, therefore, have equal honor. Paul also legislates chastity with this example. How? In what way? He says, "This mystery is great; but I am speaking with respect to Christ and the church."[14] It is good for the wife to reverence Christ through her husband, and it is also good for the husband not to dishonor the church through his wife. "Let the wife," he says, "show reverence for her husband,"[15] for in this way she shows reverence for Christ. But the husband should also treat his wife with honor, even as Christ does the church.
>
> 8. . . . Now the law grants divorce for any reason at all, but Christ does not. He only allows separation from one who is unfaith-

ful, while in all other cases he commands patience. He allows one to divorce an unfaithful wife, because she corrupts the family; but in all other matters let us be patient and practice restraint—or rather you be patient and practice restraint, who have accepted the yoke of matrimony.

The contents of this passage have been discussed elsewhere as the expression of an early Christian attitude on the relationship of male and female and on the equality of the sexes.[16] That is not the perspective of this study. When contrasted with Gregory's consistently traditional approach outlined above, this text reveals a new and important aspect of his thought, character, and personality: he does not feel compelled to defend the traditional position at all times; nor does he hesitate to reject social, cultural, or theological ideas that are almost universally accepted, even by himself, if he feels that they are the source of injustice.

Historically, this passage seems to indicate the continued existence in the fourth century of an early Christian practice, based on an interpretation of the "except" clauses in Matthew 5:32 and 19:9, which not only allowed the divorce of an adulterous spouse, but at times even demanded it.[17] It has already been noted that Gregory is, in principle, opposed to divorce, and he clearly considers infidelity a serious sin. But he is aware that laws and custom allowed a husband to divorce an unfaithful wife easily and punished her harshly with severe penances for adultery, while at the same time they made it almost impossible for a wife to divorce an unfaithful husband, and imposed on the latter light penances, not for adultery, but for the lesser sin of fornication.[18] Gregory finds this situation intolerable, and, to his credit, actually attempts to do something about it. That his words had little effect on subsequent attitudes was not his fault.

Gregory clearly places the blame for this injustice where he believes it belongs: "the lawmakers were males." It is noteworthy to see that his sympathies are with women and that he criticizes men, a position that was surely unpopular with contemporary men, both lay and ecclesiastical. Furthermore, in rejecting these laws and customs, Gregory also repudiates a tradition, and at the same time offers an all but explicit criticism of his close friend and ecclesiastical patron, Basil of Caesarea, whom he loved and admired, but with whom he came into conflict on more than one occasion. In letters 188.9 and 199.21,[19] where Basil describes penitential practice with respect to divorce and infidelity, he raises the issue of the differing types of penalties imposed on men and women. In the first letter he says that the scriptural legislation of Matthew 5 and 19 should apply equally to men and women, but custom declares otherwise; the examples he offers give women almost no rights or protection against infidelity, personal and financial exploitation, and even physical harm. In the second letter he touches on the same general issue and concludes by saying "the argument is not easy, but this is the custom." Basil sees and even articulates the problem, but, unlike Gregory, does not criticize or attempt to resolve it.

Gregory goes even further in his open attack on the double standard that exists in Christian legislation and customs on marriage, when he expresses shock that men demand from women a fidelity that they themselves are not prepared to give. This is a sensitive aspect of human relationships, and his frankness in criticizing male attitudes toward women must have touched, disturbed, and perhaps angered many a man in his audience.

The issues just discussed—legislation, custom, and the attitude of men toward women—stem primarily from personal, social, or cultural factors. But Gregory turns to the religious foundation beneath many of these factors and contradicts certain traditional theological doctrines, including some which he himself normally held. Thus he says that Adam and Eve sinned equally, that neither was stronger or weaker, and that the devil deceived them both; Eve is not accused of seducing Adam or of being the primary cause of the fall. Christ died for both the male and the female, and both of them are represented in aspects of Christ's life and activity. In this way Gregory gives the equality of male and female a theological basis that it does not normally have in the early church or even in his own thought. In speaking, as he does here, of the weaker sex, he shows that he has not abandoned all of his presuppositions about men and women; but he transcends them because of a quality that not only enables him to perceive injustice inflicted on fellow human beings and Christians and to sympathize with them, but also moves him to try to rectify the situation by speaking freely about the problems and uprooting their causes, whatever the cost to himself.

The last comment on this passage relates to its closing words. In explaining Christ's attitude toward divorce, Gregory urges patience and restraint toward one's spouse, and then, in a final touch that may be the product of rhetoric, but is nonetheless significant, he addresses his audience directly by changing the subject of his exhortation from the first person to the second. This would seem to indicate, first, that Gregory is not himself married, and, more to the point, that he is aware of a certain incongruity in including himself in the plea to show patience and restraint toward a spouse's faults. By correcting himself and saying, "or rather you be patient," he is responding, perhaps consciously, to the complaint that celibates should not be so quick to advise married people on marriage; he appears at least to sense the issue, and, by shifting to the second person, he emphasizes the point that the advice he is offering comes, not from himself, but from Christ. There may indeed be a rhetorical flourish involved here, but Gregory has used it, because of his personal sensitivity, to touch and motivate his audience in a personal way.

Gregory displays similar attitudes on the relationship between the sexes in his funeral oration for his sister Gorgonia, an example of true and deep emotion expressed in a clearly rhetorical vehicle. He praises his sister for entering marriage with the attitude appropriate to a woman of her time,[20] and goes on to portray her as an independent person who achieved a high level of holiness; at the end he emphasizes her virtue by describing the effect she had on her husband: "Do you wish me to describe her husband briefly? [He was] her husband, and I do not know what more one can say."[21] In eulogizing his brother Caesarius, Gregory echoes this thought with respect to the influence of their mother on his brother and himself. After saying that she was so holy that "some people both believed and said that her husband's perfection was the work of no one but herself," he adds parenthetically, "I shall make this assertion, even though it is a bold one."[22]

One must, of course, allow for personal prejudice in favor of his family, but the fact remains that, despite his stated belief that the husband is the head of the house, Gregory attributes great influence and power to the wife; this perception undoubtedly expresses an aspect of family life that was often reality, but rarely acknowledged. Gregory states this openly; he does not feel constrained to exalt men over women, nor does he feel that the men in question have their honor or memory dimmed by this revelation of their relationship with their wives. By speaking in this way, Gregory reveals a dimension of his own commitment to unmarried life that sees great value in the marriage relationship, but does not appear when he says simply that celibacy is better than marriage.

Another example of Gregory's attitude toward the sexual realities of life appears in Oration 39, "On the Holy Lights," delivered on the feast of the Epiphany; while urging people to be baptized because of the forgiveness baptism brings, he turns to a discussion of an opponent of Cyprian of Carthage, Novatus, whose rigorist approach to repentance, forgiveness, and baptism was a major element in the third century controversies in the churches of Carthage and Rome, and between the two churches as well.

Gregory says that he agrees with Novatus, insofar as the latter refused forgiveness to people who did not truly repent:

> But if he refused those who were worn out with weeping, I shall not imitate him. What kind of law for me is the hatefulness of Novatus? He did not punish covetousness, which is a second form of idolatry, but so bitterly condemned sexual sin, as though he were a person who had no flesh or body. What do you say? Are we persuading you with these words? Come, stand here with us human beings. Let us glorify the Lord together. Let no one of you dare to say, even if he dared to say it to himself, "Let no one touch me, for I am pure, and who is so pure as I?"[23]

This passage reveals the extent of Gregory's compassion for human weakness, both in himself and in others. He is a celibate who preaches the value of chastity; but he does not stress sexual sins as the only, or even the most terrible sins. Thus he criticizes Novatus for his harshness, for not condemning covetousness, and for ignoring the shortcomings of his own humanity. Gregory is clearly aware of his own defects and rejects every form of hypocritical self-righteousness, as he exhorts his audience to "Come, stand here with us human beings."

Returning to the subject of panegyrics on family members, one must take careful note of Gregory's attitude while preaching on the death of his father. As he is in the act of praising both his father's zeal in combating heresy and the way in which he transmitted that zeal to his children, he suddenly addresses his mother who is present:

> I blame both of you for one thing; and please do not be annoyed at my frankness, for I shall pour out my grief, even if it is hard to bear. I was disgusted with life's evils and I longed for solitude in a way that none of my contemporaries did; I was struggling to get away, as quickly as possible, from the storms and dust of this life and to escape to security. In the midst of this struggle, somehow or other you handed me over to this wearisome and treacherous market-place of souls through the glorious name of the priesthood. As a result terrible things have already happened to me, and others are still expected. . . .[24]

Gregory's frankness here seems to be the product of self-pity and an insensitivity to his mother's grief that present a less appealing side of his character; on the other hand, it is clear from this homily and the ones on his brother and sister that he loved his parents, and this passage could be interpreted as the cry of a sensitive individual who felt that he had suffered because of a decision that changed his life radically, but which was made for him by others, not by himself.

He voices the same complaint in his long panegyric on Basil of Caesarea, who is also portrayed as a guilty party. After describing how Basil's political activity successfully defused a volatile political situation in the church, he adds:

> I fear that I myself was made a kind of incidental accessory to this plan. There is no other way that I can properly describe the situation. For even though I admire everything about him to such an extent that I cannot even express it properly, I cannot approve this one single case—for I will say how I feel—which is not unknown to most of you from other sources. I am referring to the change in his attitude toward me and the consequent faithlessness with which he treated me; even time has not done away with the pain it caused. For that was the source of all the disquiet and confusion that came into my life. . . .[25]

In this passage, as in those immediately preceding, Gregory reveals a self-centered side of his personality that clashes with the openness and concern for other people that have appeared here so often; it may help explain the conflict and torment he says he experienced in meeting the responsibilities of his office. He is clearly not a person who readily forgave other people for problems he felt they had caused him.

Oration 40, "On Holy Baptism," was delivered on the day after Oration 39. Gregory addresses the practice of delaying baptism until late in life and urges his audience to repent and be baptized while there is still time; he presses his point with a variety of arguments, some of which display his understanding of human nature and are expressed with touches of irony and common sense that one rarely finds in early Christian writers.

Thus Gregory recommends baptism while one is still in good health; after detailing the religious and familial aspects of one's last hours, he describes the final moments as a struggle between doctor and priest, each offering a particular service:

> [Be baptized] before the physician, unable to do anything for you, gives you only hours to live (hours which he does not control), puts your salvation in the balance with a nod of his head, holds learned discourses about your disease after your death, increases his fee by

> draining your bodily fluids, or hints that you had despaired. [Be
> baptized] before the battle begins between the one who is to baptize
> you and the one who wants your money; the former struggles to
> provide for your journey, while the latter strives to be written into
> your will as an heir—but there is not enough time for both of
> them.[26]

Because this scene is in many ways so realistic, the macabre and
almost ludicrous tone that pervades it raises the question if he has not
shaped it deliberately to make his point more forcefully. There is
rhetorical influence here; but it serves to personalize the thought,
and while the passage's contents are neither particularly charming
nor humane, it does appear to reveal another aspect of Gregory's
personality.

He goes on to provide a list of possible causes of sudden death
that is such a mixture of the awesome and the trivial that he cannot
have been totally serious:

> [The evil one says,] give the present to me and the future to God;
> give youth to me and old age to God; give pleasures to me and your
> uselessness to God. How much danger surrounds you! How many
> unexpected disasters there are! War consumed you; earthquake
> buried you; the sea welcomed you; a wild beast carried you off;
> sickness killed you; a crumb went the wrong way and killed you (it is
> a totally insignificant thing, and yet what is easier than for a human
> being to die, even though you pride yourself on the [divine] image).
> You were killed by excessive drinking; by a wind that threw you
> down; by a horse that ran away with you; by a drug that acted with
> malice aforethought, or by one that happened to turn out to be a
> poison instead of a remedy; by an inhuman judge; by a pitiless
> executioner; or by any one of those things that cause the change
> that is instantaneous and beyond the possibility of human help.[27]

The content of this list is most likely drawn from rhetorical sources,
but Gregory was too skilled a rhetorician and knew human nature too
well to think that the serious presentation of such an odd and lengthy
list would move people to action. He shows himself as one who can
lighten even the most grim discussion by the content and tone of his
discourse.

In speaking to those who are actively engaged in business or
politics, Gregory says that the best way to avoid sin after baptism is
simply to leave one's former occupation; but if that is impossible,
then, he maintains, it is still good to be baptized, even though the

possibility exists that one will again commit sin. His argument is based on a pragmatism and a sympathy for human weakness that are uncommon in the early church; he replaces the normal idealistic exhortation to seek absolute perfection by avoiding sin with the suggestion that it is better to be purified once and for all in baptism, and then do one's best, even when one knows that one will sin again. His main point is the need for baptism, but he also appears to believe that those who do their best in difficult situations are better people, even if they sin, than those who live perfect lives, but were simply free of problems and temptations:

> The better way is to do both, i.e., grasp the good and preserve the purification. But if one cannot do both at once, then it is better to be stained while in public life than to be deprived totally of grace. . . . Do not, therefore, be too afraid of the purification. For the good we do is always judged by our just and loving judge in connection with the circumstances of our life. And one in public life who has done good in some small way is often better off than another who was not so involved and did not do everything right. In the same way, I think it is more remarkable for one in chains to take just a few steps forward than for one who is not carrying any weight to run; and it is more unusual to be spattered only a bit when walking through mud than to come out clean when walking on a clean roadway.[28]

Gregory's view that God's judgment takes into consideration the "circumstances" of life would both console and encourage those members of the congregation who felt that they were "in chains" or "walking through mud"; for they could see in Gregory one who perceived the complexity of human life and who preached a God that shared the same understanding.

The material still to be discussed deals primarily with issues of theology or ecclesiastical life and practice; these passages are not all of equal significance, and they consequently vary in tone. Several of them reflect the critical frankness that appeared in his attitude toward his family and Basil of Caesarea.

In Oration 41, "On Pentecost," Gregory offers a long exegesis of the text of Acts 2:8, which states that all of those present at the first Pentecost heard the words of the apostles in their own language; he sums up his explanation and then, with disarming frankness, says, "But if somebody does not accept this interpretation because it is too elaborate . . . and wants a more plausible one, it would perhaps be better to understand it as follows. . . ."[29] This is an approach taken by few ancient exegetes.

Oration 21 is a eulogy of Athanasius of Alexandria. Gregory takes the occasion to comment on the state of the church and theology: "He is raised to the throne of Mark, therefore, in this way and for these reasons, by the vote of the whole people, not by the evil procedure that prevailed afterwards. . . ."[30] "It was a period in which our [form of life] was in full bloom and prospering, when this strange way of teaching about God in complex and artificial language had not yet entered the schoolyards of religion. . . ."[31] Even as he praises Athanasius, Gregory speaks, directly and frankly, to his own church, and his appraisal of the ecclesiastical machinery and of theological instruction in his day was not calculated to please those involved. In a passage on the outstanding way in which Athanasius exercised his priesthood, Gregory contrasts him, at great length, with priests who fall short of the sacerdotal ideal; the negative details which he includes must have been intended to move those members of the clergy from whose lives they were drawn. If they were as ill-suited to the priesthood as Gregory says, they cannot have been happy with his evaluation.

The same is true of a passage from his panegyric on Basil, in which he compares Basil's advancement in the church, based on spiritual qualifications, with the situation in his own day:

> I do not praise the lack of discipline among us, even occasionally in the case of those who preside over the sanctuary. . . . There is a danger now that the most sacred rank of all is our most ridiculous one. For the presidency depends, not on virtue, but on wickedness, and the thrones belong not to the more worthy, but to the more powerful.[32]

Since Gregory had resigned as bishop of Constantinople, his attack on the problem of power in the church rings true. Even the emperor, presumably Constans, who had alternately exiled and honored Athanasius, is not spared: "[Athanasius] wins over to his side [the emperor's] simplicity; for, with all due respect to his piety, that is what I call his instability."[33] Finally, in praising Athanasius' orthodoxy concerning the Holy Spirit, he says, perhaps with tongue in cheek, that this was an area of theology in which, at that time, "being only slightly heretical was considered orthodox."[34]

In Oration 45, "On Easter," Gregory turns to the ransom theory of redemption and the circumstances under which Christ's blood was shed for humanity. Gregory rejects outright the belief that Christ's blood was given in payment to either the devil or God, although he finds the idea of paying the devil especially repugnant. This interpretation had a long history in both east and west, and Gregory surely invited criticism by repudiating the traditional position and adopting one through which he parted company with Basil's brother, Gregory of Nyssa, and implicitly criticized his predecessors. The relevant text follows:

> There is, then, an issue and a doctrine to examine, which is disregarded by most, but which I examine very carefully. To whom and for what reason was the blood, the mighty and famous blood of God, high priest, and sacrifice, shed for us? We were held captive by the evil one, since we were sold into sin, and received pleasure in return for evil. But if the ransom belongs to no one else than the captor, I ask to whom and for what reason was this ransom offered? If the ransom goes to the evil one, then it is an outrage, for the robber would not only receive a ransom from God, but would be given a ransom which actually is God, and would thus have for his tyranny a remarkable reward, that by itself would have justified his sparing us. But if it goes to the Father, my first question is, how can this be, for we were not in captivity to him. Second, for what reason does the blood of an only begotten Son give pleasure to a Father who did not even accept Isaac, when he was offered by his father, but exchanged the sacrifice, substituting a ram for the human victim? It is obvious that it is the Father who receives [the blood], not because of a demand or a need, but because of the divine plan [of the Incarnation], and because humanity had to be sanctified by the humanity of God, so that God might actually deliver us, after conquering the tyrant, and lead us back to God through the Son, who acted as mediator and arranged this for the honor of the Father, whom he is seen to obey in all things.[35]

The doctrine was not, as Gregory tactfully says, "disregarded" by others; it had, according to his interpretation, been handled erroneously. His initial approach to the subject is, therefore, cautious, perhaps to show deference to the tradition. But when it comes to the heart of the teaching, Gregory is forthright: it is an "outrage" to believe that the blood of God was given to the devil as ransom; and he implies that it is a bloodthirsty God who would desire or need the blood of one who is called God's own Son. Gregory's explanation, that it was God who received the blood, not because of demand or need on God's part, but as part of God's plan to save humanity through the humanity assumed by the Word of God in the Incarnation, is based on a humane and common-sense understanding of God and God's activity.

It has not been the intention of this study to draw a definitive picture of Gregory as bishop, rhetorician, theologian, or homilist, or even simply as a human being. One can envision possible objections to the methodology of this discussion and the conclusions drawn from it, and it may perhaps be useful to adapt Gregory's approach in Oration 41, 17,[36] by stating some of them and indicating a response. Rhetoric did play a role in the composition of certain texts, but it should be clear that this does not preclude the possibility of Gregory's revealing an aspect of his true character through such texts. Since there are no "cues" in written texts, one can never determine with absolute certitude the exact original tone or spirit of a particular passage; in the text, however, there are indications of Gregory's intent, and serious analysis attempts to base an objective evaluation on them. Ancient sensitivities differ from modern ones, and care must be taken, therefore, not to attribute to the one attitudes or ideas proper only to the other.

The personality that emerges from this study, then, belongs to a complex person who reveals himself as he speaks on a wide variety of topics. As a homilist, his primary object of concern is his congregation. As a bishop, he is an authority figure, a guardian of tradition, and a teacher of religious truth and moral action. Because he is sensitive and has experienced personal suffering, he is also sensitive to the concerns and problems of his audience, and he sincerely seeks to deal with them; for the same reasons, he is also deeply concerned about himself. In his orations he speaks candidly, without worrying whether his words will offend others; this frankness can be refreshing and is effective in fighting injustice, but it leads at times to a certain insensitivity, especially when he is talking about relatives or friends, and, even more, when he is speaking to them.

However one finally judges Gregory's character, there can be no doubt that he is an intriguing person and was a highly effective homilist; for those of his audience who were seeking the truth would surely react positively to this man of compassion, who admits his own weakness, fights against injustice, and invites them to "Come, stand here with us human beings."[37]

NOTES

1. See Rosemary Radford Ruether, *Gregory of Nazianzus: Rhetor and Philosopher* (Oxford: Clarendon Press, 1969).

2. See Antonio Quacquarelli, *Reazione pagana e trasformazione della cultura (fine IV secolo d.c.)* (Bari: Edipuglia, 1986) 172–77.

3. See, for example, the extensive quotations in Theodoret's *Eranistes*, composed in 447: Gerard H. Ettlinger, ed., *Theodoret of Cyrus: Eranistes* (Oxford: Clarendon Press, 1975).

4. PG 37.245–248. New translations have been made for this paper; references are to texts in SC, PG (where a critical edition was not available), and CSEL.

5. See or. 37.10 (SC 318.292).

6. See, for example, the funeral oration for his sister: or. 8.8 and 14 (PG 35.797, 805).

7. SC 318.282–288; the paragraph numbers here correspond to the divisions in the Greek text.

8. The Greek word here is *andres*, which can mean both "male" and "husband." The issue is not, therefore, simply a contrast between divine and human law.

9. Eph 6:2 (and Ex 20:12).

10. Ex 21:17.

11. Sir 3:9 (LXX 3:11).

12. Rom 1:3.

13. Gen 2:24.

14. Eph 5:32.

15. Eph 5:33.

16. See Gerard H. Ettlinger, "*Theos de ouch houtōs* (Gregory of Nazianzus, *Oratio XXXVII*): The Dignity of the Human Person according to the Greek Fathers," *SP* 16 (1985) 368–72.

17. See, for example, *The Shepherd of Hermas*, Mandate 4.1 and Justin Martyr, *Dialogue* 2.2.

18. Gregory is not alone in criticizing the double standard that prevailed in marital legislation and practice. Both John Chrysostom, *Homily on 1 Cor 7:39–40* (PG 51.222), and Jerome, ep. 77.3 (CSEL 55.39), reject what Gregory deplores here on the grounds that, in Christianity, male and female should be treated equally. But neither of them goes as far as Gregory in blaming men or in linking the problem with theological interpretations of the creation and the fall as related in Genesis 1–3.

19. PG 32.677, 721.

20. See above, n. 6.

21. Or. 8.20 (PG 35.813).

22. Or. 7.9 (PG 35.760).

23. Or. 39.19 (PG 36.357).

24. Or. 18.37 (PG 35.1035).

25. Or. 43.59 (PG 36.573).

26. Or. 40.11 (PG 36.373).

27. Or. 40.14 (PG 36.376–377).

28. Or. 40.19 (PG 36.384).

29. Or. 41.17 (PG 36.452).

30. Or. 21.8 (SC 270.124).
31. Or. 21.12 (SC 270.132).
32. Or. 43.26 (PG 36.532).
33. Or. 21.21 (SC 270.152).
34. Or. 21.33 (SC 270.182).
35. Or. 45.22 (PG 36.653).
36. See above, p. 111, n. 29
37. See above, p. 108, n. 23

7

PREACHING AND PROPAGANDA IN FOURTH CENTURY ANTIOCH: JOHN CHRYSOSTOM'S *HOMILIES ON THE STATUES*
by David G. Hunter

The name "John Chrysostom" (the "Golden-mouthed") is almost synonymous with patristic preaching. No other early Christian writer produced such a vast corpus of sermons. Few preachers, ancient or modern, can rival him either in rhetorical eloquence or in passion for moral reformation and social justice. His sermons are also an invaluable mine of information on the social and cultural life of his times. In this essay I would like to discuss only one small sample of his preaching, but one that sheds special light on the character of religious life in late antiquity: the twenty-one *Homilies on the Statues*. These homilies, I will argue, show that polemics between contemporary pagans and Christians were an important concern for Chrysostom and one that shaped his preaching in a significant way.

The *Homilies on the Statues* are among Chrysostom's most famous works. Composed at Antioch during the Lenten season of 387, the discourses describe an uprising of the populace occasioned by the imposition of an unusual imperial tax.[1] While focusing on themes of repentance, Chrysostom weaves into his discussion references to the riot, the terror of the citizens, and their subsequent pardon by the emperor Theodosius. The current crisis, although it does not dominate the discourses, serves as a kind of leitmotif by which Chrysostom calls the people to conversion and trust in divine providence.[2]

Chrysostom's homilies often have been examined from the point of view of style and language and are considered "among the finest achievements of his eloquence."[3] But it is a peculiar circumstance that has attracted special notice to these sermons. The pagan orator Libanius, Chrysostom's former teacher in rhetoric, composed his own set of orations on these events.[4] Unlike Chrysostom's homilies, which were composed in the midst of the crisis, Libanius' discourses clearly were written after the fact. Furthermore, numerous similarities between the two sets of speeches have led some to believe that Libanius deliberately copied from Chrysostom's sermons.[5] Given the fact that Chrysostom's discourses are characterized by frequent outbursts against pagan contemporaries and by bold assertions of the superiority of Christianity over paganism, it is quite understandable that Libanius would have wished to respond to them.

The theory of Libanius' plagiarism has not found general acceptance among scholars.[6] Nonetheless, it is indisputable that Libanius was responding in some way to triumphalistic Christian propaganda circulating after Theodosius' reconciliation with the city.[7] My purpose here is to examine Chrysostom's orations to determine the exact nature of his polemical interests. I will suggest that Chrysostom's *Homilies on the Statues* continue a long-standing debate with his former teacher, a debate concerning the relative merits of the Hellenic and Christian traditions. Chrysostom uses the crisis to argue that Christianity, and not pagan culture, forms people in the virtues most necessary for public life. Chrysostom's sermons, therefore, serve not only as consolation and moral exhortation, but also as religious propaganda.

I will proceed in three steps. First, a brief discussion will be devoted to the riot and the subsequent proceedings in the city. Second, I will examine Chrysostom's sermons and discuss in depth his apologetic interests. Finally, Libanius' orations will be treated briefly as the pagan counterpart to the Christian preaching. My claim is not that the pagan-Christian polemic was the sole interest of either Chrysostom or Libanius. Nonetheless, attention to this dimension of the discourses will illumine both the context of religious life in fourth century Antioch and the character of Christian preaching in that context.[8]

PART ONE: THE RIOT

In February 387 John Chrysostom was beginning only his second year as presbyter and preacher at Antioch. He was, however, already skilled as a writer, having composed a series of ascetical works and apologies before his ordination, a set of discourses against the Arians in 386, and some sermons against Judaizing Christians, also in the preceding year.[9] As Lent began (or perhaps a few days before),

Chrysostom started to preach on a favorite theme suggested by his Pauline text, the suffering of the righteous.[10] After his first sermon, however, there occurred that event which seized the attention of both preacher and congregation.

During the first days of February an imperial edict arrived announcing the imposition of an unusually heavy tax.[11] This levy, which probably was connected with the tenth anniversary of Theodosius' reign to be celebrated the next year, appears to have been directed at all classes in the city. Economic discontent had been rife at Antioch and throughout the east for some time.[12] The new and burdensome tax was immediately resisted by the populace.

The trouble began peacefully enough. Members of the city council, whose task it was to represent the interests of the city before imperial officials, registered their discontent to the Syrian governor in residence at Antioch. Meanwhile, a crowd had gathered, and when the efforts of the councillors proved fruitless, the crowd marched to the house of Bishop Flavian, only to find him away.[13] The crowd returned to the city courthouse and at this point was taken in hand by the theatrical "claque." The claque was a body of professionals paid to applaud the actors and dancers in the theater.[14] In Chrysostom's day, however, the claque had become an important political voice in the Greek city. Through their "acclamations" (euphēmiai) in the theater, they gave expression to public opinion and demanded the attention even of emperors.[15]

In this instance, however, the claque incited the crowd to more violent demonstrations. The angry mob first attacked the residence of the Syrian governor, beating on the doors and railings, causing those within to fear for their lives.[16] They then rushed to the public baths and cut down the lamps hanging outside. The riot culminated in an assault on the imperial statues and images. The mob first stoned the wooden panels bearing portraits of the emperor Theodosius and his family. This was already an act of treason, since the official portraits were considered embodiments of imperial dignity.[17] Bronze statues of the emperor, his wife, and his son Arcadius were then pulled down and dragged through the streets. As the crowd set fire to the house of a prominent citizen and seemed about to commit worse acts, archers from the local police force arrived to disperse the mob and extinguish the fire.

At this point the ranking imperial official, the comes Orientis, took charge, rounded up those guilty of arson, and dispatched news of the riot to the emperor in Constantinople. Those who participated most actively in the insurrection were summarily executed, and even children were not spared.[18] The city now waited anxiously to see what the emperor's response would be. It was not impossible that Theodosius could have demanded a wholesale slaughter of the citizens, as occurred at Thessaloniki three years later. Rumor also circulated that all of the councillors would be executed, and in fact members of the council soon were rounded up and imprisoned.[19] Within a few days Bishop Flavian departed for Constantinople to attempt to intercede with the emperor, while two representatives sent by Theodosius arrived to conduct an inquiry. It is at this point that Chrysostom's preaching began.[20]

Both Chrysostom and Libanius tell us that the emperor's representatives, Caesarius and Hellebichus,[21] conveyed a preliminary judgment against the city: Antioch was deprived of the title of *metropolis,* and the hippodrome, theaters and baths were closed.[22] But many citizens did not stay to see these punishments. Immediately after the riot large numbers fled the city, the wealthy taking refuge in their country estates, the poor fleeing to nearby mountain caves.[23] As Caesarius and Hellebichus conducted their investigation, another unusual event occurred, one that Chrysostom would later use to his apologetic advantage. A group of monks from the nearby mountains came down to intercede on behalf of the city.[24] One of them, a hermit named Macedonius, delivered a speech in Syriac which was then relayed to the officials in Greek.[25]

Whether or not the officials were persuaded by these efforts, as Chrysostom tells us, we cannot say. What is clear, however, is that Caesarius and Hellebichus did recommend leniency to Theodosius. Caesarius returned to Constantinople where Bishop Flavian had been for some time making his appeal to the emperor. Theodosius yielded to their entreaties, rescinded the existing penalties, and restored all privileges to the city. A messenger reached Antioch by Palm Sunday, where the news was met with great rejoicing.[26] By Easter Bishop Flavian had returned to Antioch and was able to join his congregation in the paschal services.

PART TWO: CHRYSOSTOM'S HOMILIES
AND APOLOGETICS

Chrysostom's response to these events, as I have noted, spanned the entire course of the crisis. His second homily was delivered within a week of the riot; his last celebrated the return of Bishop Flavian.[27] Chrysostom's interests throughout were predominantly pastoral. He constantly assures his congregation that they are under the care of a benign providence and he employs the imperial threat of death and destruction to urge the citizens to detach themselves from worldly concerns and to embrace an "otherworldly" way of life. As we would expect an effective preacher to do, he puts the experience of his hearers into the context of biblical stories, hoping that they will interpret their experience within that narrative framework. The story of Jonah and his preaching to the Ninevites, for example, is one of his favorite illustrations.[28] The wickedness of a great city, the willingness of its citizens to repent, and the mercy and forgiveness of God are all themes from the story of Jonah that Chrysostom wished to impress on the citizens of Antioch.[29]

But throughout the homilies Chrysostom also reveals that he has polemical and not merely pastoral interests. This concern is evident in homily 21 where Chrysostom portrays Bishop Flavian addressing his entreaty to the emperor Theodosius: "Reflect, that the matter now for your consideration is not respecting the city only, but is one that concerns your own glory; or rather, one that affects the cause of Christianity in general" (*peri tou Christianismou pantos*).[30] Chrysostom goes on to say that if the emperor's decree is humane (*philanthrōpos*) and merciful (*hēmeros*), all people—Jews and Greeks, Romans and barbarians—will applaud the moral efficacy of Christianity:

> Heavens! [they will say] how great is the power of Christianity, that it restrains and bridles a man who has no equal upon earth . . . and teaches him (*epaideuse*) to practice such philosophy as one in a private station had not been likely to display. Great, indeed, must be the God of the Christians, who makes angels out of men, and renders them superior to all the restraining force of our nature.[31]

The foregoing sentences summarize in a useful way the thrust of Chrysostom's apologetic. The centerpiece of his argument is the claim that Christianity, not paganism, truly educates people in the virtues and schools them in "philosophy." Throughout the *Homilies on the Statues* Chrysostom asserts that Christian convictions and the stories in scripture shape in people the virtues most valuable for public life. In the remainder of this section, I would like to discuss two aspects of Chrysostom's argument. First, the virtues which Chrysostom most exalts—"humanity" (*philanthrōpia*), "magnanimity" (*megalopsychia*), and "boldness" (*parrhēsia*)—are virtues which contemporary pagans wished to ascribe to their own tradition. Thus, as I will argue, rival moral claims are also apologetic claims. Second, I will explore further the structure of Chrysostom's argument. His apologetic efforts are based on the belief that Christian convictions have an ethical relevance, that is, they shape in Christians the virtues appropriate to those convictions. Conversely, Chrysostom will argue, the presence of such virtues in the contemporary Christian community validates the truth of Christian convictions.

Christianity and the Virtues

The passage cited above from Chrysostom's twenty-first homily expressed the claim that a showing of "humanity" (*philanthrōpia*) on the part of Theodosius would redound to the credit of Christianity. Throughout the homilies Chrysostom constantly appeals to the "humanity" of the emperor as grounds on which to expect a favorable verdict.[32] Such an appeal in itself is not surprising. It was a commonplace in Greek rhetoric of this period to associate *philanthrōpia* particularly with the character of a good emperor.[33] What is significant, however, is the way in which Chrysostom argues that it is Theodosius' Christian faith which renders him *philanthrōpos*. In a speech placed on the lips of Bishop Flavian, Chrysostom begs the emperor to imitate the *philanthrōpia* of God: "Make the Judge above merciful to you by humanity towards your fellow-servants."[34] He entreats Theodosius to recognize the Christian history of Antioch: "This is the city in which Christians were first called by that name. Honor Christ!"[35] The three youths in the fiery furnace were undaunted by the wrath of the pagan Nebuchadnezzar, Chrysostom writes. "How much more ought we [i.e. Christians] to be confident, having an emperor who is humane and merciful" (*philanthrōpon kai hēmeron*).[36]

Chrysostom also appeals to Theodosius' respect for the Lenten season as further evidence of the emperor's Christian philanthropy. He recalls an edict of Theodosius granting an Easter amnesty to condemned prisoners and asks the emperor to remember his own example of humanity.[37] But, most of all, Chrysostom calls to mind the example of Christ. Again referring to the intercession of Bishop Flavian, Chrysostom writes that Flavian "will remind the emperor of the season when Christ remitted the sins of the whole world. He will exhort him to imitate his Lord."[38] The parables of Jesus regarding forgiveness and the Lord's prayer also are adduced as biblical evidence of the philanthropy and clemency required of Christians. And, when at last the deliverance of the city is won, Chrysostom attributes it to divine action, "God having softened the emperor's heart."[39]

Chrysostom clearly is attempting to establish a link between the

emperor's "piety," that is, his Christian convictions, and the virtue of "philanthropy." The Christian tradition, in Chrysostom's mind, is responsible for shaping this imperial virtue. The full significance of Chrysostom's argument is revealed only when it is acknowledged that certain contemporary pagans were making precisely the same argument on behalf of the Hellenic tradition. In the late fourth century as Christian writers began to adopt the classical notion of *philanthrōpia* and to infuse it with Christian meaning (i.e. *agapē*), pagan writers began to develop the notion of "philanthropy" as a principle of conduct which could provide a counterpart to Christian teaching.[40]

The pagan orator Themistius, for example, who also composed orations to Theodosius, developed the notion of divine and royal philanthropy as a direct response to the Christian use of the term. As does Chrysostom, Themistius stresses that royal philanthropy is but an imitation of God's philanthropy.[41] But in contrast to Chrysostom's emphasis on the role of Christianity in producing philanthropy, Themistius stresses that the emperor's virtue is shaped by classical learning. In an address to the emperor Valens, for example, Themistius attributes the formation of *philanthrōpia* to the "love of literature (*philologia*):

> I have often considered that there is no cause for that *philanthrōpi*
> of yours, which is so widely celebrated, than love of literature a
> the desire to listen to it. That man, indeed, who loves learning m
> perforce love men as well.[42]

The point of Themistius' statement, as G. Downey has rec "to show that paganism as a way of life can provide prin are as good as those of Christianity."[43]

In a similar vein the emperor Julian (whom Ch quently attacked in his early works) also made *phil* element in his pagan restoration. In his famous *Le* which he outlined his plans for a reform of the p Julian maintained that priests above all must dem of "philanthropy" to gain the favor of the gods argues, by showing philanthropy a priest can le Christianity and back to paganism. When a philanthropy, Julian suggests, he shows that truly *philanthrōpos*.[45] It is no wonder, there revival included the establishment of ch imitated those of Christianity. He wishe Christian claim to moral superiority.[46]

Closer to Chrysostom, the sophist Libanius attributes the *phi-lanthrōpia* of the emperor Julian to his formation in classical learning. "Humanity" is described as a characteristic trait of "Hellenes," that is, of those trained in Greek culture. In an oration to Julian Libanius writes, "If I consider all the qualities which make you 'humane' (*phi-lanthrōpos*), first you are a Greek and rule over Greeks."[47] Julian's formation in virtue is credited to Greek *paideia*. The poets, orators and historians all have lent a hand. Particularly the philosophers— Socrates, Pythagoras, and Plato—Libanius writes, have shaped Ju-lian's noble character:

> They have entered into it and have rendered it fine and beautiful, as physical instructors do with the bodies they train. As farmers de-mand crops of the soil, so do these demand of you clemency (*hēme-rotes*) towards us.[48]

When Chrysostom's appeal to the emperor's "philanthropy" is viewed in the light of these pagan texts, its polemical nature is clearly revealed. That virtue which Themistius, Julian and Libanius would ascribe to an education in Hellenic literature is attributed by Chry-sostom to the formation obtained from a Christian "culture." For both the pagan and the Christian, the formation and possession of virtue were considered signs of the value of a tradition. The rival ethical claims, therefore, are also apologetic claims. Each side argues that it possesses the *paideia* which can form virtue.

The same point can be made with reference to the other public virtues which Chrysostom exalts: "magnanimity" (*megalopsychia*) and "boldness" (*parrhēsia*). Both of these terms are applied to the monks who intervened before the imperial commissioners at Antioch. Both are also applied to Bishop Flavian who interceded directly with Theodosius. As with *philanthrōpia*, the terms refer to classical virtues associated with city life, and again Chrysostom argues that the posses-sion of these virtues by Christians is a sign of the superiority of Christianity over Hellenism.

Megalopsychia was a virtue with both public and private dimen-sions. According to Aristotle, "that man is thought to be 'magnani-mous' who thinks himself worthy of great things and who is truly worthy of them."[49] Associated with both "courage" (*andreia*) and "beneficence" (*euergesia*), magnanimity could refer to public acts of generosity done by a civic official or patron. A vivid illustration of this dimension of the virtue is found in a famous fifth century mosaic at Antioch which portrays *megalopsychia* as a female figure (surrounded

by scenes of civic life) scattering coins in an act of public generosity known as *sparsio*.[50] Libanius also applied the term to acts of public service, in particular to the willingness of a student of rhetoric to forego wealth and material comforts in exchange for the glory (*doxa*) of an orator.[51]

"Boldness" (*parrhēsia*) was also a virtue with a long history in the Greek tradition.[52] Originally associated with the "freedom of speech" accorded an adult male citizen at Athens, the term later was used in the moral sphere, particularly in connection with philosophical teaching on friendship. *Parrhēsia* was most often associated with the "free speech" of philosophers before kings. The Cynic Diogenes of Sinope was the most popular example of this virtue in antiquity; the example of his "boldness" before Alexander the Great was constantly mentioned in the philosophical tradition.[53]

The intercession of the monks before the imperial commissioners provides Chrysostom with a striking example of "magnanimity" and "boldness." Although under no threat themselves, he writes, the monks "showed their own true philosophy" by descending the mountain and boldly addressing the officials.[54] They "displayed such great magnanimity" when they offered to give up their own lives along with the prisoners.[55] With a clear reference to the Cynic philosophers, Chrysostom contrasts the fearlessness of the monks with the flight of pagan philosophers and distinguished citizens from the city.[56] "So great is the philosophy that was brought among men by Christ," Chrysostom exclaims, that the monks prevailed upon Caesarius and Hellebichus to defer judgment to the emperor himself. Thus the whole world will come to know "that the monks who dwell at Antioch are men who have displayed an apostolic boldness (*parrhēsian*)," he exults; "all men will admire their magnanimity" (*megalopsychian*).[57]

The same magnanimity, Chrysostom writes, also was manifested by the priests, especially Bishop Flavian.[58] When Flavian went to Constantinople he addressed the emperor with great *parrhēsia*.[59] Like the biblical Esther who made entreaty before the Persian king, Chrysostom asserts, the priest will prevail over the emperor's wrath. Indeed, the dignity of the priest is even greater than that of the emperor, he writes:

> [The priest] too has a sword, not of iron but of the Spirit. He too has a crown resting on his head. But his panoply is more splendid, his arms more august. His boldness (*parrhēsia*) is greater, his strength mightier. Thus from the weight of his authority and from his own

magnanimity (*megalopsychia*) and, above else, from his hope in God, he will address the emperor with much freedom (*parrhēsia*) and much prudence.[60]

As with *philanthrōpia* the presence of the virtues of *parrhēsia* and *megalopsychia* among Christians is cited by Chrysostom as evidence in favor of Christianity.

The Structure of Chrysostom's Argument

At this point it would be worthwhile to examine more closely the steps in Chrysostom's argument. Two points must be mentioned. First, Chrysostom assumes that Christian beliefs are ethically relevant; in other words, what Christians believe should directly shape how they live. The point is made explicit several times in the homilies. Early in the crisis Chrysostom tells his audience that Christians should distinguish themselves from pagans by their fearlessness of death. The passage is worth quoting in full, for it vividly illustrates his view that Christian convictions (in this case, belief in the resurrection) have ethical implications.[61]

> Is our doctrine, indeed, a fable (*mythos*)? If you are a Christian, believe in Christ! If you believe in Christ, show me your faith by your works. How will you show your faith by your works? By despising death, for in this we differ from unbelievers. Rightly do they fear death since they have no hope of resurrection. But you, who are travelling the road towards better things, who have the hope of philosophizing there, what excuse would you have if, while confident in the resurrection, you fear death just like those who do not believe in the resurrection.[62]

Chrysostom's point is that Christian convictions are a source of ethical as well as theological guidance. Belief in the resurrection, he argues, should imply a reevaluation of one's attachment to this life and a change in the way one lives.

The Christian monks are Chrysostom's preeminent example of those who have properly shaped their lives according to their Christian convictions. The monks, "who earnestly desire death and call it rest," are the Christians who most clearly display the eschatological orientation required of all. Their lives of fasting and mortification are a daily preparation for death.[63] The intervention of the monks before the tribunal at Antioch was possible only because they already had readied themselves for death. "If they had not previously prepared themselves for every slaughter," Chrysostom writes, "they would not have been able to speak so freely before the judges or to have manifested such magnanimity."[64]

The first step in Chrysostom's argument should be plain. The virtuous conduct of the monks, their "free speech" and "magnanimity," he suggests, is the direct result of their Christian convictions. By shaping their lives according to Christian beliefs, they are a living example of the moral efficacy of those beliefs.

There is a second aspect to Chrysostom's apologetic argument. Not only do the monks display the moral value of Christian convictions, but they also demonstrate the truth of the scriptures. The presence of contemporary examples of virtue, Chrysostom suggests, proves that the New Testament stories about the apostles are true and that the stories of pagan philosophers are false:

> These things also let us tell the Greeks, when they dare to dispute with us concerning their philosophers. From hence it is manifest that their stories of former days are false, but that the things of old reported among us are true; that is, the things concerning John, and Paul, and Peter, and all the rest. For inasmuch as these monks have succeeded to the piety (*eusebeia*) of those men, they have consequently exhibited their boldness (*parrhēsia*). Inasmuch as they were brought up in the same laws, they have consequently imitated their virtues.[65]

Chrysostom's point is that when contemporary Christians display the same virtuous deeds once ascribed to the apostles, the earlier accounts become more credible. "There is no need for writings to show the apostolic virtue," he asserts, "when the very deeds all but shout and reveal the teachers of the students."[66]

Conversely, Chrysostom maintains, the failure of pagans in the present crisis reveals the foolishness and small-mindedness (*mikropsychia*) of contemporary pagans and demonstrates the falsity of pagan claims about their own philosophers:

> We have no need of words (*logoi*) to show the foolishness of the Greeks and the small-mindedness of their philosophers. For their deeds, both now and in the past, loudly proclaim that everything on their side is a myth, a stage-play, a piece of acting (*mythos kai skēnē kai hypokrisis*).[67]

Here Chrysostom dramatically expresses his hostility to the contemporary advocates of pagan culture. He claims that Christians, by truly embodying the philosophical virtues, have proven the moral superiority of Christianity. The "Greeks" by failing to come to the aid of the city have revealed the moral bankruptcy of paganism.

PART THREE: LIBANIUS' ORATIONS ON THE RIOT

How would a devout pagan have received Chrysostom's attack on traditional Hellenism? To understand Libanius' response it is necessary to know that Chrysostom's homilies were not his first attack on the culture of the Hellenes. In his earliest work, the rhetorical *Comparison between a King and a Monk*, Chrysostom had actually plagiarized several works of Libanius in order to portray the virtue and dignity of the Christian monk.[68] In this treatise, as well as in his work *Against the Opponents of the Monastic Life*, Chrysostom had already begun to use the monastic life in apologetic argument and to attack the moral values of Hellenism.[69] Later, in his apologetic work, the *Discourse on Blessed Babylas Against the Greeks*, Chrysostom explicitly attacks the emperor Julian and Libanius, quoting long sections from an oration of Libanius and cruelly mocking the sophist's sympathy with Julian.[70] John Chrysostom, therefore, was no stranger to polemic, and it is impossible that Libanius could have been unaware of his former pupil's propaganda.

Libanius, however, had not responded overtly to any of Chrysostom's previous attacks. After the crisis of the statues and Chrysostom's homilies, however, he was unable to remain completely silent, and an indirect response to Chrysostom's polemic can be discerned in Libanius' orations. Perhaps, as Chrysostom later says, too many converts were being won over from paganism to Christianity as a result of the successes of Flavian and the monks.[71] No doubt, Libanius would have been chagrined to see a Christian bishop and some illiterate monks usurping the civic role normally assumed by councillors trained in rhetoric.[72] Libanius believed intensely in the power of rhetoric (*logoi*) to form the qualities needed for public and private life. It would have been a grave omission, in Libanius' mind, if Hellenic rhetoric had nothing to contribute in the current crisis.

Libanius' response took several forms. First, he lays the blame for the riot squarely on the Christians. The charge is made several

times, but it is especially in oration 22, addressed to the pagan Hellebichus, that Libanius' bitterness is fully expressed.[73] Describing the
start of the riot, he writes:

> First of all, near the throne and gaze of the governor they broke out
> into disorderly cries. Ostensibly it was a cry of supplication, but, in
> reality, one of disobedience. In our times of dire trouble we usually
> call upon the gods and beg them to help us. In the same way on that
> occasion the rowdies called upon their god to pity them for reaching
> such a pitiable plight because of these decrees.[74]

By thus blaming the Christians for the riot, Libanius hoped to tarnish
some of Chrysostom's assertions of moral superiority.

Libanius then proceeds to ignore entirely the role of Bishop
Flavian and the monks.[75] Like Chrysostom, he praises the *philanthrōpia* of the emperor, but, unlike the Christian apologist, Libanius attempts to give a pagan interpretation of this virtue.
Pardoning offenses, Libanius writes, is among the "ways of the gods";
to pity is a peculiarly Greek virtue.[76] For Theodosius to apply some
remedial punishment to the city, rather than the death penalty, would
display "a gentleness which attempts to equate itself with the gods."[77]
The gods observe all from heaven and, although they have the power
to punish, they usually refrain from doing so. Thus the emperor
"believed that he would reveal himself as a peer of the gods,
truly nurtured of the divine, if he did not delight in merited
punishments."[78]

Besides characterizing philanthropy and forgiveness as pagan
virtues, Libanius also appeals to his own version of divine providence:
the goddess *Tuchē* ("Fortune"). Fortune was a tutelary deity of Antioch and an object of Libanius' personal devotion.[79] In his address to
the Christian Caesarius, whom he credits with persuading Theodosius
to be clement, Libanius says that the commissioner's efforts would
have been vain without the assistance of *Tuchē*. Fortune provided
Caesarius with a safe and speedy journey to Constantinople.[80] She
worked in harmony with the other gods to save the city. Caesarius is
congratulated for running his race with the approval of the gods who
cared for the city. Libanius clearly is trying to counteract the Christian propaganda by emphasizing the intervention of the pagan gods
during the crisis.

Finally, Libanius takes the opportunity to praise his beloved
"eloquence" or "rhetoric" (*logoi*). The virtues of Hellenic *paideia* are
touted:

> Eloquence helps to conceal lowly origin: it hides ugliness, protects wealth, relieves penury and suffices cities for their protection, since in war it is more useful than any equipment and in battle is more potent than any superiority of numbers.[81]

Rhetoric enables its possessors to vie with oracles in their ability to see the future. "Only those who excel in education (*paideia*) can be described as immortal," Libanius writes, "for though they die in the course of nature, they live on in their fame" (*doxa*).[82]

Whereas Chrysostom explicitly attacks pagan philosophers and the contemporary advocates of Greek culture for their cowardice during the crisis,[83] Libanius exalts both his own and Theodosius' conduct and attributes it to the value of a classical education:

> And now the tale is told everywhere and at length, both of what I and of what you have done. Even in the councils of the gods, I believe, there is mention of us both, and some of them—the Muses, Hermes and Apollo—utter words of praise, while others express their opinions upon the gifts which you should receive from them. Calliope, in company with her sisters, will bring them to pass, and on behalf of her own city she will make a double repayment by instilling into your sons the love of learning and of music.[84]

CONCLUSION

This investigation into Chrysostom's *Homilies on the Statues* has shown that the young Antiochene preacher freely used the pulpit for polemical purposes. Although Christian emperors had reigned for over seventy-five years, in late fourth century Antioch pagan and Christian were still locked in struggle; it was "not yet the Christian era," as Robert Wilken recently has noted.[85] In this context preaching provided a formidable weapon in the apologist's arsenal. In these homilies Chrysostom attempted to use current events to assert the moral value of Christianity over paganism. This argument, as I have suggested, was directed against similar claims being made by contemporary pagans, most notably Libanius. Moreover, in Libanius we have an example of one Hellenist who attempted to respond to Chrysostom's propaganda.

Two conclusions can be drawn from this analysis of the rival preaching of pagan and Christian. First, the battle was engaged, at least by these two spokesmen, on the level of culture. Each side argued that it possessed the educational resources, the *paideia*, which could form virtue. Chrysostom's conflict with Libanius, therefore, was not essentially different from that "confrontation of cultures"[86] which beset the wider Roman world in the final decades of the fourth century and early decades of the fifth. For the pagans the intellectual culture itself became the true religion. The ancient tradition aligned itself against the upstart Christian novelty. In such a debate the Christian was immediately at a disadvantage; the weight of tradition was on the side of the pagans.[87] In his preaching *On the Statues* Chrysostom seized the opportunity to present the old Hellenic tradition in a new Christian dress: the Christian emperor, bishop, and monks, he argues, embody the classical virtues.

Second, I would suggest that the ethical interests which dominate Chrysostom's preaching throughout the rest of his life may have been definitively shaped by this pagan-Christian conflict. For if, as he argues, the moral virtues of Christians could be used to support the truth claims of Christianity, the reverse could also be the case: lapses in Christian morality could undermine such claims.[88] Hence Chrysostom's apologetic argument ultimately turns to moral exhortation. The pressure of pagan and Christian polemics made it imperative that Christians display the requisite virtues. Chrysostom, therefore, devoted his life to the task of urging Christians to be faithful to their convictions and thus to demonstrate the moral integrity of their tradition.

NOTES

1. The most recent discussions of these events can be found in R. Browning, "The Riot of A.D. 387 in Antioch: The Role of the Theatrical Claques in the Later Roman Empire," *JRS* 42 (1952) 13–20; P. Petit, *Libanius et la vie municipale à Antioche au IVe siècle après J.C.* (Paris: P. Geuthner, 1955) 238–45; and G. Downey, *A History of Antioch in Syria from Seleucus to the Arab Conquest* (Princeton, NJ: Princeton University Press, 1961) 426–33.

2. J.M. Leroux, "Saint Jean Chrysostome: Les Homélies sur les Statues," *SP* 3 (TU 78; 1961) 233–39, has argued that the riot was a merely peripheral concern for Chrysostom. The crisis served simply as a "pathetic illustration" of Lenten themes, in Leroux's view.

3. J. Quasten, *Patrology*. Vol. 3. *The Golden Age of Greek Patristic Literature* (Westminster, MD: The Newman Press, 1960) 457. See M.A. Burns, *Saint John Chrysostom's Homilies on the Statues: A Study of Their Rhetorical Qualities and Forms* (Washington, DC: The Catholic University of Amer-

ica Press, 1930); also M. Soffray, *Recherches sur la syntaxe de saint Jean Chrysostome d'après les Homelies sur les statues* (Paris, 1939).

4. On Libanius as Chrysostom's teacher, see A. Naegele, "Chrysostomos und Libanios," in *XPYCOCTOMIKA. Studi e richerche intorno a. s. Giovanni Crisostomo* (Rome: Pustet, 1908) 81–142. I have treated the question briefly in a recent book, *Comparison Between a King and a Monk/Against the Opponents of the Monastic Life: Two Treatises by John Chrysostom* (Lewiston, NY: The Edwin Mellen Press, 1988) 3–5, cited hereafter as *Two Treatises by John Chrysostom*.

5. This thesis was advanced by R. Goebel in his inaugural dissertation, *De Ioannis Chrysostomi et Libanii orationibus quae sunt de seditione Antiochensium* (Göttingen, 1910). Goebel was followed in this by C. Baur, *John Chrysostom and His Time* (tr. M. Gonzaga; Westminster, MD: The Newman Press, 1959) 278.

6. See the review of Goebel's work by J. Misson in *Analecta Bollandiana* 33 (1914) 222–23 and the remarks of P. Petit, *Libanius et la vie municipale à Antioche*, 238, n. 3.

7. Cf. A.F. Norman, *Libanius. Selected Works*. Vol. 2 (LCL; Cambridge, MA: Harvard University Press, 1977) 346–47, note C. Norman points out that the peroration of Libanius' oration 22 "culminates in this emphatic assertion of the virtues of the Hellenic *paideia*, as a counterblast to the Christian propaganda current following the reconciliation." Nonetheless, elsewhere (p. 239) Norman can assert that "there is no indication of any religious confrontation or co-operation at this time." It is this latter statement I wish to confute.

8. My approach stands in clear contrast to the position of Leroux, "Les Homélies sur les Statues," 234, who writes that the question of the reciprocal dependence of Libanius and Chrysostom is "question d'un mediocre intérêt pour tout lecteur attentif de ces homélies."

9. On the ascetical and apologetic works, see my study, *Two Treatises by John Chrysostom*, 44–54, and the literature cited there. The discourses against the Arians and the sermons on Judaizing Christians have been translated by P. Harkins in the FC series. On the latter set of sermons, see Robert L. Wilken, *John Chrysostom and the Jews. Rhetoric and Reality in the Late 4th Century* (Berkeley: University of California Press, 1983).

10. Homily 1 (PG 49.15–34). The text under discussion is 1 Timothy 5:23: "Take a little wine for thy stomach." For the exact date of the riot, see Downey, *Antioch*, 426, n. 27.

11. The precise nature of this levy is unknown. Browning, "Riot," 14–15, suggests that it was both a *lustralis collatio* (levied on tradesmen and merchants) and an *aurum coronarium* (levied on curials). See also Downey, *Antioch*, 427.

12. Downey, *Antioch*, 426.

13. Libanius, or. 19.28. On the whole, Libanius' accounts of the riot are more detailed and reliable than Chrysostom's. See or. 19.25–37, or.

20.3–5, and or. 21.5. In general, however, they agree on the basic course of the events. The versions in Theodoret, *Ecclesiastic History* 5.20 and in Sozomen, *Ecclesiastical History* 7.23 are of little historical value.

14. Robert Browning, "Riot," is responsible for drawing attention to the role of the claque in setting the riot in motion.

15. Browning, "Riot," 18, cites edicts of Constantine and Valentinian authorizing that reports of acclamations be sent to the emperor for review: "On the basis of these reports he would determine the promotion or punishment of the officials concerned."

16. Such fears were not unwarranted. In 353 CE a similar mob had lynched the *archon* Theophilus. See Downey, *Antioch*,, 428.

17. Only one year earlier Theodosius had granted the right of asylum to those who fled to the imperial images. See *Codex Theodosianus* 9.44.1, cited in C. Baur, *John Chrysostom and His Time*, 260.

18. Libanius, or. 19.37.

19. The fears of the citizens are related by Chrysostom in hom. 2.12, hom. 6.2, hom. 14.15, and hom. 15.2–3, 6–7.

20. Homily 2 was delivered after the riot, one week after homily 1. Homily 3.1–2 describes the departure of Flavian. R. Goebel has discussed and established the chronology of the homilies: *De Ioanni Chrysostomi et Libanii orationibus*, 51–55.

21. Caesarius, a Christian, was *magister officiorum*, head of the civil service. Hellebichus, a pagan, was *magister utriusque militiae per Orientem*, supreme military commander in the East.

22. Chrysostom, hom. 14.15, hom. 15.1, hom. 17.9–10; Libanius, or. 20.6–7 and or. 23.25–26.

23. Chrysostom, hom. 2.3–6; Libanius, or. 23 *passim.*

24. Their arrival is described in Chrysostom, hom. 17.2–3.

25. Theodoret, *Religious History* 13.7, identifies this monk as Macedonius and records a version of the speech similar to that found in Chrysostom's homily.

26. Libanius, or. 22.37; Chrysostom, hom. 21.4.

27. Only homily 19 does not fit into this period. It was delivered after the events on the Sunday before the Ascension.

28. See hom. 3.9–10, hom. 5.15 ff., and hom. 20.21.

29. Cf. Jonah 1:1–2, 3:3–10, 4:11. Other biblical stories that Chrysostom likes to use include the deliverance of the three youths in the furnace and the sufferings of Job.

30. Hom. 21.13 (PG 49.217). Translated in NPNF 1/9.486.

31. Ibid.

32. For example, hom. 3.4, hom. 4.9, hom. 6.6, and hom. 17.3, 14.

33. In general see C. Spicq, "La philanthropie héllénistique, vertu divine et royale," *ST* 12 (1958) 169–91. The crucial figure in the fourth century is the pagan orator Themistius. See G. Downey, "*Philanthrōpia* in Religion and Statecraft in the Fourth Century after Christ," *Historia* 4 (1955)

199–208, and "Themistius and the Defense of Hellenism in the Fourth Century," *HTR* 50 (1957) 259–74. See also L.J. Daly, "Themistius's Concept of Philanthropia," *Byzantion* 45 (1975) 22–40.

34. Hom. 3.3 (PG 49.48).

35. Ibid.

36. Hom. 4.9 (PG 49.66).

37. Hom. 6.6 (PG 49.84). Chrysostom may be thinking of Theodosius' decree of March 380 (*Codex Theodosianus* 9.35.4–5) in which criminal proceedings and the death penalty were suspended during the forty days of Lent.

38. Hom. 3.2 (PG 49.48).

39. Hom. 12.3 (PG 49.128).

40. This argument has been made by G. Downey, "*Philanthrōpia*," 199.

41. See G. Downey, "Themistius and the Defense of Hellenism," 267; L.J. Daly, "Themistius' Concept of Philanthropia," 35.

42. Themistius, or. 9.145a; cited in Downey, "*Philanthrōpia*," 202. Cf. L.J. Daly, "Themistius' Concept of Philanthropia," 37–39.

43. Downey, "*Philanthrōpia*," 199.

44. Ep. 89b.289b; cited in Downey, "*Philanthrōpia*," 203. See also the discussion in R.A. Pack, *Studies in Libanius and Antiochene Society under Theodosius* (Ph.D. Dissertation: University of Michigan, 1935) 70–74. On Julian's understanding of *philanthrōpia*, see J. Kabiersch, *Untersuchungen zum Begriff der Philanthropia bei dem Kaiser Julian* (Klassisch-Philologische Studien 21; Wiesbaden, 1960).

45. Ep. 89b.290b. Cf. 291b–d.

46. Julian, ep. 84.430 to Arsacius. Cf. the criticism of Julian's efforts by Gregory Nazianzen: or. 4.111–112 (SC 309.266–270). See also the comments of a modern critic, G.W. Bowersock, *Julian the Apostate* (Cambridge, MA: Harvard University Press, 1978) 88: "It is evident that the humanitarian program of Julian was a calculated part of his scheme to wipe out the Christians rather than any reflection of a basic generosity of spirit on his part."

47. Or. 15.25. Translated in A.F. Norman, *Libanius. Selected Works.* Vol. 1 (Cambridge, MA: Harvard University Press, 1969) 165.

48. Or. 15.28 (Norman 1, 165).

49. *Nichomachean Ethics* 4.3.1121b. The most thorough study of this virtue is that of R.A. Gauthier, *Magnanimité. L'idéal de la grandeur dans la philosophie païenne et dans la théologie chrétienne* (Paris, 1951).

50. See D. Levi, *Antioch Mosaic Pavements.* Vol. 1 (Princeton, 1947) 337–45, and the comments of R. Wilken, *John Chrysostom and the Jews*, 18.

51. See the discussion in B. Schouler, *La tradition héllénique chez Libanios* (Paris: Les Belles Lettres, 1984) 979–82.

52. In general see G.J.M. Bartelink, "Quelques observations sur *parrhēsia* dans la littérature paleochrétienne," *Graecitas et Latinitas Christianorum Primaeva.* Suppl. 3 (Nijmegen, 1970) 5–57, and the literature cited

there. For Chrysostom's use of the term, see Bartelink, "*Parrhēsia* dans les oeuvres de Jean Chrysostome," *SP* 16 (TU 129; 1985) 441–48.

53. See Plutarch, *Alexander* 671 and Diogenes Laertius, *Lives of the Philosophers* 6.32, 38, and 68. In his apologetic treatise, *De sancto Babyla, contra Julianum et gentiles,* Chrysostom explicitly attacks the *parrhēsia* of Diogenes, contrasting him with the bishop and martyr Babylas, who displayed the true apostolic "boldness." See *De sancto Babyla* 34–48 and the commentary on these paragraphs by M. Schatkin in her translation: *St. John Chrysostom. Apologist* (FC 73; Washington, DC: Catholic University of America Press, 1983) 95–103. In general see P.R. Coleman-Norton, "St. John Chrysostom and the Greek Philosophers," *Classical Philology* 25 (1930) 308–09.

54. Hom. 17.3 (PG 49.172–173): *meta parrhēsias dielechthēsan.* Cf. hom. 18.12 and hom. 19.3.

55. Ibid. (PG 49.173).

56. Hom. 17.5 (PG 49.173–174).

57. Hom. 17.6 (PG 49.175).

58. Hom. 17.8 (PG 49.175).

59. Hom. 3.4 (PG 49.49).

60. Hom. 3.6 (PG 49.50).

61. On the development of this theme in Chrysostom's other works, see F. Leduc, "L'eschatologie, une préoccupation centrale de saint Jean Chrysostome," *Proche-orient chrétien* 29 (1969) 109–37, especially 121–22.

62. Hom. 5.6 (PG 49.71).

63. Hom. 6.7 (PG 49.85).

64. Hom. 17.4 (PG 49.173).

65. Hom. 17.7 (PG 49.175). Translated in NPNF 2/9.455.

66. Ibid.

67. Ibid.

68. See my study of this work in "Borrowings from Libanius in the *Comparatio regis et monachi* of St. John Chrysostom," *JTS* ns 39 (1988) 525–31. The text is translated with an introduction in my *Two Treatises by John Chrysostom.*

69. I have developed the arguments for this position in *Two Treatises by John Chrysostom,* 25–36 and 43–54.

70. An excellent translation and commentary on this text can be found in M. Schatkin, *St. John Chrysostom. Apologist,* cited in note 53 above.

71. See his sermon *De Anna* 1.1 (PG 54.643).

72. See especially his oration 11, the encomium on Antioch, where Libanius exalts the power of rhetoric when exercised by curials in defense of the city.

73. Or. 22.5. Cf. or. 19.25 and or. 20.1.

74. Hom. 22.5 (Norman 2, 378–79).

75. Only very brief references to each are made and nothing is said about their intercession: or. 19.28 and or. 22.13.

76. Or. 19.12–13.

77. Or. 20.11.

78. Or. 20.13 (Norman 2, 319). Cf. or. 19.17 and or. 20.16.

79. See P. Petit, *Libanius et la vie municipale*, 192. J. Misson has discussed Libanius' special devotion to *Tuchē: Recherches sur le paganisme de Libanios* (Louvain, 1914) 50–66.

80. Or. 21.17–18.

81. Or. 23.21 (Norman 2, 261).

82. Ibid.

83. See esp. hom. 17.2 (PG 49.173–174).

84. Or. 20.51 (Norman 2, 347). Cf. Norman's comment on these lines (n. C): "The pagan terminology of the whole peroration culminates in this emphatic assertion of the virtues of the Hellenic *paideia*, as a counterblast to the Christian propaganda current following the reconciliation."

85. Robert Wilken, *John Chrysostom and the Jews*, 29–33.

86. The phrase is taken from R. Markus, "Paganism, Christianity and the Latin Classics," in *Latin Literature of the Fourth Century* (ed. J.W. Binns; London/Boston: Routledge & Kegan Paul, 1974) 8. Markus is concerned primarily with the west, but the point applies in the east as well.

87. No less a figure than the Christian Bishop Basil of Caesarea had recently defended the moral value of the Hellenic tradition, at least as a "preliminary training" before the study of scripture. See his treatise *Ad adolescentes*. Greek text and English translation by R.J. Deferrari in *St. Basil. Letters* (LCL 4; London, 1934) 249–348.

88. Chrysostom is conscious of this. See hom. 16 where he notes the failure of Christians to convert the pagan commissioner Hellebichus owing to their fear of death.

8

CHRISTIAN REACTION TO THE BARBARIAN INVASIONS AND THE SERMONS OF QUODVULTDEUS
by Robert B. Eno, S.S.

"God is punishing you for your sins." Disasters have frequently proved a boon for preachers of repentance. As Augustine noted, just the threat was often sufficient to bring people to church demanding the baptism they had put off for years.[1] Even today, in less sophisticated societies, this type of explanation may not have disappeared completely. I was told by a Colombian priest that, after the eruption of the Nevado del Ruiz volcano in November 1985 in which 25,000 people in the town of Armero were drowned in a tidal wave of mud, some local people recalled the murder of a priest in that same town some years before and looked upon the eruption as divine punishment. But in more secularized milieux, the connection of disasters with divine punishment has worn thin. The Lisbon earthquake of 1755 in which tens of thousands perished provoked at least as much questioning of divine providence as affirmation of it. It is said that when, after the great San Francisco earthquake and fire of April 1906, preachers began to speak of God's vengeance on the wicked city, skeptics pointed out that while many churches had been consumed in the flames, several distilleries had been untouched. The AIDS threat has given this type of preaching a new lease on life.

This time-honored homiletic practice of using catastrophes to scourge the faithful verbally has always been a two-edged weapon. Long ago people asked the obvious question: Do not the innocent suffer along with the guilty in such events? Preachers might then distinguish: the sufferings brought about by disasters were a punishment for the wicked but a warning to the good or perhaps a test of their patience and docility. Another approach appeared in more pessimistic theologians like St. Augustine. All are guilty. Therefore, it is presumptuous as well as ignorant for anyone to speak of himself or herself as innocent. No one has any right to complain about punishment because all deserve it. This argument in turn might provoke further discussion about degrees of guilt.

This paper will discuss the generalized historical disaster which terrified and baffled Roman Christians of the first half of the fifth century. The crisis arose from the disintegration and progressive collapse of the western Roman empire. In similar circumstances, men and women of every age have always turned to those who were supposed to be able to read the signs of the times and asked: What have we done to deserve this? But for Christian preachers seeking to answer the question at this time, the situation was more complex. Many people, including Christians, noted pointedly that the Roman empire had become great and victorious under its traditional gods and rites. Why now, when they had been abandoned and the new religion adopted, was Rome collapsing? The process of this "decline and fall" had been long in the preparation, but it was the sack of Rome by Alaric and his Goths in August 410 that traumatized many Romans. Jerome, on hearing the news, reported: "The speaker's voice failed and sobs interrupted his utterance. The city which had taken the whole world, was itself taken. . . . The world is falling in ruins. . . . The glorious city that was the head of the Roman empire has been engulfed in one terrible blaze."[2]

The longer part of this study will look at Christian responses to these fearful developments. Much of this material is not homiletic in form, though, no doubt, these authors and others used the very same arguments in their preaching. After this general survey, the paper will concentrate on the sermons of Quodvultdeus, a contemporary of Augustine and bishop of Carthage during the Vandal conquest.

THE CHRISTIAN VIEW OF THE BARBARIANS

A review of earlier Christian literature raises the question of whether theology in particular or even Christianity in general had had any influence on the way the Roman Christians viewed the barbarians. One may be chagrined to find that when mentioning these "lesser breeds without the law," Christians usually spoke with the same cultural prejudice and disdainful tones employed by their pagan neighbors and ancestors. The surprising lack of missionary élan to go beyond the Rhine or Danube to convert the heathen is also part of the picture.[3] The one successful missionary movement, connected with the name of Ulfilas, ironically had the unfortunate result for Roman Christians of converting to Arianism many of the same tribes who would later oppress them.

Tertullian began his massive assault on Marcion (c. 207) with a description of the latter's native region of Pontus in terms of its barbarity. With brilliant exaggeration, he appeared to place it on the shores of the Arctic Ocean. "Even so, the most barbarous and melancholy thing about Pontus is that Marcion was born there, more uncouth than a Scythian, more unsettled than a wagon-dweller, more uncivilized than a Massagete . . . darker than fog, colder than winter," etc.[4] To be sure, these and other patristic comments are largely literary commonplaces about the Romans' little-known northern neighbors, but why did Christianity not bring about a fresh look?

As demons destroy souls, noted Eusebius, barbarians destroy bodies. In his tricennalian oration for Constantine (336), he wrote: "Now the visible barbarians, a kind of savage nomad, no different from wild animals, roamed wildly about the domesticated flocks of men, laid fields waste, and reduced cities to slavery, coming against the citizens like fierce wolves from the desert and mauling whomever they might."[5] Somewhat later, Christian authors gave evidence not only that they were repeating traditional generalizations about the barbarians but that they had uncritically appropriated Roman chauvinism as well.

In 378, shortly before the great Roman military disaster of Adrianople, Ambrose reassured the young western emperor, Gratian, of victory over the Goths whom he identified with the apocalyptic Gog and Magog. "I must detain your Majesty no further in this season of preparation for war and the achievement of victory over the barbarians. . . . Go forth to the victory, promised of old time, and foretold in oracles given by God."[6] Gratian never made it to the battle but his uncle, the eastern emperor Valens, was killed. In reply to the request of Fritigil, queen of the Marcomanni, for instruction in the faith, Ambrose also instructed her to persuade her husband to remain at peace with Rome.

Ambrose's exegetical short-sightedness was surpassed a few years later by the Christian poet Prudentius who echoed Virgil in his prediction of Rome's eternity. "Unending sway he taught, so that the valor of Rome should never grow old. . . ." Writing c. 404, or six years before Alaric's sack of Rome, Prudentius made the foolhardy boast that nothing could happen to Rome henceforward because it was now Christian.

> Let those who din into my ears once more the story of past disasters and ancient sorrows observe that in your time, I (*Roma*) suffer such things no longer. No barbarian foe shatters my bars with his spear, nor with strange arms and dress and hair goes roving through captured city, carrying off my young men to bondage across the Alps.

His contempt for the barbarians was even more graphic than that of Eusebius: "What is Roman and what is barbarian are as different from each other as the four-footed creature is distinct from the two-footed or the dumb from the speaking. . . ."[7] In the event of the barbarian conquests, even Augustine spoke of their "brutal nature . . . their fierce and savage minds." A common lament was that they were merciless. Nearly two centuries later, Gregory the Great, writing to the bishop of Constantinople in October 596, insisted that the subjugation of the barbarian nations by the Roman empire was the condition sine qua non for Christian peace and freedom.[8]

THE TIME OF THE INVASIONS

Looking at western Christian literature of the fifth century, one inevitably finds a sense of foreboding that terrible things are threatening. The barbarians were a menace in northern Italy, and Paulinus at Nola, near Naples, composing his annual verses (for 402) in honor of Felix, the patronal martyr of Nola, wrote:

> If only the troubled times allowed such expressions of delight. . . .
> Yet even amidst battles, this day will be for us one of joy and peace.
> . . . So depressing fears must go. . . . I would gladly celebrate . . .
> even if I were an unhappy prisoner of Gothic arms or amongst the harsh Alans. . . . So now, though rumor wandering over diverse regions strikes our apprehensive ears with fearsome tidings . . . no black fear must cast its cloud over the day which God makes cloudless to give heavenly honor to Felix.

Paulinus adds as an afterthought the common view of churchmen: "Foreign races . . . are being roused by God's angry displeasure at our sins. God is trying to rouse our sluggish hearts to take thought for life by inspiring us with fear of death."[9]

GAUL

With the crossing of the frozen Rhine on the fateful last day of 406, the doom of Gaul was sealed. Wars are everywhere; peace has fled the earth, lamented the unknown author of the *Carmen ad coniugium* (c. 415). The pagan Rutilius, writing of his journey from Rome back to his native Gaul the next year, tells us that he had to travel by sea since the land routes had been rendered impassable. Writing c. 430, Orientius, possibly bishop of Auch, near Toulouse, described the universal desolation.

> Neither the wild tracts of dense woods or of lofty mountains, nor the rivers strong in their swift rapids, nor natural fortifications, nor cities protected by walls, nor the pathless sea, nor dismal wastes, nor holes, nor caverns under forbidding cliffs avail to frustrate the barbarian hordes.
>
> Throughout villages and farms, throughout the countryside and crossroads, and through all districts, on all highways leading from this place or that, there was death, sorrow, ruin, fires, mourning. All Gaul smoked as one funeral pyre.[10]

The most common theme of these reflective works is not a direct exhortation to repent but a preliminary and preparatory consideration. These writers try to take advantage of the situation to remind Christians forcefully of the fleeting nature of this life. The horrors described are reminders that life is short. Therefore, one must concentrate on the life that will never end. In his letter to Demetrias, the young Roman noblewoman who was committing herself to a life of consecrated chastity and asceticism, Pelagius used the sack of Rome in 410 and the current unsettled state of affairs to encourage her in her resolve. "What is stable in this world? What is firm? What is not short and uncertain, not subject to chance?" Recently the city of Rome was plunged into fear and sadness when the sound of the Goth's trumpets was heard. What good was nobility then? Everywhere there was confusion; all felt fear equally and mourning visited every home. What kind of fear will be felt when the final trumpet sounds?[11]

At almost the same time but in Gaul, Pseudo-Prosper, writing to his wife, drew the same lesson. This life is short; eternal life is what is truly important. Therefore, one must lead a good and modest life. If sufferings are coming, true Christians should not be surprised. On the contrary, they should be welcomed. He seems to echo the thoughts of the earlier martyrs: Christ suffered and died for us; how can we refuse to suffer for him? Orientius' words foreshadow Hobbes' description of primitive life. We now tread a path of sorrow, and life is "wanton, wretched, deceptive, brief, inconstant, and vain." There have been false friends, perjury, plots, treachery.

> What was not conquered by force was conquered by starvation. The unfortunate mother fell with her children and her husband, and the master submitted to slavery with his slaves. Some lay as food for dogs, and for many their flaming dwellings, after destroying their lives, served as funeral pyres.

Given the brutality and misery of this life, the only sensible choice is to live a life here which prepares us for death. "Happy is the one who considers death is granted to us as an end to labors and fearing it during life has acted with proper concern lest he should fear it later."[12]

Paulinus of Pella, grandson of the poet Ausonius, writing about the year 459 and looking back on the misfortunes of his life, brought about largely by the reversal of Roman fortunes, could nevertheless entitle his work the *Eucharisticus,* the *Thanksgiving.* Despite his losses and his wanderings, he thanked divine providence for having taught him "that I ought neither to love too earnestly present prosperity which I know I might lose nor to be dismayed by adversities. . . ."[13]

Paulinus of Beziers, on the other hand, writing in the immediate aftermath of the initial invasions (407–409), expressed dismay that despite God's scourges, people had changed little. They repaired the physical damage but did not correct their vices. If people would reform, they would be less frightened by the barbarian threat. A later work of this period, the *Chronicle* of the Spanish Bishop Hydatius of Aquae Flaviae restricted its comments to noting the sadness and misery of the age.[14]

Most of these works do not explicitly pose the question of why these things are happening to Christians. One that does is the *Carmen de Providentia Dei,* formerly attributed to Prosper of Aquitaine (c. 416). Amid all the destruction, the "wounds of a broken world," there are many who ask questions. Those who believe in God and divine providence are confronted with comments such as: "Why have so many cities perished together without being guilty of any crime?" or "If the entire ocean had poured over the fields of Gaul, more would have survived the vast waters." For a decade the "slaughtering swords" of the Goths and Vandals have gone unchecked. Nothing has been able to stop them. If the bulk of the dead had been older men, one might argue that they had accumulated a greater load of sins. But this was not the case. What about the children killed? What about the priests, nuns, those dedicated to God? "The same tempest destroyed both the good and the wicked."[15]

But it was not just a problem of why the good and the innocent suffered during this whirlwind of misery. This was but a small subsection of the perennial problem of evil. Why do the wicked prosper and why are the good victimized? The author launched into a full-scale theodicy beginning with the existence of God, creation, the fall, etc. Like most he must conclude, whatever his arguments, ultimately that human beings cannot understand God's ways. The human view of good and evil, sinners and innocents, is not based on a correct judgment. "We are citizens of heaven but we love the things of earth."

Punishment for some can mean a cross which can be spiritually profitable if they take it well. Whatever the losses, if you view things *sub specie aeternitatis,* you will not be overwhelmed.

> The wise servant of Christ has lost none of these things, for in rejecting them he has already transferred his true riches to heaven. And if any earthly misfortune falls upon him, and he meets with a multitude of sufferings, he faces it with courage, being sure of the glory that has been promised him, and eager with victory won to depart.[16]

SOMBER REFLECTIONS AND UNBELIEVABLE EXPLANATIONS

Whether or not this author's arguments were found convincing, his work is less well known than those which follow here. These works, of Orosius and Salvian, still moved within the traditional framework of the Roman mindset of religion as a *do ut des* relationship with God. Many Christians shared this spiritual presupposition with their pagan ancestors. The gods bless the world with peace and prosperity (the *pax deorum*) as long as they are kept satisfied by the observance of traditions and the proper rituals. Hence in earlier centuries, Christians themselves had been regarded as a menace to the well-being of society because they refused to honor the gods and observe the traditions. As Tertullian reminded us, many pagans were convinced that the Christians were the reason why disasters came upon the world (*Apology* 40.2). If many Roman Christians maintained the same expectations of the Christian God, then clearly the barbarian triumphs and the Roman defeats posed new problems for Christian thinkers. Hence the *queruli* mentioned in the *Carmen* of Pseudo-Prosper.

This, of course, was the same challenge that confronted Augustine after August 410. More disturbing were the murmured questions about the efficacy of the old gods in contrast to the apparent impotence or indifference of Christ. Orosius, the Spanish priest who had sought refuge in Africa from the barbarians in his homeland, was commissioned by Augustine in the early stages of the *City of God* to write a history which would illustrate the working out in the past of the theological views expressed in the master work. When the history was completed c. 417, well before the *City* itself (426), it met with at best a mixed reception from Augustine. As Mommsen has well shown, Augustine expressed his clear disagreement on several points.[17]

Orosius sought to counter complaints against Christianity by collecting every example of a natural disaster, plague or misfortune of any kind from historians of the pre-Christian era. In so doing, he hoped to demonstrate that if the *tempora christiana* had their difficulties, pre-Christian times were one long catalogue of catastrophes! In other words, the widespread basic presumption was kept intact: If you worship God correctly, i.e. if you are a Christian, God will bless you and the Christian empire in this life. Orosius probably got the clue for his thesis from the complaints of Augustine in the early stages of his own apologetic that educated pagans knew about the disasters of pre-Christian times but were keeping silent in order to embarrass Christians. In the interim, while Orosius was writing, Augustine's own thinking was moving in a different direction. Ironically, Orosius' history was to become an influential work for the middle ages which took it as a faithful representation of Augustine's views.

SALVIAN OF MARSEILLES

A work with similar presuppositions is the jeremiad of the Gallic monk, Salvian of Marseilles. Written after the death of Augustine in the 440s when the barbarian overlordship in Gaul was a fact of life, Salvian also sought to answer the questions of Christians. The issue of divine providence appears in the title of his book: *De gubernatione Dei*, On the Governance or Providence of God. "They say that God, since he neither protects the good nor punishes the wicked, is disinterested in all things; that in this world, therefore, the status of the good is decidedly worse than that of the evil."[18]

The question is the same: Why are the good not being rewarded now by being protected from harm? Salvian agrees with the presupposition of the question but gives an answer with a new twist. God is rewarding the virtuous—only now it is the barbarians who are more virtuous than the Romans. This was not an easy assertion to make. He was well aware that the barbarians were either pagans or Arians. He was vague about details but also knew well enough that the moral behavior of the barbarians was far from perfect. Nevertheless, he asserted that, in general, the barbarians despite their status as non-Catholics were more worthy than the orthodox Romans. So God *was* rewarding the virtuous with victory. Clearly the essential thrust of the work was not to praise the virtues of the enemy but to denounce the moral corruption of the Catholics. As such the work was a tour de force.

Speaking to Catholics, he began by reminding his readers that God's providence should not be interpreted as simply meaning protection. "God is always our judge in this life. While God governs us, he judges us because his governance is his judgment."[19] As Christians must believe in God's providence, so they cannot escape the reality of his judgment. Judgment as punishment is clearly visible in scripture.

Many Christians apparently demand that God should reward them, pay tribute to them, as it were, for their Christian faith. They expect that Christian peoples should be stronger and more powerful than others. Yes, these Catholics hold the orthodox faith but that by itself is not really to believe in God. "I think (that) . . . he is faithful to God who observes faithfully the commandments of God."[20] Christians like to think of themselves as good but they are not. They follow God only in appearance. They do not think of God or of others; they always act solely in their own self-interest. Think of how angry an insolent slave makes you. How do you think you look in the eyes of God? "The majority of Christians have not lived up to even the least and smallest of the commandments."[21]

He then turns his scorn on the church itself in this terrible indictment.

> The Church herself, which should be the appeaser of God in all things, what is she but the exasperator (*exacerbatrix*) of God? Beyond a very few individuals who shun evil, what else is the whole assemblage of Christians but a cesspool of vice? How many will you find in the Church who are not either a drunkard or a beast or an adulterer

or a fornicator or a robber or a debauchee or a brigand or a murderer? And, what is worse, they do all these things almost unceasingly. . . . Almost the whole commonality of the Church is reduced to such a low degree of morals that, among all Christians, it is the general norm of holiness to be less corrupt than others.[22]

What about those who actually attend church? Those who ask for forgiveness of their sins? In the latter case, they have hardly left the church building when they are back to their old ways. Indeed, their activities in church seem to be devoted to contemplating their future crimes.

They are setting their crimes in motion in the midst of their prayers and supplications. While their lips do one thing, their hearts do another. While they bewail their past evils with words, they are meditating future evils and thus their prayers are originators of crimes. . . . When the solemn rites are over, they all immediately scurry to their wonted pursuits, some to steal, others to get drunk, others to commit fornication, others to highway robbery. It seems to be clear that while they were inside the church they planned what they would do, once they were outside.

It should be no source of surprise, let alone of scandal, that the mere name of Christian without the substance does the Romans no good. "It is of no advantage whatsoever to have a holy name and no morals, because a life that does not harmonize with our profession cancels the dignity of a glorious title through the baseness of unworthy deeds."[23]

He went on to describe the evils of this allegedly Christian society. The Master is good and loving but Christians are wicked servants. With the *City of God* in mind, he berated the contemporary Roman state with its lack of justice as little better than a *latrocinium*. The rich are like brigands who strangle the poor with taxes. In such a society, *conversio* came to mean that when the nominal Christian (just about everybody) decided to turn to God to become a serious and committed Christian, this usually meant in practice that the *conversus* would become an ascetic. This, said Salvian the ascetic, earned that person the scorn of the "Christian" populace. Thus he could say that this Christian society forced God to punish. In fact it did not suffer as much as it deserved. Do not blame God for the present troubles; blame yourselves. The latest sin, added to all the rest, was to assert that God was indifferent and negligent. On the contrary, our sufferings show both that God is watching and that he is not indifferent. He still hopes to make us wake up and change. The barbarians are not without sin but at least they have the excuse of ignorance; the Romans know better but go on sinning anyway. "We among the whole human race have professed Christian philosophy. Because of this we must be . . . considered worse than all other peoples, because we live under the name of such a great profession, and, being placed in the midst of religion, we continue to sin."[24]

Salvian begins to detail many of the miseries and iniquities of contemporary Roman society: excessive taxation, especially burdensome on the poor; peasants reduced to serfdom; avarice, dishonesty, etc. However cruel the barbarians may seem, at least they love other members of the same tribe whereas Romans persecute one another. Things became so bad within the empire that some Romans sought out barbarian controlled areas in the hope of finding justice and honesty.

> They prefer to live as freemen under an outward form of captivity than as captives under an appearance of liberty. Therefore the name of Roman citizen, at one time not only greatly valued, but dearly bought, is now repudiated and fled from, and it is almost considered not only base but even deserving of abhorrence. They seek among the barbarians the dignity of the Roman because they cannot bear barbarous indignity among the Romans.[25]

He went on to excoriate the Roman obsession with pleasures and distractions, especially with the games in the amphitheaters. As other Christian preachers had complained before and since, the games easily outdrew attendance at church. Salvian added that some who may have forgotten about the games and gone to church, when reminded, got up and walked out of church! Looking back at the fate of Roman cities in Gaul now occupied by the barbarians, cities such as Trier and Cologne near the frontier, he recalled how mad they were for the games. "Wherever there are Romans there is much vice." Great amounts of public treasure even now are being spent so that Romans can be entertained but this has not lessened their appetite. "We are a new kind of wastrels and profligates, in whom opulence has ceased to exist but in whom evil continues to endure."[26] He mentioned the siege of Carthage and some have wondered whether he knew the sermons of Quodvultdeus.

He extended his survey to Spain and especially to North Africa which he portrayed as even more debased and corrupt than the rest of the empire. The unquenchable thirst for entertainment went on amidst society's collapse. The empire went to its death laughing. As for the North Africans, vice was their second nature. They committed every sin in the book, but in sins of "impurity and blasphemy, they had surpassed even themselves." In terms reminiscent of Augustine's *Confessions,* Salvian described Carthage as "a city bubbling over, as it were, in vice. I see a city burning with every kind of iniquity. . . ." The city was so rotten that the barbarian conquerers were scandalized and the Vandals have since tried to clean it up. He ended the book with a call to the Romans to be ashamed. "The vices of our bad lives alone conquered us."[27]

This highly heated and caricatural explanation of the barbarian invasions, like Orosius' strange history, both purported to account for the plight of the Christian empire within the traditional presupposition that the good are rewarded for their worship of the true God. For Orosius, Catholics are being rewarded even if they do not realize it because of their ignorance of history. For Salvian, on the other hand, the good are also being rewarded—only this time it is Rome's enemies. Salvian's thoughts and words are also profoundly traditional in that they portray the disasters of the times as God's punishment for sins in the hope, however forlorn, that people may be induced to repent. Salvian's picture of the state of affairs is so unrelievedly dark that he is hardly open to the objection that the innocent suffer with the guilty. In Salvian's world, all are profoundly corrupt. The factual objection that he is open to (apart from the charge of wild exaggeration) is the good face he generally puts on the barbarian adversaries.

AUGUSTINE, 410–413

Gaul was the first region of the western empire to be drastically affected by the invasions, and it is Gallic authors who both described the results and sought to explore the reasons. All Romans were affected by the sack of Rome in 410 and thus, well before the Vandal crossing into North Africa, Augustine undertook the defense of the Christian era. During the long years of reflection and writing, he ultimately came to abandon the belief that somehow Christian times will necessarily be more peaceful and prosperous than other eras. In reverting to a more exclusively eschatological solution, he finally escaped more than other Christian authors of the time from the dilemma of trying to explain what was happening solely in terms of reward or punishment for Christians in this life. But this attempt did not emerge whole and intact immediately. His initial reaction to the news of the sack of Rome in August 410 was also one of shock and some confusion. An early sermon, *De urbis excidio*, seems to show him searching in several directions for explanations. The same situation seems evident in the early books of the *City of God*. Some of his statements might be put in the category of the contemporary politician's protest when some embarrassing incident comes to light: "It did not happen but, if it did, it is not as bad as you claim."

His arguments are jumbled together in these early sermons. If the human race is chastised, some as a punishment, some as a warning, we should not complain. The just and the unjust punished together? Who is not deserving of punishment? Terrible things happened, yes. We must heed God's warning. No suffering is like hell as we shall learn to our sorrow if we do not heed these warnings and change our ways. Yes, there were fifty just men in Rome at that time, indeed many more than fifty, but not people who were not deserving of punishment for their sins. Even in the case of those who died, including monks and nuns, is death so bad? They are now safe from life's temptations. The saints who died are now glorifying God. But most people did not die, and whatever physical damage was done to the city, are not the people really the city? They survived these punishments, but what about conversion? In Constantinople a few years before, fiery clouds were seen in the east and there was a great wave of religious emotion which drove people to the churches.[28]

Do the barbarian threat and the sack of Rome represent God's wrath or God's mercy? Even the sack was not as bad as such things usually are. Compared to the destruction of Sodom in the Bible, Rome was not severely damaged. The barbarians, heretics though they are, regarded the Christian basilicas of Rome as places of sanctuary where people were permitted to seek refuge. "So Rome has endured a single tribulation in which the pious man has been either freed or corrected, the impious has been condemned." Therefore one should be neither shaken nor dismayed. It is a test that we should make the most of. It has been a *dolor utilis*. The time to fear is when God does nothing to us. This means that he has given up hope of our repentance.[29]

Other sermons delivered about this same time have similar themes: Why are you so upset? Did not Christ predict the destruction of the world? "Why did you believe when it was promised and yet are so upset when the promise is fulfilled?" Although it was still to be given a more prominent place in the course of his writing the *City of God*, Augustine's conviction all along was that it is the next life that is all important. Earthly life is the preparation, the testing ground for it.

Thus it should not be surprising if there are tests and trials for us here. If there were fewer bad people, the times we live in would not be so bad. But unfortunately such is not the case. "Evils abound in this world that the world may not be loved."[30]

In June of 411 he preached on the feast of Saints Peter and Paul. This proved an apt occasion for discussing the special objection that the disaster had befallen *Christian* Rome, site of the burial places and relics of Peter and Paul, not to mention so many other Christian martyrs. "Peter the Apostle reigns with the Lord; the body of Peter the Apostle lies in a certain place. His shrine (*memoria*) is meant to stir up in you love for the things of eternity; it does not exist that you may cling to this earth but that you may think of heaven with the Apostles." Reminiscent of the words of Plotinus which he would recall while dying in besieged Hippo in 430 are these comments: "Do you mourn and weep that wood and stones have fallen down and that those who were going to die, have died?" Or, later: "Did Peter die and was he buried (in Rome) that a stone might not fall from a theater? God is striking the playthings from the hands of spoiled children."[31] This is Augustine's ultimate consideration: what happens in this life, joy or sorrow, must be viewed in the light of our future with God.

From time to time, he also spoke of punishment for sins and repeated the whole line of arguments used by other Christian authors. But as he went on year after year, reflecting, writing and discussing these matters, he came to stress that no one was promised a happy life on earth in exchange for or as a reward for a Christian commitment. "His primary aim was to show that Christianity brings a solely eschatological good, and cannot be regarded as a totemistic guarantee of success, that the millennium cannot be realised in this transient world."[32]

QUODVULTDEUS OF CARTHAGE

Quodvultdeus[33] has been identified as the deacon of Carthage who wrote to Augustine late in the latter's life (c. 426 or 427) to request that Augustine write a brief survey of Christian heresies. In his response, ep. 222, Augustine declined but suggested the works of Philaster of Brescia and Epiphanius of Cyprus. Quodvultdeus' letter brought a renewed plea for the opusculum. Finally Augustine gave in, saying that he would see what he could do even though he was busily engaged in controversy with Julian of Eclanum.

Aurelius of Carthage preceded Augustine in death by a few months. His successor in the primatial see of north Africa was Capriolus. This, of course, was the time of the Vandal invasion and siege. The tenure of Capriolus is uncertain but he was succeeded by Quodvultdeus between 431 and 439, probably in 437. His sermons were probably preached during the time of the siege. After the Carthaginian capitulation of 439, Quodvultdeus was exiled and took refuge in Naples. Here he wrote the *Liber promissionum et praedictorum Dei.* Deogratias, the next Catholic bishop of Carthage, was chosen in 454. It is presumed that Quodvultdeus died shortly before that date, though in fact his death could have occurred earlier, since we must presume that the Vandal rulers did not allow the election of a new Catholic bishop without a good deal of hesitation.

This essay presumes the correctness of the attribution to Quodvultdeus of the works found in Réné Braun's edition of 1976.[34] Most of the works now attributed to the African bishop were up until fairly recently attributed to other authors, including Augustine. Germain Morin was one of the earliest scholars to assign the twelve sermons of Pseudo-Augustine to the single authorship of Quodvultdeus. Most like Braun have followed this judgment. One holdout is Manlio Simonetti. He points out that antiquity knew of no particular literary activity on the part of Quodvultdeus. Some of the sermons, he believes, furthermore, are not theologically coherent with some of the others attributed to the same author. In any event, we shall here follow Braun as even Simonetti now does for the sake of convenience, if not conviction on his part.[35]

Before proceeding to the two sermons *de tempore barbarico,* let us see if the themes present in the other sermons are similar. In these sermons, the issue of the barbarians' threat and presence is mentioned in passing. There is the same atmosphere of doom and foreboding. Violence, famine and disease are everywhere. "Where are the fountains of tears? . . . Some are dead; others have fled; the land has been handed over to the impious; tribulation and want have found us." Look forward to the joys of heaven where, among other things, there is no all-pervasive fear and dread of the barbarians.[36]

As an understandable part of the pastor's concerns, Quodvultdeus is indignant at the new Arian hegemony and fearful of what that may mean for the future of the church. The barbarians are doing the devil's work in destroying the church. The church has now become the disadvantaged David facing the new reality of the Arian Goliath. The new masters can easily attract converts with promises of regaining wealth and position. Will Catholics content themselves with a long-term situation of repression and inferiority? The pressure is already being felt and there have been less than subtle offers of money. The injury of conversion to Arianism is compounded by the insult of rebaptism. Quodvultdeus says that they seek to exorcise the Father, Son and Holy Spirit and introduce a "new God" from overseas. Arian religious leaders, he complained, did not appear to have done anything to restrain the savagery of the Vandals, their lust for blood.[37]

Ultimately the only immediate consolation that Quodvultdeus can offer is that one will suffer less if one puts less hope in this world which is falling into ruins. People in Africa, as in Gaul, are complaining about their situation and want to know why. The easy, if not always convincing, explanation is at hand and Quodvultdeus, like everyone else in the same position, seizes on it: "We are all sinful." We have been rightly handed over to those who afflict us. Like Salvian, he finds that the North Africans are incorrigible. When there is a choice between church and the games, the latter will always win out for the allegiance of Christians.

One should not be content to complain and lament about what is happening. Think about it seriously; discuss it with others. We are all guilty children of Adam and of wrath. This world is coming to its end, falling into ruins. There is nothing left for us here. If we stay here, we shall be caught up in the general collapse and ruin. What remains is to turn to the things that last for eternity.[38]

IN THE TIME OF THE BARBARIANS

The two sermons *de tempore barbarico*, even apart from the question of whether they are from the same author, pose a variety of problems. Were they preached during the siege as is usually asserted? Some remarks seem to presume that the Vandals' triumph was already a fact. Is the preacher describing the fall of the city? If so, then the sermon could hardly have been preached before the fall. On the other hand, one must not forget that Carthage was the final holdout against the Vandals. They had in effect already conquered and were simply waiting for the last and greatest jewel to drop into their hands. The city was no doubt filled with refugees, and Quodvultdeus had heard many tales of woe and horror from them about the earlier fall of other cities and of the Vandal and Arian policy toward the now subject Roman population.

His comments graphically portray the desolation and terror.

How does one cope with the extent of the destruction? One weeps for a single death; how mourn a whole city?

> Truth speaks to you, O lovers of the world: Where is the thing that you loved? that you were holding fast as a great possession? Where is the thing that you were unwilling to part with? Where is Africa, that for the whole world was like a garden of delights? Where are her many districts? Where are her great, most splendid cities? Was she not chastised the more sharply, the more unwilling she was to take on discipline to remedy those evils, when other provinces had reformed themselves?

No one is safe; no one is spared, not even clerics or dedicated virgins.[39]

Quodvultdeus' general concern for the Arian threat is evident throughout his works from the many passages in which he refutes Arian theology and Arian polemic against Catholic trinitarian doctrine. We have mentioned above his fear that the Vandals will take advantage of their new overlordship to pressure Catholics into abandoning their trinitarian faith. In these two sermons he mentions this also, but it does not appear as frequently. The warfare in which they live brings dangers for souls as well as for bodies. Many die without baptism. The Roman defeat enables the Arians to claim that their religious views have been proved the stronger and therefore correct. God keeps silence, say distressed Catholics. Why? If theological arguments do not convince, then worldly advantages now available to collaborators will tip the scales in favor of Arianism.[40]

By far the predominant theme of these two sermons is that God is punishing the north African Catholics for their sins. He castigates their addiction to the games. "Human blood is daily being spilled in the world and the voices of the deranged are heard in the circus." We deserve what we are getting. We preach but we do not practice. Everyone blames everyone else with good reason but none can validly excuse himself. Only God is not to be blamed. In earlier times God destroyed the world in a flood; now he chastises one region or city but not everyone. God is love but if we will not heed his warnings, he will turn away from us.

> The face of the Lord is mercy; he turns away and wrath comes upon us. The face of the Lord is salvation; he turns away and confusion comes upon us. The face of the Lord is the highest good; he turns away and every evil comes among us. The face of the Lord is peace; he turns away and where is the peace?[41]

Before they are regarded as punishments, the disasters which befall us should be understood as warnings. But do we pay attention? No. We shut our ears and go on sinning, worse than before. Yet we are foolish enough to expect that blessings will continue to come to us. The saints warn us, the church preaches to us, but they are wasting their breath. Do we repent? Instead, as in Italy at the time of Alaric, some "Christians" demand that pagan sacrifices be offered once again. People complain that the barbarians have robbed them, have stolen everything. Now they are reduced to poverty. But what did you do earlier when you were urged to help the poor? You did nothing except to go on filling up your own barns and storehouses. And who is your heir now? your beneficiary? The new barbarian masters.

Quodvultdeus seems to suggest that Catholics and Romans who have been despoiled should take comfort and satisfaction when they see their despoilers themselves eventually being despoiled by a bigger and more ruthless brigand. In the cruel sea of life, there will always be a bigger fish to swallow the smaller. But such an interpretation would be premature. Rather Quodvultdeus seems to be saying to the Roman complainers: You lived in a ruthless and pitiless world and you should not complain if others with the same ethic now devour you.

You complain of being victimized. Did you not do the same to others to amass your wealth? Do not give alms for your sins. The church does not want stolen money to atone for sins of stealing. The Vandals are the new overlords and masters, and Romans of all classes tremble at the thought of offending them. Great ladies who used to have many slaves serving them now find themselves reduced to the status of handmaidens and without even having been paid for. The victors are merciless and only hard slavery is to be expected at their hands.[42]

It all can be summarized in the old lesson, always to be relearned the hard way—do not put your hopes on this world. One simply cannot rely on this world or on worldly prosperity. Turn to your creator and repent; make satisfaction. He is kind and merciful. He is a shepherd and we are his lost sheep. "Fear the wolf. . . . Call out that the Shepherd may hear you; call out, wandering sheep." One particularly appealing theme that brings to mind the future development of the devotion to the Sacred Heart as the symbol of love and a place of refuge for the sinner is Quodvultdeus' passage at the end of the first sermon concerning the open side of Christ. Through it the good thief on Calvary entered paradise immediately. It is a place of peace, security, eternal happiness where there is no longer fear of the barbarian. "Come, all of you, enter; this is the way to enter; his side lies open."[43]

CONCLUDING REFLECTIONS

There are clearly passages and thoughts here which recall Augustinian themes. It is not surprising that Quodvultdeus, a north African and one who had corresponded with Augustine, should mirror a certain number of Augustinian ideas and arguments. For example, as we have seen, Quodvultdeus insists that all people are deserving of punishment, eliminating to some extent the objection about the suffering of the innocent. The few good people are only relatively good. He alludes to Augustine's basic belief that what you love determines what you do and, indeed, what you are. We love this world too much. If the scales of justice were brought forward, the love of the world would be found to outweigh the love of God with us. But we are not put here to find happiness in this world. He also makes use of Augustine's play on the names of the two early north African female martyrs. Why should we cling to earthly unhappiness (infelicitas) when we are meant to have *perpetua felicitas* only in heaven? I am not arguing here for or against direct Augustinian derivation, but the examples just cited are possible candidates.[44]

This essay undertook to review the work of Quodvultdeus especially the two sermons *de tempore barbarico,* in the context of Christian reflection on the disaster of the barbarian invasions. Augustine's shifting views in the *City of God* put decreasing effort into trying to explain the time of troubles in terms of God's rewarding those who worship him correctly in this world. He came to the conclusion that any such correlation of happiness for Christians in this world is a dangerously mistaken presupposition.

Quodvultdeus reminded his hearers that they were not to look for their happiness in this world. Sometimes it sounds almost like a counsel of despair. But a much larger amount of time was spent reminding people that the sufferings of the present were just what they deserved because they had been such bad Catholics. In other words, he was following the traditional homiletic theme: You are being punished for your sins. Indeed, if we took Salvian seriously, he could hardly have said anything else, given that the north Africans were such superlatively bad Christians. He has no words about any supposed superiority of virtue among the Vandals. I must conclude

that Quodvultdeus' preaching shows little influence of any new theological insights. Rather he continues in the well-worn track followed
by the less creative writers and preachers surveyed earlier.

NOTES

1. Augustine, *Sermo de urbis excidio* 6.7, ed. M. Vianney O'Reilly (PS 89;
   Washington, DC: Catholic University of America Press, 1955) 68.
2. Jerome, epp. 127.12; 128.5 (CSEL 56.154, 161; ed. Hilberg). The best
   survey of this literature remains that of P. Courcelle, *Histoire littéraire des
   grandes invasions germaniques* (3rd ed.; Paris: Etudes Augustiniennes,
   1964).
3. *Kirchengeschichte als Missionsgeschichte*. Band 1: *Die alte Kirche* (ed. H.
   Frohnes and U.W. Knorr; München: C. Kaiser, 1974).
4. Tertullian, *Adversus Marcionem* 1.1, ed. Ernest Evans (OECT; Oxford:
   Clarendon Press, 1972) 2–4.
5. *Laus Constantini* 7.2, tr. H.A. Drake in *In Praise of Constantine* (University
   of California Classical Studies 15; Berkeley: University of California
   Press, 1976) 95. Greek text edited by I. Heikel in *Eusebius' Werke*. Band 1
   (GCS 7.212).
6. Ambrose, *De fide* 2.16.136 (CSEL 78.104); ep. to Fritigil: *Vita Ambrosii*
   36 (PL 14.39). On the God-Magog identification with the Goths, Augustine clearly disagrees with Ambrose: *De civitate dei* 20.11; Quodvultdeus
   is non-committal: "ut quidam dixerunt." See *Dimidium temporis* 13.22.
7. Prudentius, *Contra orationem Symmachi* 1, vss. 542–3 ("Empire without
   end"; LCL 1.390); other citation: 2, vss. 690–95; 816–17 (LCL 2.60,
   70).
8. Augustine, *De civitate dei* 1.7 (CCSL 47.6); Ambrose, *De officiis clericorum*
   2.15.71 (PL 16.121; merciless barbarians); Quodvultdeus, *Sermo de tempore barbarico* 2.5.13 (CCSL 60.477); Hydatius, *Chronicum* 46 (SC
   218.116); Gregory the Great, ep. 7.5 (CCSL 140.452).
9. Paulinus of Nola, *Carmen* 26. vss. 4–6, 12, 22–23, 29–30, 33–34, 71–73
   (CSEL 30.246–48); tr. P.G. Walsh (ACW 40; Westminster, MD: Newman
   Press, 1975) 254–56.
10. Pseudo-Prosper, *Carmen ad coniugium*, vss. 27, 30 (CSEL 30.344–45);
    Rutilius, *De reditu suo*, vss. 37–38, in J.W. and A.M. Duff, edd., *Minor
    Latin Poets* (LCL, 766); Orientius of Auch, *Commonitorium* 2, vss.
    167–72, 181–84, ed. M.D. Tobin (PS 74; Washington, DC: Catholic
    University of America Press, 1945) 94.
11. Pelagius, *Epistula ad Demetriadem* 29, 30 (PL 30.43–44).
12. *Carmen ad coniugium*, vss. 53–54, 61–91 (CSEL 30.345–47); Orientius,
    Commonitorium 1, vs. 11 (PS 74.52), 2 vss. 173–74, 176–80 (PS 74.94), 2,
    vss. 255–56 (PS 74.98).
13. Paulinus of Pella, *Eucharisticus*, Pref. 3 (SC 209.56).

14. Paulinus of Beziers, *Epigramma*, vss. 24–25, 89–93 (CSEL 16.504, 507); Hydatius, *Chronicum*, Pref. 5, 7 (SC 218.102, 104).

15. Michael McHugh, ed., *The Carmen de Providentia Attributed to Prosper of Aquitaine* (PS 98; Washington, DC: Catholic University of America Press, 1964) 260, 262: "wounds," vs. 17; "so many cities," vs. 25; "entire ocean," vss. 27–28; "older men," vss. 40ff; "same tempest," vs. 52.

16. Ibid. 302, 304: "things of the earth," vs. 859; "wise serpent," vss. 908–12.

17. On Orosius, see Theodor E. Mommsen, *Medieval and Renaissance Studies* (Ithaca: Cornell University Press, 1959): "Orosius and Augustine," 325–48; "St. Augustine and the Christian Idea of Progress: The Background of the *City of God*," 265–98. See also B. Lacroix, *Orose et ses Idées* (Paris: Vrin, 1965) 199–210.

18. Salvian, *De gubernatione Dei* 1.2.6 (SC 220.106); tr. J. O'Sullivan (FC 3; Washington, DC: Catholic University of America Press, 1947). For a comparison of Salvian with other Gallic authors, see J. Badewien, *Geschichtstheologie und Sozialkritik im Werk Salvians von Marseille* (Göttingen: Vandenhoeck und Ruprecht, 1980) 167–76.

19. Ibid., 1.4.18 (SC 220.118).

20. Ibid., 3.2.6–7 (SC 220.190).

21. Ibid., 3.6.26 (SC 220.206); 3.8.30 (SC 220.210), citation.

22. Ibid., 3.9.44, 46 (SC 220.220). The latter part of the citation is reminiscent of Tertullian, *De pudicitia* 1: "He is considered sufficiently chaste who is not too unchaste."

23. Ibid., 3.9.48–49 (SC 220.222); 3.11.60 (SC 220.230).

24. Ibid., 4.2.10 (SC 220.238–40; good master); 4.6.30 (SC 220.254, 256; brigands); 4.7.33 (SC 220.258; conversion needed); 4.8.36 (SC 220.260, 262; we are to blame); 4.12.54–55 (SC 220.276, 278; God is trying to wake us); 4.12.57 (SC 220.278; no excuse of ignorance); 4.12.59 (SC 220.280), citation.

25. Ibid., 5.5.22–21 (SC 220.328).

26. Ibid., 6.7.38 (SC 220.386; leave church); 6.8.39–40 (SC 220.388; vices, Cologne and Trier); 6.9.52 (SC 220.396; wastrels); 6.12.60 (SC 220.406; Carthage).

27. Ibid., 7.1.6 (SC 220.434; dying laughing); 7.13.57 (SC 220.470; second nature); 7.15.64 (SC 220.476; impurity); 7.16.70 (SC 220.480; bubbling); 7.21.89 (SC 220.494; barbarian cleanup); 7.23.108 (SC 220.508; vices have conquered).

28. *De urbis excidio* 1.2 (PS 89.54; punishment for all); 3.2 (PS 89.58; terrible things); 5.5 (PS 89.62; fifty just men); 6.6 (PS 89.66; city-people); 7.6 (PS 89.68; Constantinople, as in note one).

29. Ibid., 2.2 (PS 89.56; Sodom); 9.8 (PS 89.72; *dolor utilis* and citation). Cf. sermo 296.12 (=Bib. Cas. 1.133, *Miscellanea Agostiniana* 1.410): "Qui tollit correptionem, parat damnationem."

30. Sermo 81.8 (PL 38.504; why did you believe); ser. 80.8 (PL 38.498; evils abound).

31. Ser. 296.7 (MA 1.405; burial place of Peter); ser. 296.12 (MA 1.409; spoiled children).

32. Citation from Elizabeth Allo Isichei, *Political Thinking and Social Experience. Some Christian Interpretations of the Roman Empire from Tertullian to Salvian* (Christ Church, NZ: University of Canterbury, 1964) 80. Augustine may have had public readings of earlier drafts of books of the *City of God.* Cf the new letter to Firmus, ep. 2*.3: "Among these, of course, is that eighteenth book which you listened to with us so intently for three afternoons running."

33. For Quodvultdeus, see A. Mandouze, ed., *Prosopographie chrétienne du Bas-Empire.* vol. 1. *Afrique* (Paris: Centre nationale de recherche scientifique, 1982), sv. "Quodvultdeus, 5," 947–49. Augustine, epp. 221–224 (CSEL 57.442–54).

34. *Opera Quodvultdeo Carthaginiensi episcopo tributa* (CCSL 60; ed. R. Braun). Braun had earlier edited the *Liber promissionum* in SC 101–102. In the introduction of volume 1, 13–113, Braun gives a survey of the question of authorship.

35. See also A. di Berardino, ed., *Patrology,* vol. 4. *The Golden Age of Latin Patristic Literature* (Westminster, MD: Christian Classics, 1986): "Quodvultdeus," 501–03 (by V. Grossi). Simonetti summarizes his objections in *La Produzione letteraria Latina fra Romani e Barbari (sec. V-VIII)* (Sussidi Patristici 3; Rome: Augustinianum, 1986) 35–39; bibliography, 226.

36. *De accedentibus ad gratiam* 2.4.2 (CCSL 60.461; violence, famine); *Adversus V haereses* 6.5 (CCSL 60.280), citation; *Contra Iudaeos, paganos, et Arrianos* 21.5 (CCSL 60.256; no fear of barbarians); *De cataclysmo* 6.17 (CCSL 60.419; no fear of barbarians).

37. *Dimidium temporis* 13.22 (CCSL 60.207; Devil's work); *Adversus V Haereses* 1.6 (CCSL 60.261; David and Goliath); *De tempore barbarico* 2.14.7 (CCSL 60.486; David and Goliath); *De symbolo* 1.13.6 (CCSL 60.334; offer of money); *Adversus V Haereses* 7.38 (CCSL 60.299; rebaptism, exorcism); *Dimidium temporis* 8.16 (CCSL 60.201; new God); *De accedentibus ad gratiam* 2.13.10–11 (CCSL 60.470; restrain Vandals).

38. *De symbolo* 3.1.19 (CCSL 60.350; no hope here); ibid., 3.2.16–18 (CCSL 60.352; question Providence); *De ultima quarta feria* 7.2 (CCSL 60.405; rightly handed over); *De accedentibus ad gratiam* 1.5.4 (CCSL 60.444; games over church); ibid., 2.3.6 (CCSL 60.461; think it over); *De cantico novo* 2.2–3 (CCSL 60.383; things that last).

39. *Sermones de tempore barbarico* 1.1.9 (CCSL 60.423–24; mourn a whole city); 2.5.4 (CCSL 60.476–77; citation); 2.6.4 (CCSL 60.478; clerics and nuns).

40. Ibid. 2.5.16 (CCSL 60.478; danger for souls); 2.6.2 (CCSL 60.478; dying without baptism); 2.14.4 (CCSL 60.486; God is silent); 1.8.7 (CCSL 60.436; worldly advantages).

41. Ibid. 1.1.11 (CCSL 60.424; blood spilled); 1.1.12–13, 17–19 (CCSL

60.424; all are to blame); 2.6.5–7 (CCSL 60.478; flood); 2.2.8–9 (CCSL 60.474; citation).

42. Ibid. 1.1.1–2 (CCSL 60.423; shut ears); 2.10.2 (CCSL 60.482; saints); 2.3.2 (CCSL 60.474; offer sacrifice); 2.6.9, 11 (CCSL 60.478; robbed); 2.8.1–2 (CCSL 60.480; bigger fish); 2.8.7–8, 11 (CCSL 60.480; almsgiving); 2.5.9, 11, 13 (CCSL 60.477; new masters).

43. Ibid. 2.5.4 (CCSL 60.476; no hope in this world); 2.9.6 (CCSL 60.481; can't rely on world); 2.1.2 (CCSL 60.473; turn to Creator); 2.13.1 (CCSL 60.484; fear the wolf); 1.7.32 (CCSL 60.435; side of Christ).

In his article in *Heart of the Saviour* (ed. J. Stierli; New York: Herder and Herder, 1959), Hugo Rahner speaks of Quodvultdeus (p. 55), but only in terms of the connection between the blood and water from the side of Christ and the sacraments of baptism and the eucharist. He does not speak of this passage (1.7.32) which does not fall into the sacramental context. See Hugo Rahner, "The Beginnings of the Devotion in Patristic Times," 37–57.

44. *Sermones de tempore barbarico* 1.3.1 (CCSL 60.426; relatively good); 2.5.4 (CCSL 60.476; amor meus, pondus meum); 1.3.10 (CCSL 60.427; scales of justice); 2.7.4 (CCSL 60.479; happiness in this world); 2.12.4–5 (CCSL 60.484; perpetua felicitas). For a translation and commentary, see R. Kalkman, *Two Sermons: De Tempore barbarico attributed to St. Quodvultdeus, Bishop of Carthage. A Study of Text and Attribution with Translation and Commentary* (Unpublished Ph.D. Dissertation; The Catholic University of America, 1964).

9

THE EUCHARISTIC GIFT: AUGUSTINE OF HIPPO'S TRACTATE 27 ON JOHN 6:60–72
by Edward J. Kilmartin, S.J.

Around the year 400, a certain Januarius asked Augustine about the basis for diversity of liturgical practices in the various churches. One question concerned the custom of an additional eucharistic celebration on Holy Thursday. The bishop's response shows that his mind was turned in another direction: "Now we do not dispute how it is done, but how the sacrament is to be understood."[1]

How Augustine himself understood this sacrament has been a matter of controversy since the ninth century. From the nineteenth century beginnings of critical history of dogmatic theology, scholarly opinion, for the most part, has held that Augustine never fully affirmed that the humanity assumed by the Word is communicated in, and by, the consecrated elements of the eucharist. However the yield of contemporary research on the subject of the evolution in Augustine's christology seems to indicate a tendency in the direction of sacramental realism.

Among all the works of Augustine that might shed more direct light on this problem must be counted his longest treatment of the subject of the eucharistic food and drink in his mature years: Tractates 26.11–20 and 27.1–11 of the *Commentary on the Fourth Gospel.* All authors who have attempted a comprehensive presentation of his eucharistic doctrine refer to this source. However few attempts have been made to provide a complete commentary on either of these tractates. In this century the exception is Fr. Marie-François Berrouard, the well-known Augustinian scholar. His detailed analysis of Tractate 27.1–6, 9–11,[2] led him to the conclusion that Augustine taught a sacramental realism that conforms to the popular north

African and Greek conviction. However the proof he offers may not settle the question, in the judgment of this writer.

ANALYSIS OF TRACTATE 27

This essay offers an interpretation of Tractate 27,[3] which takes into account Tractate 26.[4] It is taken for granted that the close link between these sermons, delivered within a short time of one another, requires that Tractate 26.11–20 (on John 6:49–59) be continually brought into play. Tractate 27 contains an exposition of John 6:60–72 (numbering of verses: Vulgate edition), prepared for the feast of St. Lawrence, August 10, 414.[5]

[27.1] At the outset Augustine observes that a commentary on this text is not out of place on the feast of the saint because it is "about the body of the Lord, which he was saying that he himself gives to eat for eternal life."[6] On the presupposition that this exposition was to be delivered at the celebration of the eucharist, the mild excuse is probably required because the acts of the martyrdom usually took the place of a homily. Why it is fitting to comment on this particular text becomes clear at the end of the sermon. In the meantime Augustine sets about his task by referring to what he said in the previous sermon.

The initial statement quoted above is a concise summary of John 6:51–56, already explained in 26.13–17. More space is given to the previous commentary on v. 57 in 26.18. Augustine recalls how Jesus "explained the manner of attribution of this his gift, how he would give his flesh to eat, saying: "Who eats my flesh and drinks my blood, abides in me and I in him" (v. 57). Augustine has two observations to make on this verse.

The first relates directly to what he will say about St. Lawrence in the peroration: "The sign that one has eaten and drunk is this: if he remains and is abided, if he dwells and is indwelt, if he adheres in order that he be not forsaken." This observation implies that the eating and drinking, when it occurs, has the effect of securing the abiding and being abided. But how is this eating and drinking actually done? Augustine views v. 57 as a direct response to this question. In other words, only those who abide and are abided actually eat and drink the body and blood. For he adds: "Therefore he taught us this, and admonished with mystical words, in order that we might be in his body under him as head among his members, eating his flesh, not abandoning his unity." From what has been said up to this point, it seems that "eating his flesh" is confined to believers who are truly members of the body of Christ. This understanding is confirmed by 26:18, where it is said that "whoever does not remain in Christ, and in whom Christ does not remain, without any doubt neither eats his flesh, nor drinks his blood, but eats and drinks the sacrament of so great a thing for judgment unto oneself. . . ."

The preacher continues with the remark that many of those present "not understanding were scandalized; for hearing this they thought only of the flesh, that they themselves were." Augustine seems to be referring back to 26.13, the commentary on v. 52. Christ had said that the bread he would give is his flesh. Augustine remarked: "The flesh is named, that flesh does not comprehend, and all the more so, flesh does not comprehend, because flesh is named." The preacher then pointed out that the Jews "were shocked . . . they thought it could not be done."

The consequence of this unbelief is now unfolded in 27.1 on the basis of Romans 8:6: "To discern according to the flesh is death."[7] This text is applicable to what Augustine had said in 26.14–15 on the subject of the unbelieving Jews. Their question, "How can this one give us his flesh to eat?" (v. 53), was interpreted in 26.14 as a query of unbelievers: ". . . they did not understand, nor wish to receive the bread of concord," namely, participation in the mystical body of Christ.[8] The result of this unbelief is death of the soul, as Augustine stresses in 26.15 by connecting the question of the Jews: "How the Lord was able to give his flesh to eat," with John 6:54–55. These verses show without doubt that "whoever does not eat this bread, nor drink this blood, does not have this (eternal life); for human beings can have temporal life without it, but they are not able at all (*omnino*) (to have) eternal (life)."[9]

Now in 27.1 the same thing is expressed explicitly by applying 1 Corinthians 8:1: "The Lord gives his flesh to eat, and to discern according to the flesh is death, since he said concerning his flesh that therein is eternal life." In other words, those who discern according to the flesh will reject what Christ said, will not come to believe and know, to eat and drink "spiritually,"[10] and on that account will be deprived of eternal life.

[27.2] Having recalled salient features of the previous sermon, Augustine begins his exposition of John 6:60–72. An example of discerning according to the flesh is also found among "many . . . not of his enemies, but of his disciples, who said: 'This talk is hard; who is able to hear him' " (v. 61). They should have been open in simplicity of faith to be taught by the Lord. But "they did not believe him saying a great thing, and concealing a very great grace by his words." The term "grace" seems to be related to what was said in 27.1 about the "manner of distribution of this his gift," namely "his flesh." For Augustine paraphrases the latter saying in 27.11 as "the grace of his distribution" with reference to "his flesh and blood." Further light is shed on the meaning of "grace" in 27.3.

"Rather," the preacher continues "as they wished so they understood,[11] in the manner of humans, that Jesus was able, or that Jesus ordained this, to distribute the flesh wherewith the Word was clothed, as if cut into pieces, to those who believe in him." Here Augustine insinuates that these disciples are like heretics who deny the inseparable unity of the humanity and divinity in Christ. To think that Jesus was able to give the flesh wherewith the Word is clothed is a heretical opinion. For, as was already pointed out in 26.19: ". . . he himself is both God and man, the Son of God and Son of Man, the one Christ Jesus." Those who really believe in him know that this is impossible because of the unity between the humanity and divinity.

[27.3] In the response of Jesus to the disciples, "This scandalizes you" (v. 62), Augustine allows Jesus to add: "because I said: I give my flesh to you to eat, and my blood to drink, it is this, is it not, that scandalizes you." In this way the preacher identifies very clearly the source of the scandal. But he remarks that the saying about the ascension of Jesus (v. 63) should have removed the scandal "if they understood. For they thought that he would divide his body for distribution; however, he said that he would ascend into heaven, indeed integral (*integrum*)."

A further significant remark is made on v. 63, where Augustine himself addresses the unbelieving disciples: "When you see the Son of Man ascending where he was before, certainly, at least then, you will see that he does not divide his body for distribution in the way you think; certainly at least then you will understand that his grace is not consumed in morsels." It is noteworthy that Augustine says that there will be a distribution of his *body*, but not in pieces. Second, "his body" is identified with "his grace." Hence "this his gift . . . his flesh" (27.1), or "the grace of his distribution . . . his flesh and blood" (27.11) is identified with "his body . . . his grace" in 27.3. In other words, Augustine does not seem to have gone beyond the idea that the gift of the eucharist is deeper insertion into the body of Christ, the holy church: the only point of view explicitly mentioned in 26.14–15.

[27.4] Augustine now quotes v. 64a: "It is the Spirit who vivifies, the flesh profits nothing." However he does not immediately comment on this verse. Rather he returns to v. 63: "Before we explain this (v. 64a), as the Lord grants, it is not to be passed over negligently, that he said: 'If therefore you were to see the Son of Man ascending where he was before.' "

The rest of this pericope explains why the saying does not furnish the basis for the opinion that the Son of Man was *not in heaven* when he was on earth. The problem is this: "Indeed this one said: 'where I was before,' as though at that time he was not there, when he was saying these things." The relatively long exposition cannot be described as a "digression." If the subject of the sermon is "the body of Christ," nevertheless Augustine is commenting on a passage of scripture. He would never pass over lightly a verse of this type with its obvious christological implication, especially in a series of sermons in which the bishop intends to refute all christological heresies as occasion is offered by the text of scripture.[12]

The saying about the Son of Man ascending "where he was before" is linked with John 3:13: "No one ascends into heaven, except the one who descended from heaven, the Son of Man who is in heaven." The verses need an explanation. The Son of Man began to exist on earth through the incarnation. Yet Christ says the Son of Man ascends where he was before. This seems to mean that he was in heaven previously, and that he is not now in heaven. On the other hand, in John 3:13, Christ says that the Son of Man descended from heaven, and therefore was in heaven before, and, at the same time, affirms that he is now in heaven. Both sayings are explained on the basis of the unity of person:

> Where does this tend, except that we understand what I also commended to your charity in a previous exposition: Christ, God and man is one person, not two, lest our faith be not Trinity, but quaternity? Accordingly Christ is one: the Word, soul and flesh, the one Christ; the Son of God and Son of Man, the one Christ. The Son of God always, the Son of Man out of time, yet the one Christ according to the unity of person.

On the ground of this reasoning, Augustine concludes the pericope: "He was in heaven, when he was speaking on earth. Thus he was Son of Man in heaven, the same way he was Son of God on earth; Son of God on earth in the assumed flesh, Son of Man in heaven in the unity of person."

The interpretation of these verses, and the verbal correspondence with Hilary of Poitiers' commentary on the same verses in *De*

Trinitate 10.54,[13] suggests that Augustine may have been inspired by Hilary's use of John 3:13 in connection with John 6:63 to refute various heresies which deny that the man Jesus Christ is truly God and man.[14] He seems to have the same heretical tendencies in mind, especially the Apollinarists. The reference to "one person . . . not two," "soul" and "quaternity," recalls Augustine's criticism of the Apollinarists. These heretics held that the Word assumed a human body and irrational soul, the Word himself becoming the rational principle of this body. They reasoned that if Christ was true God and true man, he would be two persons. Augustine, on the other hand, argued that if the Word took the place of a human soul, the Word would be changed. Only because the Word entered into a hypostatic union with a fully constituted humanity would the Word lose nothing of his perfection.

Augustine rejected the position of the Apollinarists on the grounds that it implies a deterioration of the divine nature. For example in *Epistula* 140.4 (12), written in 412, with an eye to the Apollinarist position, he affirms that the Word was not changed for the worse because he united himself to the humanity through a rational soul.[15] The objection that the assumption of a fully constituted humanity would make two persons in Christ is answered with a reference to Philippians 2:8b–c:

> You see what care the apostle takes to make us see that the one Jesus Christ, God and man, makes only one person, for fear that we would introduce a quaternity in the Trinity. In effect, just as the union of soul and body does not double the number of persons, and constitutes only one man, likewise the union of man and Word does not destroy the unity of Jesus Christ, and constitutes only one and the same Christ.[16]

[27.5] Following this confession of the unity of humanity and divinity in Jesus, Augustine repeats v. 64a. He had remarked already, at the outset of 27.4, that special divine assistance is needed to interpret this saying ("as the Lord grants"). But now he invites his hearers to join him in asking for the Lord's help: "Let us say to him (for he allows us not contradicting, but seeking to know): O Lord, good master, how 'does flesh profit nothing,' when you said: Unless one eats the flesh of the Son of Man and drinks his blood, that one will not have life in oneself (v. 54)?" It is customary with the most difficult texts of scripture for Augustine to ask the Lord himself, and to invite his audience to ask with him, for enlightenment.[17]

Augustine is going to treat the last part of v. 64a first: "The flesh profits nothing." He asks: "Does life not profit?" The answer is obvious. The preacher then refers to John 6:55, where the life Jesus is talking about is identified as eternal life. But not everyone eats and drinks this food and potion. Only those who are in the body of Christ really eat and drink. Augustine alludes to this notion in the question: "And for what reason are we what we are, except that we should have eternal life, that you promised by your flesh?"

The phrase "we are what we are" harkens back to what was said in 26.13 about the faithful being "the body of Christ."[18] Subsequently, in 26.15, the "flesh" referred to in vv. 54–55 is identified with the "holy church," in which the members of Christ participate through the sacrament by eating spiritually. Through the sharing of this eucharistic gift, namely, the "unity of the body and blood of Christ," the deepening of the life in the body results.[19] Consequently, one lives from the Spirit of Christ who works in the body of Christ.[20]

In the light of 26.13 and 26.15, it is difficult not to conclude that the ecclesial outlook obtains in 27.5. Therefore Augustine is affirming that this kind of flesh profits, namely, the body of Christ, the holy church. But what kind of flesh does not profit? Flesh of a corpse profits for temporal life, not for eternal life. Hence the saying about "flesh profiting nothing" refers to flesh as "they understood it . . . as cut from a corpse. . . ." The "they" are the same ones, however, who understood that Jesus intended to distribute "the flesh wherewith the Word was clothed just as though cut into pieces to those who believe in him." Hence this saying also refers to the flesh of Jesus when considered by itself alone.

The flesh that profits is now identified as flesh "quickened by the spirit." Since it is a question of eternal life, that spirit can only be the divine Spirit. But the "flesh quickened by the spirit" is not to be identified only with the flesh of the Word of God. The rest of the pericope offers a set of examples of the usefulness of fleshly, or non-spiritual, beings when employed by the divinity.

The first example is the effect of charity, the gift of the Spirit, on knowledge acquired by individual effort. Here Augustine appeals to 1 Corinthians 8:1: "Knowledge inflates, but charity upbuilds." Since knowledge has this detrimental side, the preacher asks: "Should we hate knowledge?" Not at all, he responds. In fact Augustine is on record as recommending the pursuit of various sciences.[21] Why? To gain a clearer perception of the signs found in holy scripture. But the value of the knowledge of the sciences depends on the use made of them. When sciences are self-seeking, ruled by cupidity, then they are tools of self-destruction, and damage to others. But when ruled by charity, they are useful to oneself and benefit others. Science profits when ruled by love, that is, employed out of love of God, and love of neighbor for the love of God.

Hence Augustine says that science alone, and therefore ruled by cupidity, does not profit. But "add charity to knowledge, and knowledge will be useful; not by itself, but by charity." In other words, even when knowledge is ruled by charity, it does not take on an independent value with respect to the true life.

This example is especially suited to the context. Augustine has already discussed how the unbelievers, depending on their own powers, cannot understand what Jesus is talking about. They are those who "as they wished so they understood." But here Augustine seems to choose this example with an eye to what he will say, in 27.6, about charity as a gift of the Spirit in the sphere of the corporate life of the members of Christ's body, the church.

Augustine now establishes an analogy between the effect of charity on knowledge, and the effect of the spirit on flesh. "Thus also now, 'the flesh profits nothing,' but flesh alone; let the Spirit be added to flesh, as charity to knowledge, and it profits very much." Obviously the preacher is referring to the divine Spirit because he is talking about profiting "very much" for eternal salvation. However one should not jump to the conclusion that the preacher is confining his remarks only to one specific "flesh." The statement is put in general terms. Then the application is made to christology in two ways: The Word would not have become flesh to no purpose; Christ profited us much through the flesh.

In the first step, Augustine says: "For if the flesh profited nothing, the Word would not have become flesh in order to dwell among us." This statement points, in a general way, to the fact that the incarnation was for our benefit: "in order to dwell among us." Then Augustine adds: "If Christ profited us very much through the flesh, how does the flesh profit nothing?" But how did Christ profit us through the flesh?

In 26.8 Augustine explained that the Father teaches through his Word. But he asks: "How may a human being, constituted in the flesh, hear such a Word? Because the Word was made flesh and dwelt among us."[22] Also Augustine refers to the goal of the incarnation in 26.20: "This is the bread that descended from heaven in order that by eating him we might live. . . ."[23]

A new idea is conveyed in the next sentence of 27.5: "Rather through the flesh the Spirit worked something great for our salvation.

The flesh was a vessel; attend to what it contained, not what it was."
In the first place, this passage is talking about the incarnation.
"Spirit" refers to the divinity of the Word who assumed the flesh. The
use of the "Spirit" in this sense is not surprising, since both the Greek
and the Latin fathers, including Augustine, favor the word "spirit" to
express the nature of divinity.[24] It is true that Augustine underscores
the view that the Son of God in the form of God is not the source of
salvation for humanity. Rather the mediation of salvation is based on
the humanity which the Son of God assumed. In short, it is the Son of
God in the form of servant who, without losing the form of God, is
mediator.[25]

However, according to Augustine, the abasement of the Son in
the form of servant can have true meaning for salvation only in the
measure where the permanence of the divine dimension of the Word
in the being itself of the act of abasement is assured. The role of the
Son of God at the heart of the redemptive work of the Son of Man is
expressed in 26.19, where Augustine comments on John 6:58. Here
Christ is allowed to say: "My abasement in which he sent me brought
about that I live 'with a view to' the Father, that is, I refer my life to
him as greater than I."[26] The choice of "Spirit" for Word is possibly
influenced by this consideration, but one must also reckon with the
context in which the theme of dead flesh and flesh animated by the
spirit is central.

The notion that the flesh alone does not profit is expressed by
the image of "vessel." Most frequently Augustine uses the image of
"vestment" to describe the relation between the changeable humanity and the unchangeable divinity. But he uses several images to con-
vey the same idea. The intention is to affirm that the humanity
assumed by the Word remains a perfect humanity. In short, Augustine says that the flesh of the Incarnate Word, despite its humble
status, comparable to a "vessel," was the docile instrument through
which the Son of God in the form of servant "worked something
great for our salvation." He accomplished, in principle, the redemption of humanity.

What the Son of God effected concretely in the form of servant
was succinctly summarized in 26.10: "Eternal life assumed death.
Eternal life wished to die . . . for thee. . . . For he assumed flesh
from human beings. . . . Therefore life assumed death, in order to
kill death. . . . Eternal life, the Word . . . also gave eternal life to the
assumed flesh."[27] This passage reflects Augustine's understanding
that the assumption of a human nature by the Word is the assumption
of all human nature; that is, it establishes an ontological identity

between Christ and all human nature. The idea that the assumption of a human nature entails a divinization of all human nature that must be actualized through the free response of faith is expressed in this pericope by the reference to the need for belief: "For 'who believes in me,' he said, 'has eternal life,' not what lies open to the light of day, but what lies hidden."[28]

The next example of flesh profiting is that of the apostles. "The apostles were sent; is it perhaps that their flesh profited us nothing? If the flesh of the apostles profited us, was the flesh of the Lord able to profit nothing? For whence comes the sound of the word to us except by the voice of the flesh? Whence the writing, whence the composition? All these are works of the flesh, but by the spirit agitating the flesh as its organ."

In this example, Augustine refers explicitly to the "flesh" of the apostles as distinguished from their "spirit." It was the souls of the apostles that ruled their bodies, employing their voices to preach the good news of salvation, and their hands to write the scriptures. However because the apostles "were sent" by the Lord they were able to contribute to the work of salvation. In Augustine's view, the spoken words and writings of the apostles are the voice of God, insofar as given to the apostles' souls. For this reason, their activity has a special role to play in the actualization of revelation.[29] What Augustine expresses here is spelled out more fully in his remark on 1 Corinthians 1:21 in *Enarratio in Ps.* 103, ser. 1.8, written in 411: "All that the apostle did . . . is work of the body, but the soul commanded the body, and God commanded the soul."[30]

Why has the preacher compared the bodies of the apostles with the "flesh" or humanity of the Word? He could have said that the bodies and souls of the apostles, creaturely beings, served as instruments of God. For example, sermon 78.4 (no date) employs imagery that brings the function of the apostles as such more in line with the description of the humanity of Christ as a "vessel." In this text, Augustine says that Christ himself speaks through the prophets: ". . . the Lord as Lord . . . these ones as vessels (*vasa*); himself as fountain (*fons*). Moses and the prophets were speaking and writing; but they were filled by him, when they poured forth."[31] Perhaps the choice was made because, in Augustine's view, a hypostatic union exists between the human soul and body that is comparable to the union between the Word and his humanity. By employing this analogy, the instrumentality of the flesh of Christ is seen more clearly to have an exceedingly efficacious role in the redemptive work.

This consideration explains why Augustine asks: "If the flesh of the apostles profited us, was the flesh of the Lord able to profit nothing?" In both cases the present perfect tense is used (*profuit. . . potuit*) to denote the permanent state resulting from completed acts. What the apostles did for us through the flesh profits us now. But how much more must be counted what the flesh of the Lord accomplished for us because it was the flesh of the Word of God!

Having cited these examples of flesh profiting, drawn from the history of salvation, Augustine ends the pericope by quoting v. 64a and making this comment on "the flesh profits nothing": "as they understood flesh, not in the manner I give my flesh to eat."

The original question of 27.5 was: ". . . how does 'the flesh profit nothing'?" The answer was: It profits as "quickened by the spirit." But now the acceptable alternative is: It profits "as I give my flesh to eat." If the argument of the pericope was intended to insinuate that the flesh assumed by the Word continues to function as medium of communion with the risen Lord, and so "participation of the Son,"[32] one might have expected the preacher to close the passage by repeating the original response, which is summarized in the saying: "It is the Spirit who vivifies, the flesh profits nothing." However the final statement evokes the question: How does Christ give his flesh to eat? This question is answered in 27.6. However before taking up this passage. It is time to review briefly the interpretation that M.-F. Berrouard has given to 27.3–5.

He argues plausibly that there is a *systematic* development in these three passages, which excludes the opinion that 26.5 is precisely a "digression" aimed at refuting heterodox christological interpretations of John 6:63. His thesis can be quickly summarized. The Son of Man ascends integral (27.3). This means that Christ is, and remains, one: Word, soul and body. Augustine stresses this unity of Christ as the basis for the explanation of how the eating of Christ's flesh, the flesh assumed by the Word, can be a means of communication of eternal life (27.4). In 27.5 Augustine shows that the flesh of Christ has been profitable for eternal life because it was instrument of the divinity ("Spirit"). Therefore, Augustine is implying that this flesh is still exceedingly useful for the communication of eternal life, since it remains united to the divinity. In other words, Augustine is saying: "It is necessary to maintain that Christ is going to give his flesh to eat, not the flesh such as these disciples conceived it, and which would be a flesh impotent and dead, but as living flesh, become spiritual by the resurrection and ascension, and which holds its power from its personal union with the divinity of the Word."[33]

Berrouard agrees that Augustine does not hold the position of

Cyril of Alexandria, a contemporary, who teaches that the Spirit mentioned in John 6:63 refers to Christ's divinity, and that Christ's humanity is so divinized by the union with the Word that it becomes divinizing itself.[34] But his conclusion suggests that Augustine has come around to a position akin to that of John Chrysostom, expressed in his Homilies 46 and 47 (on John 6:41–71), who is not quite so explicit as Cyril of Alexandria on the subject of the divinizing power of the risen Lord's humanity considered by itself.

It is not unlikely that Augustine was influenced to some degree by John Chrysostom's *Homilies on the Fourth Gospel*. Evidence was cited at the beginning of this century by Karl Adam to establish that Augustine had at hand this commentary of the patriarch of Constantinople as he undertook the refutation of the Pelagian heresy.[35] While the proof Adam offers is slim, a detailed comparison of homilies 46 and 47 with Augustine's Tractates 26 and 27 shows many similarities. One example is Chrysostom's teaching about the necessity of reception of the eucharist for salvation in his commentary on John 6:53–55.[36] It corresponds to Augustine's similar and more protracted emphasis in Tractate 26.15.[37] But there are also noteworthy differences in the presentation of eucharistic theology. One very significant one is found in 27.5, and precisely in two passages where there is a verbal correspondence with some of Chrysostom's remarks on John 6:63(64) in Hom. 47.2.

I. Augustine: "How 'does the flesh profit nothing,' when you said: (John 6:54 paraphrased)? Does life not profit? And why are we what we are, except that we should have the eternal life, that you promised by means of your flesh?

Chrysostom: "If one does not eat his flesh, nor drink his blood, that one does not have life in oneself (paraphrase of John 6:54). Therefore how does it not profit, without which we cannot live?[38]

What is noticeable in these two texts is how Augustine has changed the orientation from the individual communicants to the identification of the communicants as the body of Christ ("Why are we what we are . . . .") as was noted previously.

II. Augustine: "Therefore what does it mean: 'The flesh profits nothing'? It profits nothing, but as they understood . . . not as it is quickened by the spirit."

Chrysostom: "How therefore did he say, 'the flesh profits nothing'? He spoke not of his own flesh—let it not be said—but about those who receive his words carnally."[39]

In these two passages there is also a striking difference. Chrysostom speaks only of the flesh of Christ itself as profiting. Augustine views it as profiting insofar as vivified by the spirit, and, as the rest of the pericope shows, the flesh is viewed as a docile instrument of the spirit.

Between Chrysostom and Augustine there is a world of difference. Whereas Augustine never makes it absolutely clear, Chrysostom explicitly teaches that the flesh of Christ is a means of union with the risen Lord. Augustine, on the other hand, speaks consistently of the union with Christ effected through union with Christ's body, the holy church.

[27.6] Augustine begins this pericope with v. 64b: "The words I have spoken to you are spirit and life. . . ." In this way the preacher links up what he said at the end of 27.5: ". . . not as they understood." In other words, what Jesus is saying must be understood spiritually. This is explained at the end of 27.6: "They are to be understood spiritually." This, of course, does not mean metaphorically. Rather, "The words I have spoken to you" are to be interpreted as referring to spiritual realities. They open the way to benefiting from these spiritual realities, if properly understood. But if understood "carnally," they remain " 'spirit and life,' but they are not for you." In 27.11, it is made explicit that this saying refers to "spiritual things" (*spiritualia*).[40]

After the quotation of John 6:64b, the last statement of 27.5 is developed, namely, ". . . not as I give my flesh to eat." The exposition begins with a reference to v. 57, which, as we have seen, was explained in 26.18, and again in 27.1.

27.6 recalls the interpretation of v. 57, found in 27.1: "For we said . . . ." Following this the preacher calls attention to the communitarian dimension of the abiding and being abided, explaining how we remain in Christ, and he remains in us—namely, "when we are his members . . . when we are his temple." The image of temple highlights the fact that the faithful are one unique temple in which Christ dwells. But the thought that we are his members is also situated in the relation between Christ and his church.

Elsewhere, as we have seen, Augustine is unable to think of the relation of believers to Christ without, at the same time, thinking of the relation of believers to one another. In effect, believers are defined as embedded in the relation Christ–church. In 26.13 the necessity of belonging to the body of Christ in order to be vivified by the Spirit of Christ was developed. Now the preacher adds the consideration that one is able to be a member of Christ only on condition that the "unity," the quality of unity, links a believer to Christ and to the other members: "However in order that we be his members, unity structures us."

The principle of unity is identified as *charity*. It is love that establishes the vital link of dependence on the head and binds the members who belong to his body to one another: "In order that unity structure us, what does this except *charity*?" The source of *charity* is identified as the Spirit: "And whence the love of God? Ask the apostle! 'Love,' he says, 'of God is diffused in our hearts by the Holy Spirit who is given to us' (Rom 5:5)." On this account the preacher concludes that the saying, "It is the Spirit who vivifies," refers to the Spirit who "makes living members."

A further consideration is also added to explain the full role of the Spirit. Here the analogy with the human soul is used. The human being is constituted as such by the soul (*anima*). This soul forms the body, and confers on it unity to the end that it may give the body life and bestow life on each of the members of the body. The Spirit of Christ plays a similar role. In other words, the unity produced by charity, the gift of the Spirit, defines the organism at the interior of which the Spirit works. Hence, Augustine can say, in general: "Nor does the spirit make living members, except those which it finds in the body which the spirit itself quickens." Applied to the Holy Spirit this means: "If one is separated from the body of Christ, he is not his member; if he is not his member, he is not quickened by his Spirit." But because the Spirit is the "soul" of the body, it also holds that if one is not quickened by the Spirit of Christ, he is not a member of Christ. Hence the word of the apostle holds here: " 'Whoever . . .' says the apostle, 'does not have the Spirit of Christ, that one is not his' (1 Cor 8:9)."

In 26.13, the argument was this: The body of Christ is the *exclusive* sphere in which the Spirit of Christ vivifies.[41] At the same time, the body of Christ is *exclusively* vivified by the Spirit of Christ.[42] Correspondingly, members *alone* are vivified by the Spirit of Christ,[43] and members are *only* vivified by the Spirit of Christ.[44] In 27.6, the argument is this: The Spirit of Christ vivifies *exclusively* in the body of Christ.[45] The Spirit of Christ *exclusively* vivifies the body of Christ.[46] Correspondingly, the spirit makes living members *exclusively* in the body of Christ,[47] and the Spirit *exclusively* makes living members of the body of Christ.[48]

The relation between the sacrament of the eucharist and the participation in the body of Christ, together with the sharing in the Spirit and his gift, is not developed in 27.6. However in 26.13 the link was made. In the latter pericope the explanation of the intimate connection between the body of Christ and the working of the Spirit of Christ closed with this statement: "The body of Christ is not able to live except from the Spirit of Christ."[49] The implication is this: If one wishes to be in the body of Christ as a living member, one must be open to receiving the gift of the Spirit of Christ, and to live a life conformed to that gift.

In this connection, Augustine recalls how the apostle Paul explains that the unity of the eucharistic bread signifies the unity of the body of Christ: "Whence it is that the apostle Paul, explaining *this bread*, said, 'One bread, we many are one body' (1 Cor 10:17)." Then Augustine refers directly to the sacrament of the eucharist: "O sacrament of piety! O sign of unity! O bond of love! Whoever wishes to live, has where he may live, has whence he may live. Let him approach, let him believe, let him be incorporated, in order to be vivified."[50]

Augustine calls the sacrament of the eucharist "sacrament of piety," that is, the outward sign of piety that points to the reality found only in the true body of Christ. The sacrament is a sign of unity because the bread is made into one thing from many grains, the wine from many grapes. This symbolism is mentioned in 26.17, where it is said that the Lord "commended his body and blood in these things which are made into one thing from many. For the one is made from many grains, the other poured into one from many berries."[51] The reference to "bond of love" refers to the gift of the Spirit that is bestowed in the body of Christ, which is signified by the sacrament of unity. In the next sentences Augustine refers to the connection between eucharist, body of Christ and Holy Spirit. If one wishes to live, the place is the body of Christ ("where"), and the source is the Spirit of Christ ("whence"). The wishing to live, the not "neglecting to be the body of Christ," becomes more than wishful thinking by receiving the sacrament of the eucharist ("Let him approach") and eating and drinking spiritually ("Let him believe"), and thus becoming more deeply inserted into the body of Christ ("Let him be incorporated"), in order to share more fully in the vivifying action of the Holy Spirit ("in order to be vivified").

[27.9] An additional reference is made to the eucharistic gift in 27.9. Peter is said to speak "for all, one for many, unity for the totality." Clearly Augustine sees Peter as a symbol of the body of Christ, the faithful who confess Christ. His confession: "You have the words of eternal life" (v. 69) receives this comment: "For you have eternal life in the ministration of your body and blood."[52] The additional affirmation of Peter: "that you are the Christ the Son of God" (v. 70) is interpreted in the same direction: "That is, that you are eternal life itself, and you do not give us in your flesh and blood except what you are."[53]

In 27.9 Augustine has returned to the peroration of the previous sermon. The interpretation of the confession of Peter is to be understood in the light of 26.19. In that passage Augustine explained the meaning of John 6:58b: "Who eats me, lives because of me," as follows: "By participation of the Son, through the unity of his body and blood, which that eating and drinking signifies, we are made better. Therefore we live because of him, eating him; that is, accepting eternal life itself."[54] At the end of this pericope, Augustine remarked that the saying "who eats me, lives because of me" can be referred also to "the grace of the mediator."[55] The "grace" of the mediator, in the context of 26:19, refers to the "unity of his body and blood," through which we have the participation of the Son.

The first saying of Peter, referred to above, has to do with the mediatorship function of Christ, the head of his body the church. Christ is identified as eternal life: To have eternal life means to be eternal life, as 26.10 makes clear.[56] "In the ministration of your body and blood" relates to 27.1, where the subject of the sermon is announced: "concerning the body of the Lord, which he said that he would give for eternal life. This communication happens in the reception of the "sacraments of Christ"[57] by those who are in the "unity of his body and blood."[58]

While the first saying of Peter refers to who it is that distributes his "body and blood," the second saying of Peter identifies what Christ gives in the distribution. It comes close to being a paraphrase of 26.19 quoted above: ". . . by participation of the Son . . . ."

The idea of "accepting eternal life" is expressed in the preacher's introduction to Peter's second statement: "What have we believed, and what have we known?" In effect Peter, as representative of the believing church, is saying this: Christ does not give in his body of which he is head, i.e. "in your flesh and blood," "except what you are." Since Christ is both Son of Man and Son of God, in the body of which is he head, he gives participation of the Son of God; or since the Son of God is "eternal life itself," eternal life is communicated. This was already said at the outset of the sermon: "The Lord gives his flesh to us to eat . . . he speaks about his flesh, that therein is eternal life."[59]

[27.11] At the end of the sermon on the "body of the Lord," Augustine offers a brief summary of the main points.[60] (The parenthetical remarks indicate how the quotations are to be understood in light of the interpretation given in this essay):

> All this that the Lord said about his flesh and blood (about the body of Christ); both that he promised eternal life to us in the grace of his distribution (participation of the Son of God though the being in the body of Christ); and that by this he wished the eaters and drinkers of his flesh and blood to be aware that they should remain in him and have himself remaining in them (and that he wished those who are in the body of Christ, and truly share in the gift of unity of the body, to be aware that only by remaining in the body is the sharing of the unity of the body possible); and that they did not understand who did not believe (and that only through the gift of faith can one discern the mystery of the body of Christ); and that discerning the spiritual things carnally, they were scandalized (and that failing to go beyond the literal meaning of the words of Christ to grasp in faith the mystery of the body of Christ they were scandalized) . . . therefore all this ought to influence us . . . to the end that we do not consume the flesh of Christ and the blood of Christ only in the sacrament, which many evil people do (that we do not receive only the sign of the mystery of the body of Christ); but that we eat and drink up to participation of the Spirit (that we eat and drink spiritually in faith and love so as to be animated by the Holy Spirit), in order that we may remain as members in the body of the Lord (*corpus Domini*), in order that we may be quickened by his Spirit (the eating and drinking of the sacrament spiritually is necessary in order to preserve oneself in the body of the Lord, and be animated by the Spirit), and not be scandalized, even if many now with us eat and drink the sacraments in a temporal way, who will have in the end eternal torments (even if many approach the sacraments of Christ without faith and love, and therefore will draw down on themselves the judgment of Christ who is present at the breaking of bread). For now the body of Christ (*corpus Christi*) is mixed as on a threshing floor . . . all we who are in the body of the Lord (*corpus Domini*), and remain in him, in order that he remain in us . . . must live among evil ones (for the true body of the Lord is mixed up with those who are juridical members of the visible body of Christ, the *ecclesia catholica,* but not members of what the visible church signifies).

[27.12] In the peroration St. Lawrence is offered as the example of what it means to abide and be abided. The source of his constancy under torture is explained: ". . . because he had eaten well and drunk well, as though satiated by that food and inebriated by that cup. He did not feel the torments."[61] In other words he ate and drank the sacraments of Christ spiritually, and so was continually fortified by the gift of the unity of the body of Christ. As a consequence, in the hour of need Christ the head of the body did not desert him: "For he was there who said: 'It is the Spirit who vivifies,' and, as mediator, bestowed the Spirit. Hence although the martyr's flesh burned, the Spirit quickened the soul."[62]

CONCLUSION

It cannot be concluded from Tractates 26 and 27 that, as Berrouard thinks, Augustine understood that the sacrament of the body and blood of Christ has so real "a participation in the risen Lord that it merits in all truth to be called the body and blood of Christ, to such a degree that those who receive it . . . receive, with him and in him, the Holy Spirit and the eternal life."[63] At the same time, it has not been shown from these tractates that Augustine did not believe in a sacramental realism.

In 414 it is possible that Augustine's conviction concerning the profound soteriological consequences of the incarnation[64] had not led him to take this step. But since this theology implies "a veritable ontological unity between Christ and humanity,"[65] the way was open to an understanding of the eucharistic food and drink as a means by which the essentially relational humanity of Christ actualizes its finality in favor of those who believe in him.

NOTES

1. Ep. 54.5, 6 (CSEL 34/2.165, 10–11).
2. "L'être sacramentel de l'eucharistie selon saint Augustin: Commentaire de Jean VI. 60–63 dans le *Tractatus* XXVII, 1–6 et 11–12 *in Iohannis Evangelium*," NRT 99 (1977) 703–21.
3. CCSL 36.270–277. All references to "Tractates" are to the Tractates on the Fourth Gospel.
4. CCSL 36.259–269.
5. The chronology of Augustine's Tractates on the fourth gospel, used here, follows M.-J. Berrouard, "La date des 'Tractatus I-LIV in Ioannis Evangelium' de saint Augustin," *Rech. aug.* 7 (1971) 105–68: Tractates 1–13 (406–407); 17–19 (414); 20–22 (418–419); 23–54 (414); 55–124 (after 419–420).
6. 270, 4. The meaning of "body of the Lord" is ambiguous at this point. It is used in 27.11 for the ecclesial body twice, to distinguish the members

of the true body of the Lord from those who are merely in the visible *corpus Christi mixtum,* but not really members of Christ.

7. 270, 16. This is not the Vulgate version ("The prudence of the flesh is death"), employed by Augustine elsewhere (ser. 155. 10, 10 [PL 38.846], dated 418). But Augustine uses this version often (e.g. *Contra Faustum* 12.2 (CSEL 25.341), dated 397–398).

8. 267, 3–4. The "bread of concord" refers to the ecclesial body of Christ, as Augustine makes clear by referring to 1 Corinthians 10:17 in 26.14.

9. 267, 13–16.

10. In 26.11 (265, 12–27) and 26.12 (266, 20–30), Augustine has already developed the idea that one must eat and drink in a spiritual way, if one is to profit by the participation in the sacrament of the altar. Those who approach the sacrament unworthily only bring judgment on themselves.

11. The phrase "as they wished, so they understood" is a way of characterizing heretics (Tractate 36.6 [328, 22]—here Augustine refers to "many heretics" who "understand as they wish," and lists a number of christological heresies). The phrase is used for the unbelieving Jews in 26.14 (267, 4).

12. Augustine's intention in this matter is made explicit in Tractate 47.9 (409, 23–24): "Therefore on this occasion, I call to the attention of your charity, that as we have sufficiently instructed you in the previous readings against the Sabellians and Arians . . . Photinians . . . Manichaeans . . . we instruct you . . . against the Apollinarists. . . ."

13. CCSL 62A.509–510, 9–25.

14. Augustine frequently cites John 3:13 to prove that Jesus is in heaven, namely that he is divine: Tractates 12.8; 14.7; 31.9 (125, 3–4; 145, 4; 298, 33–44).

15. CSEL 44.163.

16. CSEL 44.164.

17. For example, ser. 290.4 (PL 38.1314), dated 412–416.

18. 266, 10–11: "The faithful know the body of Christ, if they do not neglect to be the body of Christ."

19. In 26.15 (267, 27–37), concerning the "body and blood of the Lord," which must be eaten and drunk to have eternal life, Augustine says: "He wished this food and drink to be understood as the society of his body and members . . . the holy church. . . ." And he adds that the "sacrament of this thing, that is, of the unity of Christ's body and blood . . . is prepared on the dominical table, and received from the dominical table: by some unto life, some unto destruction."

20. 26.13 (266, 11–13): "(The faithful) become the body of Christ, if they wish to live from the Spirit of Christ. Only the body of Christ lives from the Spirit of Christ."

21. *De doctrina christianorum* 3.15.23 (CCSL 32.91, 1–5), dated 397.

22. 263, 15–17.

23. 269, 1–3. Augustine teaches that Christ assumed all humanity in the

incarnation, and in virtue of the redemptive work became head of the church, able to draw all humanity into his body. Cf. ser. 191.2, 3 (PL 38.1010), dated 411–412: "For the only-begotten Son of God deigned to unite to himself a human nature, in order to associate to himself as immaculate head the immaculate church."

24. In Tractate 99.7 Augustine remarks: "We are not able to call both the Father and Son except spirit, because God is spirit, that is, God is not body, but spirit" (CCSL 36.586, 15–18).

25. A. Verwilghen, *Christologie et spiritualité selon saint Augustin: L'Hyme aux Philippiens* (Théologie Historique 72; Paris: Beauchesne, 1985) 271–78.

26. 269, 24–26.

27. 264, 7–16.

28. 264, 12–13.

29. Tractate 41, 5 (360, 8–11); Tractate 30, 1 (289, 9–10).

30. PL 37.1342.

31. PL 38.491.

32. 26.19 (269, 5).

33. "L'être sacramentel," 711–12.

34. "L'être sacramentel," 714–15.

35. *Eucharistielehre des hl. Augustin* (Paderborn: F. Schöningh, 1908) 43–46.

36. Hom. 47.1 (PG 59.262).

37. 267, 13–26.

38. PG 59.265, 46–49.

39. PG 59.265, 38–40.

40. 276, 6.

41. "Only the body of Christ lives from the Spirit of Christ" (266, 12–13).

42. "The body of Christ is able to live only from the Spirit of Christ" (266, 23–24).

43. "Dost thou, even thou, wish to live from the Spirit of Christ? Be in the body of Christ" (266, 21–23).

44. "(The faithful) become the body of Christ, if they wish to live from the Spirit of Christ" (266, 11–12).

45. "For if one is separated from the body of Christ, he is not his member; if he is not his member, he is not animated by his Spirit" (273, 20–22).

46. " 'Whoever however,' the apostle says, 'does not have his Spirit is not his' " (273, 22–23).

47. "Nor does the spirit make living members, except those which it finds in the body that is animated by the spirit itself" (272, 11–13).

48. "For the spirit makes living members" (272, 11).

49. 266, 23–24.

50. 266, 26–29.

51. 268, 8–11.

52. 274, 12–13.

53. 274, 18–20.

54. 269, 5–10.

55. 269, 31–33.
56. "Whoever believes in me has me. For Christ himself is true God and eternal life. Therefore, whoever believes in me has me . . . eternal life" (264, 3–7).
57. 26.18 (268, 110).
58. 26.15 (267, 34–35); 26.19 (269, 6–7).
59. 27.1 (270, 16–18).
60. 275–276, 1–27.
61. 276, 11–13.
62. 276, 13–15.
63. "L'être sacramentel," 720.
64. T.-J. Van Bavel, *Recherches sur christologie de saint Augustin. L'humaine et le divin dans le Christ d'après saint Augustin* (Paradosis 10; Fribourg [Suisse], 1954) 53, 76.
65. Verwilghen, *Christologie et spiritualité,* 491.

10

THE SERMONS OF
POP LEO THE GREAT:
CONTENT AND STYLE
by Francis X. Murphy, C.SS.R.

It is perhaps temerarious to suggest an alignment between the homiletic accomplishment of Pope Leo the Great and that of the distinguished Jesuit, Walter Burghardt, in this well-deserved tribute to Walter's eminent career as priest, preacher and theologian. But a *fundamentum in re* underlies this suggestion. It is based upon the fact that both men are theologians of no mean stature, and meticulous stylists as well as highly accomplished churchmen. While Walter eschews ecclesial preferment, and Leo experienced the height of hierarchical eminence, this fact, and the diversity of centuries and cultures that separate the two men, does not negate their propinquity as effective heralds of the word.

It is the fifth century chronicler, Prosper of Aquitaine, Leo's confidant and amanuensis, who informs us that:

> Upon the death of Bishop Xystus (August 29, 440) for more than forty days, the Roman Church was without its bishop, awaiting, with wondrous patience and peace, the presence of the Deacon Leo whom Gaul detained on a mission to restore harmony between Aetius and Albinus (the Roman patricians). It was as if he were held away for so long that both the merit of the one elected and the judgment of the electors might be put to the test. And thus the Deacon Leo, summoned by public legation and presented to his joyful fatherland, was ordained the forty-third bishop of the Roman Church.[1]

In the exquisite homily with which he inaugurated his pontificate, Leo confirms this information by thanking the faithful "whose holy affection considered him present when the necessity of a long journey rendered him absent."

Leo confesses that it is not a sign of humility but of an ungrateful mind not to acknowledge divine benefits. Hence, he asserts it is proper to inaugurate the office of a consecrated pontiff with a sacrifice of praise of the Lord. Giving condign thanks to God, Leo acknowledges "how much the zeal of your reverence, love and faith proceeds from your affection, you who have conferred on me, without previous merit, so sacred a favor."[2]

Of Leo's background and education we know nothing. But there is an unabashed Roman mentality behind his theology that reflects the judicial mind of a Tertullian while drawing more immediately on the reflections of Cyprian, Hilary of Poitiers and Augustine, though he makes no mention of these predecessors of his.

I

As bishop of Rome, Leo devoted himself assiduously to the priestly duty of preaching. A representative selection of his sermons for the whole liturgical cycle has been preserved: ten for Christmas, eight for Epiphany, twelve for Lent, nineteen on the passion, two for Easter, two for the Ascension, three for Pentecost, one for the feast of St. Peter, another for Sts. Peter and Paul, one on the Beatitudes, and another for St. Lawrence, twenty-three for the ember days which, he says, are celebrated four times in the year when the faithful fast on Wednesday, Friday and Saturday, and then celebrate the vigil of Sunday at St. Peter's.[3]

Five sermons commemorate his consecration as pontiff, and six sermons describe the distribution of alms to the poor as of apostolic origin and to offset pagan superstition. They advise the almsgiver to be conscious of the poor who do not come forward out of shame or modesty. A sermon on Rome's deliverance, apparently from Gaiseric in 455, testifies to the survival of astrology, the circus and pagan spectacles.[4] Leo reproved the custom of bowing toward the sun from the steps of St. Peter's Basilica, and condemned as *paganitatis spiritu* ("in the spirit of paganism") the notion that December 25 marked the rise of the new sun rather than the birth of Christ.[5]

Following Roman legal tradition, as the heir of Peter's person and office, Leo identifies himself with his predecessor, *cujus vice fungimur*—"in whose place we function." He thus maintains:

If there is anything we do properly, or rightly discern, if there is anything we obtain from God's mercy by our daily supplications, his is the deed and the merit, whose power lives on in his see where his authority prevails.[6]

II

Leo's theological competence reflects a thorough knowledge of the sacred scriptures that he demonstrates continually in his sermons and letters. While still a deacon, he was apparently responsible for Pope Celestine's *Syllabus on Grace,* citing previous synods and papal decisions to settle the Pelagian controversy, and John Cassian's *Tract on the Incarnation* for which he supplied material from the papal archives. He was likewise the recipient of an appeal from the formidable patriarch of Alexandria, Cyril, against the alleged political ambitions of Bishop Juvenal of Jerusalem, foreshadowing, after a fashion, their future involvement in the great christological controversy of their age.

On one truth Leo is absolute and unbending—that Jesus Christ was of two natures, the divine and human, unconfusedly united in the person of the Word. This theological insight underlies his every thought and is immediately and essentially connected with his doctrine of the redemption.

III

What Leo brings to the elucidation of the truths of revelation is a clear-cut, structured Latinity and a paradoxical manner of expression that frequently requires some mental jousting to fully comprehend his insights.

His sermons are chiseled with great care, so meticulously that at times he seems to be indulging a penchant for ingenuity rather than straight doctrinal elucidation. Nevertheless, when dealing with the delicate and abstruse mysteries of the faith, he weighs his words with invariable precision. He speaks with authority bordering on the majestic, conscious of the dignity of his pontifical office. Leo frequently exhibits a joyful enthusiasm in explaining the intricacies of the faith; and in his cautions against the temptations of the evil one, or his stimulation to almsgiving and charity, there is a realism that reveals the depth of his own feelings and the perspicacity of his psychic understanding of human nature.

Leo's Latinity is a grand parade of rhythmic alliteration and assonance employing sonorous and majestic word patterns, interrogative and emphatic as well as discordant phrase-making, that utilizes the Latin language's inestimable power and regal as well as pathetic potentiality.[7]

Beginning with the *immarcescibilem veritatem*—"the unyielding truth"—of the gospels, he marches serenely through the scripture narratives, pausing occasionally, as he does in a sermon on the passion, to remind his listeners that not only have they heard the sacred story, but they have witnessed a *quaedam facta sit visio*—in a certain fashion, they have experienced a vision of these happenings.[8] This observation is in keeping with his conviction that, though a Roman of the Romans, he lived a life in direct contact with Christ and the apostles.

> We see what they saw, touch what they touched. Not in history alone do we perceive these things but in virtue of their current enactments.

> We are led to faith as it is proclaimed in the gospel narrative by prophetical instruments, in that we cannot treat as ambiguous what has been put before us by so many (prophetic) oracles.[9]

IV

A key to Leo's theological preoccupation throughout his sermons is supplied by his constant reference to the redemption which he sees as applied to the whole of mankind from the first man Adam down to the *eschaton* and the terrestrial end of mankind.[10]

Leo's soteriological approach is binomial. In what appears as simplistic, he plays out the charade of a duel between Christ and Satan in which strict justice demands that the devil be given his due. Leo asserts that, while occasioned by the astute blandishments of the evil one, Adam's fall was actually a free-will decision. It thus merited the human race the penalty of mortality, subjection to the dominance of the devil, and required a ransom through the shedding of Christ's blood, his death and resurrection.

In buttressing this concept, Leo insists that the redemption flows essentially from the incarnation, and that it is only by acknowledging the two natures in Christ that one can comprehend the mystery of the overpowering of the evil one and the restoration of the human race to God's grace.[11]

He maintains that co-terminous with the fall of Adam, God chose from among a number of possibilities the way of strict justice (*ratio justae severitatis*) as the proper means to man's restoration; that as mankind had been freely captivated by the blandishment of the evil one, Satan could only be justly disconcerted by a man who shared human nature in all its aspects, sin alone excepted, but who at the same time was divine in order to satisfy the divinity's demand for justice.[12]

Leo maintains that Christ's birth of the virgin was necessary both as the beginning of a new order of human comportment, and as a mystery concealing his true origin from Satan. The latter, convinced that Christ was an ordinary mortal since he was subject to the ills of the human condition from birth to death, subjected Christ to the buffetings of diabolical contumely. In so doing, Satan violated the pact or charter (*chirograph*) of his dominion over mankind by demanding of one not subject to sin the penalty of sinfulness. He thus lost his dominance over the human race.[13]

Leo's construct is based on a title of strict justice. He extracts the notion of a ransom (*lutron*) from Mark (10:45), payment with the blood of Christ from 1 Peter (1:18), captivity and slavery to sin from Romans (7:1 and 23), and subjection to the power of darkness, death and sin from Colossians (1:13 and 2:13).

While criticized roundly for its simplicistic contours from the fourth century *Dialogue of Adamantius* to J. Rivière's *Doctrine of the Atonement*,[14] this teaching was propagated by Origen, Gregory of Nyssa, Ambrose and others. While scattered through his sermons, frequently in off-hand references to the power of the evil one behind Christ's sufferings and death, this theory does not represent the whole of Leo's thinking.

V

Current theological speculation sees the incarnation as a new act of creation when God chose to renew all things in Christ, a theme common to Paul and John. Christ's life is thus a totality of redemptive actuality.[15] Leo seems to anticipate this concept. He states that from the moment of man's transgression, God had prepared the remedy, prophetically announced in the enmity placed between the woman and the serpent (Gen 3:15). He asserts that

> much more wonderful is the second generation of mankind than its first condition; for it is a greater thing that God did in repairing what was lost than in creating what did not exist.[16]

Current thinking likewise contends that Christ had entered a world formed by alienation from God, and that this aberration confirmed the justice of the human condition whereby mankind was subject to sin and death. Leo supports this observation:

> Justice being unpursued, and the whole world lapsed into vanity and evil-doing, unless the divine power had deferred its judgment, the whole of mankind would have received the sentence of damnation.[17]

Leo observes further that the redeeming act of Christ was not a single, static action. It is a continual irruption into history from the moment of the promise of the incarnation that coincided with man's fall, through the Old Testament history, down to the final existence of mankind.

> This sacrament of the redemption, he says, is constructed from the beginning in mysteries. The blood of the just Abel bespeaks the death of the highest Shepherd, and in the parricide of the Jews, Cain the murderer of his brother is recognized. The flood and the ark of Noah manifest what will take place in the renovation of mankind through baptism and the salvation to be discovered in the tree (of the cross). Here Abraham the father of all nations acquires his promised heredity and in his seed, not the germination of the flesh, but the propagation of the faith is blessed . . . so that in Him in whom the world received its beginning, in the same the Christian creation would have its rise.[18]

Leo then asserts that the Christian faith in no way diverges from the ancient Hebrew prophetic dispensations, despite the God-willed variety of their appearances, since Christ has assured us that he did not come into the world to abolish but to fulfill the ancient law. He maintains that the ineffable mercy of God made Israelites of the peoples of all nations; after softening their stone-like hearts, he has raised up true sons of Abraham from those very stones.

Commenting on the Lord's prophecy, "When I am exalted, I will draw all things to me," he maintains that the redeemer thus indicated that all the institutions and prophecies of the old law had passed over into the sacrament of Christ.[19]

In his commentary on the fact that Christ reigned from the cross, Leo explained that the cross was a true and predicted sacramental altar where the oblation of human nature was celebrated by a salvation-bearing Host.

> For there the blood of the Immaculate Lamb wiped out the pact of the ancient prevaricator, and the iniquity of diabolical domination was counteracted. A victorious humility was triumphant over the elation of the evil one's pride. So swift was the effect of faith that, of the thieves crucified along with Christ, he who believed in the Son of God was justified and immediately entered the kingdom of heaven.[20]

VI

In turning to the pastoral aspects of his redemptive teaching, Leo indulges a favorite contention. He maintains that everything that the Son of God both did and taught for the reconciliation of the world is known by us not only in the history of past activities, but by virtue of Christ's current actions. It is Christ who, having come forth from his virginal mother through the action of the Holy Spirit, has made his uncontaminated church fecund through the inspiration of the same Holy Spirit, so that by the parturition of baptism an innumerable multitude of the sons of God are born.

Leo then rises to an almost mystical fervor as, paraphrasing the baptismal ritual, he asserts that when someone renounces Satan, believes in God, and transfers from the old way of life to the new, dispossessing himself of the image of the terrestrial man to take on that of the celestial, he undergoes a certain kind of death and a certain similitude of the resurrection. Taken up by Christ, and in turn accepting Christ, one is not the same after the washing as he was before baptism, for the body of the one regenerated becomes the flesh of Christ.[21]

Stressing the universal efficacy of the redemption, Leo assails those querulous murmurers who complain about the tardiness of the incarnation as if what has now taken place in these times, did not affect previous generations.[22] He counters the complaint by asserting that the promise of the incarnation of the Word had accomplished what was to be done, so that the sacrament of human salvation was never without its effect on antiquity. What the apostles preached, the prophets had announced; nor was that late in its fulfillment that had always been believed.

The wisdom and benignity of God exercised the delay of this salvational work to make us more capable of its effect. Thus, what had been announced by so many signs, by so many voices and so many mysteries for so many ages could not be misunderstood in these days of the gospel. Thus, the nativity of the Savior that was to excel all miracles and all measure of human intelligence might engender in us so great a constancy in faith as its prediction was more ancient and more frequent. It was not by a new decision in human affairs or a late mercy that God decided; but from the constitution of the world he had instituted one and the same way of salvation for all.[23] Leo then assures his auditory:

> The grace of God through which the universe of the saints has always been justified has been increased with Christ's birth, not begun. This mystery of great mercy with which the whole world is filled was so great in its intimation that it was no less effective for those who had believed it as a promise than for those who received it as a gift.[24]

Leo completed his consideration of the effects of the redemption by exhorting his listeners:

> Consider, and in keeping with the illumination of the Holy Spirit, prudently reflect on who it is who has taken us to himself, and whom we have received within us. For as the Lord Jesus has become our flesh by being born, so we have become his body by being reborn. Thus, we are members of Christ and temples of the Holy Spirit.[25]

VII

In his sermons covering the whole of the liturgical year, Leo demonstrates his deeply spiritual and humane pastoral concern for his own flock as well as his solicitude for all the churches.[26] Covering themes and topics as diverse as the relations between the Old and the New Testaments, the length of Christ's stay in the tomb, and Mary Magdalene's witness to Christ's resurrection, he manifests both a singular ingenuity and a depth of theological perception that render him truly an omnicompetent churchman.

Leo provides an unchallengeable consciousness of the papacy as a continuation of the Petrine power and presence, and the indestructibility of an institution intended by its divine founder to persist until the end of time. Leo is not concerned with history as such. He does respect tradition. But in his pastoral insights and doctrinal decisions it is as Peter *redivivus* that he functions.

Discussing the relations between the two Testaments, Leo says:

> Everything that has gone before according to the Law, whether in the circumcision of the flesh, or in the diversity of burnt offering, or in the observance of the Sabbath, all testify to Christ, all are predictions of the grace of Christ. And he himself is the end of the Law, not by emptying out its significances, but by fulfilling them.

> The same one who is the author of the Old is the author of the New. He has changed the mystery of the prefigured promises by fulfilling them; and has put an end to the predictions by becoming himself the predicted.[27]

VIII

Leo maintains that of the old dispensation, none of its decrees were reprobated. Actually many were made more forceful by the gospel teaching. Those things giving salvation were more perfect and more lucid than those promising the Savior.[28]

Commenting on the Transfiguration of Christ with Moses and Elias on Mount Tabor, Leo muses:

> These things, dearly beloved, were not enunciated for the sake of those who heard them with their own ears, but in the three apostles (Peter, James and John) the whole church shared in what they experienced by sight and received by hearing. Thus, the faith of all is to be confirmed according to the preaching of the Holy Gospel.

> No one should be ashamed of the Cross of Christ through which the world has been redeemed. Nor, therefore, should anyone fear to suffer for justice sake, or doubt the retribution promised, since by work one goes over to rest, and by death to life.

> He has taken on the weakness of our humility, in whom, if we remain in his confession and his love, we will conquer what he conquered and receive what he promised. Because whether we are keeping the commandments or putting up with adversity, the voice

of the Father should be ringing in our ears saying, "This is my beloved Son . . . hear him."[29]

In his concern for orthodoxy Leo is continually warning his faithful against the contamination of the Manichean heresy which, he maintains, is the work of the devil:

> Constituted in this hope, dearly beloved, avoid all the sly doings of Satan who is insidious not only in carnal concupiscence or corporeal evils, but in the very seeds of the faith, spreading the works of falsehood, attempting to prevent the growth of truth; and those whom he cannot violate in evil actions, he subverts by impious errors. Flee, therefore, the arguments of mundane doctrine and the viperous speech of heretics. You have nothing in common with those who, by opposing our Catholic faith, are Christians in name only.[30]

In discussing the formula for daily Christian living, Leo advises:

> There are three things that greatly pertain to religious behavior, namely prayer, fasting and almsgiving. By prayer, God's mercifulness is sought; by fasting, the concupiscence of the flesh is mastered; and by almsgiving, sins are remitted.[31]

Later, he assures his listeners that they are to:

> Imitate what he has accomplished; love what he loves. Finding the grace of God within you, you are to reanimate your nature by this love. For as he did not abandon his riches in his poverty, nor diminished his glory in his humility, nor lost his eternality by his death, so you are to follow in his same steps and grades and paths so that you may attain to the heavenly and despise what is of the earth. Taking up his cross is to destroy your cupidities, bringing death to vice, a toning down of vanity and an abdication of error.[32]

IX

Leo's ingenuity is displayed in his solution of the problem posed by the three days Christ is reported as having stayed in the tomb over against the actual time he spent there.

Hence lest an extended sorrow should further disturb the troubled minds of the disciples, he abbreviated the announced three-day stay by a wonderful celerity, so that while the last part of the first day and the first part of the third day were joined to the whole second day, a short space of time was lost but not the number of days. The resurrection of the Lord, therefore, did not delay his soul in hell, nor his body in the sepulcher. So swift was the revivification of his incorrupt flesh that it seemed to have been rather a sleep than a death; because the deity that did not recede from either side of the assumed manhood joined by his power what he had divided by his power.[33]

Again in dealing with the witness given to the resurrection by Mary Magdalene, Leo's ingenuity comes to the fore. Describing the more sublime faith made achievable by Christ's resurrection, Leo advises that Mary Magdalene represents the person of the church. Hence, on approaching to touch Christ, she was told, "Do not touch me. I have not yet ascended to the Father" (Jn 20:17).

That is I do not want you to approach me corporally, nor to recognize me with your carnal senses. I am putting you off for higher things, and preparing greater things for you. When I ascend to my Father, then you will touch me more truly and more perfectly, about to comprehend what you do not touch, and to believe what you do not see.[34]

X

Throughout his sermons Leo's social consciousness (*socialis animus*) is unmistakable. In homilies on the collects, on fasting, on Lent and the ember days, he is constantly emphasizing the need for penance, abstinence and almsgiving on the part of individuals as well as the whole church, stressing the obligations of both rich and poor to care for the deprived, widows and orphans, the sick and the destitute. Leo maintains that the penitential collections were instituted by the apostles to counteract the pagan Apollonarian games presumably during the first week of July.

Keeping the ordinances of apostolic tradition, and with a shepherd's care for his flock, we exhort you to celebrate with zeal of religious practice the day which our predecessors cleansed from

pagan superstition and dedicated to works of mercy. . . . For it is
not only spiritual wealth and heavenly graces that are received from
God's hands. Earthly and material riches also flow from his bounty.
Therefore, it is with justice that he will demand an account of them.
He has not so much given them to be possessed as put them in trust
to be administered. . . . In their own nature, in their own kind,
riches are good and most useful to human society. I mean when they
are handled by men of good and generous heart; when they are not
squandered by the prodigal or hidden by the miser. . . .[35]

Leo condemns usury outright and warns the rich:

But though it is praiseworthy to shun intemperance and avoid the
wastefulness of unworthy pleasures, and though there are many
people given to magnificence who live lavishly, disdain to conceal
their wealth, and shrink from petty and sordid meanness, yet there
is no merit in such thrift and no happiness in such affluence if their
riches serve themselves alone—if the poor are not helped by their
money, if the sick are not cared for, if out of all their abundance,
the captive finds no ransom, the stranger no comfort, the exile no
aid. . . .[36]

Warming to his subjects, he continues:

But perhaps there are some rich people who, without assisting the
Church's poor by alms, nevertheless keep other commandments of
God. Having merits of faith and uprightness, they think they will be
pardoned for the lack of this virtue. But this virtue is such that
without it other virtues—if indeed they have them—can be of no
avail. . . .

At the great and final day of judgment such value will be set on the
liberality of giving or the wickedness of avarice that they outweigh
all other virtues and all other sins.[37]

Leo's appreciation of the vagaries of human nature comes out in
a sermon for Epiphany:

Our inner peace, dearly beloved, has its own perils. In vain do they
feel themselves free in the faith, who do not resist the blandishments
of vice. The heart of man betrays itself by its quality, and the kinds
of one's actions make known the qualities of one's thinking. For
there are some, as the Apostle says, who profess they know God, but
deny it by their actions (Tit 1:16). Truly guilty of this negation is he

who does not have in his conscience the good he announces with his voice. The fragility of the human condition easily slips into evil-doing, and since there is no sin without delectation, one easily acquiesces in deceptive pleasure.

Finally he warns:

Let God's patience be good for us, so that continuing in evil-doing will not be cultivated, nor making amends put off. No sinner is secure in his impurity, for if he passes up a time for penance, he will not have time for forgiveness. He who finds the reparation of self-correction difficult, let him flee to the assistance of a helping God, asking him to break the bonds of his evil-doing. The prayer of one so confessing will not be empty, for God is merciful . . . and he gives what is requested who gives when it is asked.[38]

XI

At once formal and familiar, Leo's preaching projected his deeply spiritual and consciously humane involvement with the lives of his flock both in his position as bishop of Rome, and in his pontifical solicitude for all the churches in his Petrine incarnation. Describing the church as constituted by its pontiffs, its priests, the ministers of the sacraments as well as the faithful, he exhorts all as the body of Christ to exhibit a social consciousness (*socialis animus*) in striving for holiness. He is convinced as he assures his *splendidissimam frequentiam venerabilium consacerdotum*—this most splendid gathering of his venerable fellow priests—that:

Not only Peter's apostolic but his episcopal dignity is subjected to the rule of our solemnity, since Peter never ceased to preside over his see and obtained an invincible consortium with the Eternal Priest.[39]

XII

What should be evident from this brief excursus on Leo's homiletic omnicompetence is the loss suffered by the Roman church in the abolition of Latinity in its liturgy and the neglect of Latin in its schools. By a curious accident, Vatican Council II unwittingly contributed to this debacle. Its leaders apparently applied the axiom, "unless the grain fall and die in the ground, no new life will come forth," to achieve an uncontroverted emplacement of the vernacular liturgies.

With that mutation now fully achieved, there appears to be the possibility of a remedy through the revival of interest in Latin and Greek studies, particularly in the secular universities. It is to be hoped that a reincarnation of Leo's *immarcescibilis veritas* within the vernacular liturgies can be accomplished, thus reinvigorating the church's spiritual life with new ingestion of its Leonine heritage.

NOTES

1. Prosper, *Epitoma chronicon* a. 440 (MGH auc. antiq. 9 [Chronica minora 1]; ed. T. Mommsen) 478. Cf. T. Jalland, *St. Leo the Great* (London, 1941) 38–40; F.X. Murphy, "Leo I," *NCE* 8 (1967) 637–39.

2. Sermo 92 (i) (SC 200.246). I have followed the numbering of Leo's sermons found in the edition of R. Dolle, SC 22 bis, 49 bis, 74 bis, and 200. The Roman numerals in parentheses are those of the sermons found in the PL of Migne.

3. Sermo 89 (xix) (SC 200.210).

4. Sermo 71 (lxxxiv) (SC 200.66–71).

5. Sermo 7 (xxvii).4 (SC 22b.158).

6. Sermo 94 (iii).3 (SC 200.258). Cf. 94 (iii).4 (SC 200.260). See W. Ullman, *The Growth of Papal Government in the Middle Ages* (2nd ed.; London, 1962).

7. W. Halliwell, *The Style of St. Leo the Great* (Washington, DC: Catholic University of America Press, 1939).

8. Sermo 57 (lxx).1 (SC 74b.228).

9. Sermo 51 (lxiv).1 (SC 74b.164).

10. H. Turner, *The Patristic Doctrine of the Redemption* (London, 1952); J. Riviére, *Le dogme de la rédemption dans la théologie contemporaine* (Albi: 1948); id., "Redemption," *DTC* 13.2 (1937) 1912–2004; E.L. Peterson, "Redemption (Theology of)," *NCE* 12 (1967) 147–49.

11. Sermo 38 (li).1 (SC 74b.22).

12. Sermo 2 (xxii).1 (SC 22b.76).

13. Col 2:14; cf. sermo 40 (liii).1 (SC 74b.48) and sermo 48 (lxi).4 (SC 74b.136).

14. Adamantius, *De fide orthodoxa* 1.27 (GCS 4.53–54); J. Riviére, *Doctrine of the Atonement* 2.112–13.

15. S. Lyonnet, "De notione redemptionis," *Verbum Domini* 36 (1958) 129–46; 256–69.

16. Sermo 53 (lxvi).1 (SC 74b.184).

17. Sermo 14 (xxxi).1 (SC 22b.228). See P. de Letter, "Theology of Satisfaction," *Thomist* 21 (1958) 1–28.

18. Sermo 47 (lx).3 (SC 74b.124).
19. Sermo 53 (lxvi).2 (SC 74b.186).
20. Sermo 42 (lv).3 (SC 74b.68).
21. Sermo 50 (lxiii).6 (SC 74b.160).
22. A similar complaint had been registered in the second century *Letter to Diognetus*, but there is no evidence for Leo's acquaintance with that document.
23. Sermo 3 (xxiii).4 (SC 22b.102).
24. Sermo 3 (xxiii).4 (SC 22b.104).
25. Sermo 3 (xxiii).5 (SC 22b.104).
26. M.G. De Soos, *Le mystère liturgique de s. Léon le Grand* (Münster, 1958).
27. Sermo 50 (lxiii).5 (SC 74b.156).
28. Sermo 50 (lxiii).5 (SC 74b.156–158).
29. Sermo 38 (li).8 (SC 74b.34).
30. Sermo 56 (lxix).5 (SC 74b.224–226).
31. Sermo 82 (xii).4 (SC 200.158–160). See A. Guillaume, *Jeune et charité chez s. Leon le Grand* (Paris, 1954).
32. Sermo 59 (lxxii).5 (SC 74b.262).
33. Sermo 58 (lxxi).2 (SC 74b.246).
34. Sermo 61 (lxxiv).4 (SC 74b.282).
35. Sermo 24 (x).1 (SC 49b.48–50).
36. Sermo 24 (x).2 (SC 49b.50).
37. Sermo 24 (x).2 (SC 49b.52).
38. Sermo 17 (xxxvi).4 (SC 22b.272–274).
39. Sermo 96 (v).4 (SC 200.282).

11

THE BIBLE IN EARLY
MEDIEVAL IRELAND
by Joseph F. Kelly

Walter Burghardt is a scholar who has had a significant effect on the life of the non-scholarly Christian world. His sermons have reached a wide popular audience, and his editorship of *Theological Studies,* which has a large audience among non-specialists who are interested in theology, has helped to keep many *au courant* with scholarly developments. In this honorary essay, I would like to take a somewhat different approach from my earlier articles on Christianity in early medieval Britain and Ireland, and to concentrate on how the Bible became part of the faith of the early Christian Irish *in toto* and not just for the scholars.

THE SPREAD OF CHRISTIANITY IN THE ROMAN WORLD

The progress of Christianity in the ancient world was achieved largely by the efforts of preachers and missionaries and by the heroism of martyrs and confessors, but they did not work in a vacuum. There were many cultural factors which aided the progress of the faith. These are familiar, but worth recounting. The widespread use of Greek facilitated missionary work; for example, Luke tells us that even in areas where native dialects survived, Paul and Barnabas could preach in Greek (Acts 14:8–18). The career of Alexander and the efforts of Hellenistic monarchs to promote Hellenistic culture brought into focus the idea of one world or at least of one force uniting the world. Stoic and Epicurean philosophers stressed the oneness of all people in their common situation. The Roman empire was to many people the political realization of the unitive ideal. Literacy was widespread in urban areas, and the Roman empire was very much one of cities. The extensive Jewish diaspora had spread the notion of sacred books available to all literate males. The mystery religions provided the notions of separation from the mass of people by participation in a sacred cult, and these cults had their special initiation rites. The list is long enough. Suffice it to say that many factors, cultural, psychological, social, political, aided the spread or at least eased the reception of Christianity in the Roman world.

This situation guaranteed that the initial Christian successes were all in a Roman framework. The non-Romanized successes were few and small. It is likely that Christian missionaries went to the large Jewish community in Babylon, but that is currently unprovable. Some Christians made it to India, and there were Christians in Persia for the Sassanian kings to persecute in the fourth century, but these were never large or influential communities. Christian missionaries worked successfully in Ethiopia in the sixth century, but by that time the Roman empire was largely a memory in the west. Germanic tribes were converted in the fourth and fifth centuries, but this happened as these tribes, as *foederati,* entered the empire. In sum, where we find a large and successful Christian mission, we find a Roman framework —except in one place.

THE IRISH BACKGROUND

Ireland was never part of the Roman empire, even though Tacitus tells us that the Roman governor of Britain, Agricola, contemplated an invasion. Archaeological evidence has proved conclusively that the Romans, that is, Romano-British merchants, traded with the Irish. In the fourth century these mercantile contacts were joined by and at times replaced by piratical ones. Indeed, the Roman writer Ammianus Marcellinus says that in the 360s the Irish (*Scotti* in Latin) joined the Saxons and the Picts in a three-pronged invasion of Roman Britain. This would have meant the accumulation of booty, slaves included, so the *realia* of Roman culture were known to the Irish, and presumably the Roman citizens among the captives would have told the Irish something about the empire. Some Irish settled in parts of Wales and southwest Scotland in the fourth and fifth centuries, where at least some contacts were peaceful; again some knowledge of Rome would have been gained. But when all the rather meager evidence is sifted, the inescapable conclusion is that the Irish, especially in Ireland, remained little affected by Roman, and thus by classical, culture.

The differences between Ireland and Rome were significant. Irish society was tribal. There was a sense of being Irish, but no sense of political unity. Despite the claims of later vernacular epics, there was no high king. There were petty kings who ruled over *tuatha* or small tribal areas; the first high king appeared in the eleventh century. Ancient Irish society was also rural. There were no cities on the island. The Irish cities such as Dublin, Wexford, and Waterford had to await the coming of the Vikings. Hilltop meeting places were the only political centers, trading posts the economic ones, and the noble houses the cultural ones. As for Irish culture, it was oral, not literate. It was, to be sure, an impressive culture, and twentieth-century scholars have been particularly appreciative of it, but it differed significantly from that taken for granted even by illiterate citizens of the empire.

Even this brief sketch will illustrate to the reader how different was the Irish world from that in which Christianity had grown. In literally innumerable ways, Christianity had matched its environment. Julian the Apostate might call it the religion of the Galilean, but, in fact, most Romans considered this *quondam* near eastern cult quite Romanized by the fourth and fifth centuries. Christianity had proved itself a very adaptable religion in the conversion of Rome, but Ireland was a completely different situation. Here was a land with not even a Roman veneer. Led by Saint Patrick and other missionaries, in the fifth century, this literate, urban religion from a classical culture with a strong central government which ruled over a sunny, warm, Mediterranean-based empire went to a damp, chilly Atlantic island with no cities, no central government, and no literacy. All the rules had changed.

EARLY CHRISTIANITY IN IRELAND[1]

When Christianity came to Ireland is uncertain. The first evidence comes from a sentence in the works of the Gallic chronicler, Prosper of Aquitaine, who says that in 431 Pope Celestine I sent as *primus episcopus* Palladius, and he was sent *ad Scotos credentes in Christum*.

Whatever Palladius did in Ireland, he was completely eclipsed by the next bishop, Patrick. This great saint and best known figure in Irish history, who ironically was never called Patrick once in his life

(Patrick is an Anglicization of the Latin Patricius and the Irish Padráig), left behind two writings, a *Confessio,* in defense of his mission, and an *Epistola ad Milites Coritici,*[2] this Coroticus being a British princeling who had kidnaped some of Patrick's converts in order to enslave or sell them. These works are difficult to understand and often difficult to read, but scholars have worked to establish Patrick's chronology. He was a missionary who worked primarily among pagans, in contrast to Palladius who was sent to a Christian community. His career probably fell in the middle third of the fifth century, and the traditional Irish date for his death, 461, is more or less correct. The same can be said for the traditional date for his arrival, 432.

As the first person to write anything in Ireland, Patrick provides us with the first evidence of the Bible's role in Irish Christian life. The great Latinist Christine Mohrmann once called Patrick a *homo unius libri,*[3] and the book was the Bible. A recent study of Patrick's spirituality has confirmed his total immersion in the scriptures.[4] Patrick's use of the Bible was hardly remarkable for the fifth century, but it is significant that his spiritual life was biblically-centered and shows no signs of the then new devotion to Mary or the saints. His mission put the Irish church on a firm biblical footing.

After the career of Patrick, the Irish church—indeed, Ireland itself—disappears into history until the latter half of the sixth century. There is, in fact, copious information about the immediate post-Patrician period in collections called the Irish annals, but scholars cannot take these seriously before 585. There is no literature at all which dates from the period.

I mention this because we will at this point largely abandon chronology. The period from the sixth century to the Viking invasions of the ninth century has a number of epithets—the golden age, the age of the saints, and the like—and justly so. In those two and a half centuries the Irish church produced a remarkable culture which planted Christianity firmly among the Irish people and which spread to Britain and Europe as well. There are, of course, chronological distinctions to be made, but, for cultural and literary purposes the period may be treated as a whole.

By the late sixth century a majority of the Irish were Christian, and paganism was definitely on the defensive. Monasticism was firmly ensconced on the island, and most of the great names of the period were monks—Columcille, Columbanus, Brendan, Bridgit, Finnian, Ciaran et al. In imitation of Abraham, the Irish had devised a particular devotion, the *peregrinatio pro amore Dei,* a wandering from home as a spiritual act, an intentional exile. Following that principle, many Irish monks, in contrast to the *stabilitas* of the Benedictines, chose to leave their abbeys to travel, sometimes wherever the Lord willed, other times to particular places. Irish monks could be found in England, Scotland, Wales, Gaul, Spain, Switzerland, Germany, and Italy. As a result of this and of the depredations which plagued Ireland throughout its history—only ten manuscripts dating before the year 1000 remain on Irish soil[5]—much of what we know about Irish Christianity and culture comes from continental sources. Included in these are art works, Latin writings, and vernacular writings. Just as we made no chronological distinction in treating the early medieval Irish, so we will make no geographical distinction. Irish materials from any and all locations will be included to present our portrait.

WRITTEN REVELATION

The scholar must look not only at the remnant of Irish Christian civilization, but also the mentality of those who produced them. When Christianity first moved out of Palestine, the Jewish diaspora had already prepared much of the theoretical way for it. It is a commonplace to note that the Jewish monotheism and piety influenced their pagan neighbors; we should also note that the Jewish belief in revealed scriptures which provided daily guidance for the believer also paved the way for the new faith. Pagans knew of oracular revelations, astrology, and various forms of divination—dreams, animal entrails, flights of birds, and the like—and they even knew of inspired books, like the divine Homer—properly allegorized—or the Sibylline books, but use of inspired literature with a corps of interpreters was something quite different. Indeed, C.H. Roberts has suggested that the late antique popularity of the handy codex over the cumbersome roll among the Christians resulted from the intense Christian citing of biblical passages.[6] But at least the pagans knew about books, and the concept of the Bible was not completely foreign to them.

In Ireland this type of revelation meant nothing, because the Irish did not use books. There is evidence of some written business records, but true literacy, the daily and indispensable use of writing, did not exist. The medium may not always be the message, but that was certainly the case in Ireland. Nothing in Irish paganism prepared the people for the notion that this new form of communication, writing, was also the conduit to the Christian deity. This cannot be overstated. Accepting a new god was difficult enough, but along with this new god came a whole new value system. This god could be reached by prayer, and he was pleased by good works, but his actual revelation to human beings was in writing. This made an enormous and indelible impression on the Irish.[7] In the words of the late Robert McNally, S.J., a good friend of Walter Burghardt as well as my own friend and teacher, ". . . the Irish Christians placed a maximum emphasis on the written word as a sacred sign, for the Christian God was himself the veritable author of a book."[8]

The Irish overcame the cultural difficulties, and they learned to accept and understand this religion of the book, but they always kept a veneration of the Bible which was unmatched by any other Christian people. They made it a part of their lives, and its influence is felt in almost every aspect of Irish Christianity. We will consider its influence in their art, spirituality (especially hagiography), and theology.

ART[9]

The Irish Christian art of the early medieval period is remarkable for being almost totally biblical. No other themes appear, except occasionally, and on minor works. The two best-known genres of Irish art are illuminated manuscripts and sculptured high crosses, genres which rather obviously could not have existed before the coming of Christianity; there is also a great deal of metalwork which deserves attention.

When the Irish began to illuminate manuscripts is unknown. The earliest known illuminated manuscript is the Book of Durrow, which dates c. 675, and which is a masterpiece. It is inconceivable that such a work could have been the first Irish effort, so likely decades of craft stand behind it. Illuminated manuscripts are known from both pagan and Christian antiquity, so the Irish probably first got the notion from books brought by missionaries, possibly even by Patrick himself.

An enumeration of the various themes in Irish manuscripts requires a much longer piece than this. Suffice it to cite the best-known Irish manuscripts to prove our point. As just noted, the earliest is the Book of Durrow, an *evangelium* or book containing the four gospels in the Latin, usually the Vulgate with some Old Latin elements. Durrow is either from Ireland or an Irish center in Britain. The MacRegol Gospels date to the eighth century, coming from an Irish center in England; as the title indicates, the book is an *evangelium*. The Books of Mulling and Dimma also both date to the eighth century; both are from Ireland; both are *evangelia*. The best known and most accomplished example of Irish manuscript illumination is the Book of Kells, prepared by at least four artists, and finished in the ninth century. This awesome manuscript, with literally hundreds of illustrations, is likewise an *evangelium.*

For the Irish, the Bible contained the *ipsissima verba Dei,* and they felt that those words, especially the gospel words, deserved the best. Illuminating manuscripts was not art for art's sake; it was a Christian duty. To be sure, the artists must surely have taken satisfaction from a job well done—or, in the case of the Book of Kells, in a job magnificently done—but self-satisfaction was never their intention. There is a simple but effective proof of this. There are no early medieval Irish illuminated manuscripts which are not *evangelia.*

The other great monuments of this period are literal monuments, the high, circled stone crosses which were constructed as burial markers for prominent Christians, such as an abbot of Monasterboice north of Dublin. Some of these crosses are more than twenty feet high, and they are usually in three parts—a pyramidal base, the shaft and wings, and a cap in the shape of an early medieval Irish church. Because these are burial monuments, the art often reflects Christian notions of death and resurrection, but most of the illustrations of those notions are biblical such as the crucifixion and the last judgment. There are also many other biblical scenes, such as Adam and Eve, Cain and Abel, Jacob wrestling with the angel, Moses striking the rock, David and Goliath, the adoration of the Magi, the flight into Egypt, and the baptism of Jesus.

The metalwork is perhaps less striking than the manuscripts and the crosses, but it too witnesses the popularity and the popularization of biblical themes. Some of the best pieces are crucifixes, including one showing Christ with a large, detached head and an impassive look, a clear merging of a basic gospel theme with the ancient Celtic cult of the head.

SPIRITUALITY

Irish spirituality of the early medieval period likewise reflects a bibliocentric faith. To be sure, it was far more than that. Since many Irish spiritual writers were also monks, there is a strong monastic bent to the literature; indeed, much of it deals only with the spiritual life of the monk. Many other pieces demonstrate a delightful folk-wisdom approach to the spiritual life, for example, this one on the value of pilgrimages:

Who to Rome goes,
Much labor, little profit knows;
For God, on earth though long you've sought him,
You'll miss at Rome unless you've brought him.[10]

Much of the spiritual writing dealt with the natural world, and the rejoicing of the Christian in God's creation. Some superb vernacular poetry reflects this attitude; here is one example of it.

That's the blithe cuckoo chanting clear
In mantle grey from bough to bough!
God keep me still! for here I write
A scripture bright in great woods now.[11]

A more specifically Christian prayer invokes Jesus under the following titles:

O Starry Sun!
O Guiding Light!
O House of the Planets!
O Fiery, Wondrous Comet!
O Fruitful, Billowy, Fiery Sea!
—Forgive![12]

Bibliocentric spirituality does, however, figure largely, and the greatest collections of homilies in Latin, or, more properly, Hiberno-Latin, all deal with scriptural themes. The following is from the Crakow homilies, which originated in an eighth century Irish circle in Italy:

Tribus ergo personis nativitas commendatur ut, quomodo in principio mundi a tribus personis vita nostra perdita fuerat, sic iterum et in fine saeculi tribus personis repararetur. Ibi diabolus per serpentem hominem decepit. Hic Christus per hominem homines liberavit. Ibi virgo seducta est. Hic virgo peperit. Ibi Adam uxori consensit ut periret. Hic Ioseph consentiendo virgo permansit, ut ex virginali coniugio virgo filius nasceretur.

This same author later explains why the shepherds were informed of Jesus' birth:

Vere dignum erat ut pastor ab angelis pastoribus praedicaretur, qui ait: Ego sum pastor bonus. Apte agnus gregibus effulsit de quo Iohannis Baptista testatur: Ecce, agnus Dei! Ecce, qui tollit peccata mundi! Recte quoque pastores vigilant quos bonus pastor informat. Quis ergo per pastores [significatur] nisi principes et praedicatores ecclesiae? Quid per gregem nisi sanctae ecclesiae populus obediens? Quid per noctem nisi praesentis vitae tenebrae et caecitas significatur?[13]

This is a very effective homily; it uses the scriptural text but interprets it in a way any audience could follow.

In the west, thanks largely to the efforts of Sulpicius Severus, Gregory the Great, and Gregory of Tours, hagiography became a major Christian literary genre and, simultaneously, a prime vehicle for spirituality. Modern Christians may want historically reliable lives of the great men and women of the Christian past, but early medieval writers saw the matter quite differently. Some, like Jerome in his *De Viris Illustribus,* wanted to show the pagans that the church had produced its great men (there were no women in his catalogue of Christian worthies). Sulpicius Severus was a monastic propagandist who presented his hero, Martin of Tours, as the monastic and thus the Christian ideal. Gregory the Great was motivated by patriotism; his *Dialogues* presented a catalogue of Italian saints. The late seventh century hagiographers of Saint Patrick made the case for the primacy of the see of Armagh in the Irish church. Bede's account of Benedict Biscop was a memorial to a revered mentor.

But the one element all these *vitae* have in common was the intent to present someone worthy of imitation. Since the task of every Christian is the *imitatio Christi,* it is not uncommon to find parallels drawn between the saint's life and that of Christ. For example, the earliest known example of the genre, the mid-second century *Martyrdom of Polycarp,* tells us that Polycarp has a vision of his death, he makes no attempt to escape, he is arrested by a pagan named Herod, he is silent before his accusers, and one of his executioners pierces his side. In sum, biblical elements are unavoidable in hagiography. The Irish followed in this mode and with the inevitable embellishments. But they also introduced a new wrinkle.

As noted earlier, for the Irish, the Bible meant writing per se. References to books or "the book" are usually references to the Bible. It was quite common in Irish hagiography to stress the saint's devotion to scripture but, more frequently and more picturesquely, to have saints perform miracles with their Bibles.[14]

In the prose *vita* of Saint Kevin, the holy man dropped his psalter into a lake, but an angel comforted him, and soon an otter retrieved the book unharmed. In his metrical *vita,* Kevin experienced the same

misfortune but with the same happy results. Saint Ciarán of Clonmacnoise had a stag which carried his psalter in its antlers; when the
stag was not about, Ciarán got a fox to carry the book in its teeth. (He
preferred the stag because the fox used to gnaw the book's bindings.)
He even used the stag's antlers as a bookstand. The animal ran off
with the book one day, but it was found unharmed.

   "Saint Mochua likewise performed a miracle with a book and an
animal, albeit on a much smaller scale since the animal was a fly. The
fly used to walk along each line of Mochua's psalter as he read it.
When the saint finished chanting his psalms, the fly would remain on
the line where he left off until he returned to read and chant again.
Presumably the saint never closed the book."[15]

   Book production in the period before printing was a long and
very laborious process. Fortunately for Saint Columcille a miraculous
light from heaven allowed him to copy the entire Bible in a single
night, while the Welsh writer Giraldus Cambrensis told of seeing an
illustrated *evangelium* at Kildare which had been copied *angelo
dictante*.

   Kevin used his psalter to drive a dragon out of a lake; Saint
Moling used a gospel book to drive away a demon.

   The last example is the touching story of Saints Bridget and Aed.
Once when Bridget prayed, a gospel book came forth from her breast
and entered his; the implication is that the word of God ultimately
dwells within.

   The Irish saints certainly had no monopoly on Bible reading; nor
did their hagiographers on this theme. But alone of the early medieval Christians the Irish made this a major theme. The saints were the
ideal Christians, and their lives had to reflect the ideals of their
co-religionists. Because the Irish as a group put such emphasis on
written revelation, the hagiographers expatiated upon its thaumatur-
gical significance.

EXEGESIS

   Early medieval, that is, pre-scholastic, theology was largely exegetical in form. There are occasional treatises on individual topics,
but anyone glancing at the contents of Migne's *Patrologia Latina* for
the period from 500 to 1200 will see that more than three-fourths of
the entries deal with scripture.

   I mention this in order to situate Irish exegesis properly. The
Irish fondness for scripture and the wonderment at a written revela-

tion guaranteed that they would do exegesis, but, for their time period, that hardly made them unique. Yet their unabashed enthusiasm for the scriptures did result in a number of particular emphases and themes which, if not unique to the Irish, could certainly be called characteristic of them.

This last point might sound like begging the question, and it calls for some explanation. When the Irish were being Christianized, some attitudes and approaches to the Bible were taken for granted in the western church. First and foremost was the use of Latin translation for exegesis. Westerners like Ambrose and Jerome were fluent in Greek, but the great Augustine's knowledge of it was spotty. Indeed, Augustine carried out most of his exegesis with a Latin text, including his famous anti-Pelagian exposition of the epistle to the Romans. Gregory the Great, who was the papal *apocrisarius* to Constantinople from 578 to 585, knew no Greek and was almost proud of the fact. He was the great western exegete of Job and Ezekiel and for many gospel passages, and Jean Leclercq has proved that this first pope from the ranks of the monks was more influential with early medieval exegetes (most of whom were monks) than were Jerome and Augustine.[16] This use of the Latin Bible was not something one would question, and, in fact, while the Irish were doing their exegesis, Jerome's Vulgate was achieving the status of an inspired translation. Irish exegesis was Latin exegesis, although that did not exclude attempts to use Greek or even Hebrew if the opportunity presented itself.

The second approach taken for granted in this period was the citation of the fathers. The first great patristic exegete, Origen, had virtually no predecessors and could be as original as he wanted—which, in Origen's case, was considerable. Tertullian was in virtually the same situation in the west. The fourth century theological controversies produced an enormous amount of literature, much of it exegetical and, because of new questions which had been raised, much of it quite pioneering. Augustine's reinterpretation of so many theological themes for the western ecclesiastical mind also produced much original work. But when the Irish were being Christianized, originality was widely discouraged in theological matters. The fathers had become the *auctoritates* to whom all should look. This tendency can be found earlier, for example, the insistent fidelity of the eastern Nicenes to Athanasius, of the Egyptian Monophysites to Cyril, of both the African Catholics and Donatists to Cyprian, but the tendency was magnified in the west in the pre-Carolingian age. The fathers belonged to a golden age when the Roman empire was alive and flourishing; they were the great saints who battled the insidious heretics, they were the great scholars who read Greek and Hebrew. No early medieval exegete, Irish or otherwise, could expect to match their achievement, and none did. Thus, every exegete began his work by consulting the patristic work on the topic—if such a work were available in the monastery library, which often it was not.

The third point to be taken for granted was multiple-sense exegesis. The Irish were not immune to attractions of the Antiochene approach, but, like most fathers and almost all medieval exegetes, they favored the Alexandrian approach. Origen was known in Latin translation, but the real allegorist was Gregory the Great, and in back of him stood Augustine and a host of other lesser names. Multiple-sense interpretation was not a possible form of interpretation; it was the only way to make sense out of the text. This, it should be noted, did not preclude a straight historical interpretation where the text warranted that; it simply means that virtually every prominent Latin exegete except Jerome looked for spiritual meanings. The Irish simply would not have questioned such an approach.

In this sense, we can speak of the characteristics rather than the uniqueness of Irish exegesis. A Hiberno-Latin writer would get out his Vulgate, consult the patristic exegete who had written about the book in question, and then go from there. A characteristic Irish interpretation was usually patristic in origin but heavily developed and widely used by Hiberno-Latin exegetes.

Having said that, I list as my first characteristic something independent of the fathers, namely, mass production. The modern study of Irish exegesis began in 1954 with a pioneering article by the German scholar Bernhard Bischoff,[17] who produced a catalogue of thirty-nine Irish exegetical works, most of them anonymous or pseudepigraphal. Other researchers, especially Robert McNally, S.J., followed his lead, and the number of known Irish works has grown considerably. This writer has catalogued the known Hiberno-Latin exegetical works, and their number is 114,[18] a remarkable figure for a not very numerous early medieval people living literally on the fringe of Christendom. Since, as noted earlier, only ten manuscripts dating before 1000 survive on Irish soil, catalogues of Irish works depend largely on texts surviving in England and Europe; given the flourishing state of native Irish monasteries before the Viking period, the original number of Hiberno-Latin exegetical works could easily have been double.

Two kinds of exegetical texts survive, commentaries and compendia, with the former being far more common. In general, a verse was cited, and then the exegete commented upon it. In the larger commentaries, this method was applied to an entire biblical book.

Since exegesis in Ireland began as oral teaching, the commentaries sometimes used a question-and-answer method, a technique known from the fathers. Ironically, the modern scholar is never sure who is asking the question. The texts use capital M and the Greek delta, but whether to symbolize the Latin *Magister et Discipulus* or the Greek *Mathētēs kai Didaskalos* is unknown, and the questions do not really help in solving this. The person giving the answer often starts with *Non difficile!*—a Latin translation of the Old Irish *Ni anse*, a response found in vernacular texts. The questions often deal with language, for example: What is the book's name in Hebrew, Greek and Latin? Not difficult! *Nebel* in Hebrew, *Psalterium* in Greek, *Laudatorium* or *Organum* in Latin.[19]

This procedure carries over into other commentaries, where comments on the text begin with expressions like *Dic mihi, Quaeritur, Quare, Quid est inter, Quibus modis,* and the like.

A firm pedagogical device is categorization; teachers use it and students expect it. The Irish used this practice *ad nauseam.* In their attempt to learn everything about a biblical text, they evolved categories of understanding.

One category has been mentioned already, language, or, more particularly, the *tres linguae sacrae* of Hebrew, Greek and Latin, although almost all Irish knowledge of the first two was taken from patristic sources, such as Jerome's *Liber Interpretationis Hebraicorum Nominum* for the Hebrew and Isidore of Seville's *Etymologiae* for the Greek.[20]

A second favorite was actually a triad, *locus, tempus, et persona,* a theme found in the homilies of Gregory the Great. These three categories were often linked together. An eighth century Lukan commentary explains the angel's visit to Mary in Nazareth in the sixth month with: *Tempus, per mensem. Locus, per civitatem. Per virginem, persona.*[21]

Not all authors showed such restraint. A ninth century catechism, claiming to be *Ex dictis sancti Hieronimi,* asks: *Quot sunt res quae evangelium deforis monstrant? XIII. Quae? Nomen, locus, tempus, persona, causa, lingua, regula, ordo, auctoritas, figura, prophetia, significationes, demonstrationes conventionesque.* An eighth century gospel primer investigates the gospel by using fourteen categories: *locus, tempus, persona, lingua, regula, ordo, auctoritas, causa, figura, demonstratio, conventio, qualitas, numerus et documenta.* A massive eighth century commentary on the entire Bible suggests sixteen categories for understanding the New Testament, and, having established those, the author suggests that to understand the *materia narrationis*, there are forty-two more categories.[22] Surely even the most pedantic exegete, medieval or modern, would blanch at the thought of applying fifty-eight categories to a scriptural verse!

Naturally few exegetes could take this kind of thing seriously, and most simply settled for the categories which appealed to them. As monks, they were regular readers of the psalms, and this in turn meant that they were regular readers of the greatest of the psalter commentators, Augustine, the champion par excellence of numerical interpretation. For the exegete looking for hidden meanings in a verse, numbers were a godsend because any use of a number could refer to the almost limitless use of the number in other circumstances. Much Irish speculation about numbers ended up in the *Liber de Numeris*, an eighth century work from the circle of the Irish bishop Virgilius of Salzburg, which explained all the numbers in the Bible from one to eight and, claimed the author, would eventually cover every other number as well, a claim which went mercifully unfulfilled.[23]

Examples abound in stultifying amounts. Let me quote just one example to demonstrate how easily the process works. In Luke 16:27, the rich man (*dives*) in hell tells Abraham that he has five brothers. An eighth century exegete says they represent the *populus quinque librorum* or *qui quinque sensibus non bene utuntur*.[24]

Like many people who have approached the scriptures enthusiastically, the Irish were keenly disappointed at the lack of information therein about so many biblical characters, especially their names. The Irish, like other ancient and medieval Christians, did not hesitate to search through apocryphal literature for information, and they made a very thorough search. Martin McNamara, M.S.C. catalogued medieval Irish apocrypha, and he listed 108 separate works cited or preserved or created;[25] the last category included many items about the other world, especially the seven heavens. No other medieval people appears to have preserved and clearly to have enjoyed such an apocryphal variety.

The "names for nameless" phenomenon was particularly popular. The Irish knew the standard ones. For example, Longinus was the Roman who pierced Jesus' side, Dismas and Gestas were the two thieves—good and bad—who were crucified with Jesus. But they also added to the tradition. For example, an eighth century Irish text from Saint Gall in Switzerland says that the two thieves were also named Chacham (for Dismas) and Chamna (for Gestas), these names possibly deriving from the Hebrew word *hakam* for wise man, and Cham, the son of Noah who was cursed by his father (Gen 9). On the topic of Noah, everyone knows the names of the four men in the ark; the Irish provided the names of the four women: Olla, Oleva, and Ollina for the three sons's wives and Percova for Noah's wife. The names were rather popular because another Irish work says Olla and Oliba (= Oleva) were the names of Lot's daughters. Perhaps the most unique reference is to Mog Ruith, an Irish druid who was the executioner of John the Baptist. If the modern reader insists on being picky and on wondering what Mog Ruith was doing in Judea in the first place, he was there to study wizardry with Simon Magus.[26]

The Irish were the first people in history to doodle, that is, to put in *marginalia* which have no relevance to the text or at least which do not elucidate it. Some of these are truly charming. Let me just cite two, which reflect scribal indignance. In the margin of the gospels in the ninth century Book of Armagh, next to the word Judas, someone wrote in Irish "Wretch!"[27] In a Lukan commentary, a marginal comment on Luke 2:51, *et (Iesus) erat subditus illis (Maria et Ioseph)*, has been incorporated into the text: *Qua fronte audet aliquis contradicere parentibus dum is, cui angeli et archangeli subiecti sunt, humanis parentibus subditus fuit!*[28]

It would be grossly unfair to the Irish exegetes for this to be the final word about them. For the most part, they were scholarly and careful, they used the fathers, and they adhered to that most basic of hermeneutical principles, *scriptura interpres scripturae*. I have emphasized here the ways in which their enthusiasm for the Bible caused them to go beyond the standard western modes of interpretation and to reflect a more popular Christianity.

Let me close by thanking David Hunter for inviting me to take part in this *Festschrift*, and, of course, by thanking Walter Burghardt for all he has done and meant to so many people. I hope he will find this discussion of how much the scriptures meant to one Christian people a suitable sign of my gratitude.

NOTES

1. The coming of Christianity to Ireland is always treated in the context of Patrick's mission; cf. R.P.C. Hanson, *Saint Patrick: His Origins and Career* (Oxford, 1968), and E.A. Thompson, *Who Was Saint Patrick?* (London, 1986).
2. Edited by R.P.C. Hanson (SC 249; Paris, 1978).

3. Christine Mohrmann, *The Latin of St. Patrick* (Dublin, 1961) 8.
4. Noel O'Donoghue, *Aristocracy of Soul: Patrick of Ireland* (The Way of the Christian Mystic 1; Wilmington, 1987).
5. James F. Kennedy, *The Sources for the Early History of Ireland, I: Ecclesiastical* (New York, 1929; reprinted 1966) 9.
6. C.H. Roberts, "Books in the Greco-Roman World and the New Testament," in *The Cambridge History of the Bible,* 1 (ed. P.R. Ackroyd and C.F. Evans; Cambridge, 1970) 48–66.
7. For an account of literacy and Christianity in Ireland, cf. J.F. Kelly, "Christianity and the Latin Tradition in Early Mediaeval Ireland," *BJRL* 68 (1986) 410–33.
8. R.E. McNally, "Old Ireland: Her Scribes and Scholars," in *Old Ireland* (ed. R.E. McNally; New York, 1965) 122.
9. The basic study of early Christian Irish art is the magisterial, three-volume work of Françoise Henry, *Irish Art* (London, 1965, 1967, 1970); for the manuscripts, cf. also Carl Nordenfalk, *Celtic and Anglo-Saxon Painting* (New York, 1977); for the most recent view of the dates and provenances of the manuscripts, cf. Michael Lapidge and Richard Sharpe, *A Bibliography of Celtic-Latin Literature, 400–1200* (Dublin, 1985), *sub nomine*.
10. Quoted in Robin Flower, *The Irish Tradition* (Oxford, 1970) 39.
11. Quoted in ibid., 40.
12. Prayer attributed to Ciarán of Clonmacnoise in Charles Plummer, ed., *Irish Litanies* (Henry Bradshaw Society 62; London, 1924) 46.
13. Crakow, Domkapitel MS 43, saec. viii–ix, fols. 33r–v, 40r.
14. Cf. J.F. Kelly, "Books, Learning and Sanctity in Early Christian Ireland," *Thought* 54 (1979) 253–61; most of what follows is taken from this essay written in memory of Robert McNally.
15. Ibid., 256.
16. Jean Leclercq, "The Exposition and Exegesis of Scripture, 2: From Gregory the Great to Saint Bernard," in *Cambridge History of the Bible,* 2 (ed. G.W.H. Lampe; Cambridge, 1969) 196.
17. Bernard Bischoff, "Wendepunkte in der Geschichte der lateinischen Exegese im Frühmittelalter," *Sacris Erudiri* 6 (1954) 189–281.
18. This catalogue will be published in two parts in *Traditio*.
19. "The Old Irish Treatise on the Psalter," in *Hibernica Minora* (ed. Kuno Meyer; Oxford, 1894) 20–21.
20. R.E. McNally, "The *Tres Linguae Sacrae* in Early Irish Bible Exegesis," *TS* 19 (1958) 395–403.
21. Gregorius Magnus, *Homiliae in Ezechielem* 1.2.1 (PL 76.795cd); *Commentarius in Lucam,* ed. J.F. Kelly (CCSL 108C; Turnhout, 1974) 7.
22. Cf. J.F. Kelly, "Hiberno-Latin Theology," in *Die Iren und Europa im früheren Mittelalter* (ed. Heinz Lowe; Stuttgart, 1982) 561; idem, "*Das Bibelwerk:* Organization and *Quellenanalyse* of the New Testament Section," in *Irland und die Christenheit* (ed. Próinséas Ní Chatháin and Michael Richter; Stuttgart, 1987) 114–15.

23. For a study of that very curious book, cf. R.E. McNally, *Die irische Liber de Numeris* (Munich, 1957).

24. *Commentarius in Lucam* (CCSL 108C.90).

25. Martin McNamara, *The Apocrypha in the Irish Church* (Dublin, 1975).

26. Ibid., *sub nomine*.

27. Charles Plummer, "On the Colophones and Marginalia of Irish Scribes," *Proceedings of the British Academy* 12 (1926) 11–44; many entries are quite humorous.

28. *Commentarius in Lucam* (CCSL 108C.22).

THE CONTRIBUTORS

AGNES CUNNINGHAM, S.S.C.M. is Professor of Patristic Theology and Early Christianity at Mundelein Seminary, University of St. Mary of the Lake, Mundelein, Illinois. She was the first woman president of the Catholic Theological Society of America (1977–78). Her publications include: *The Early Church and the State* (Fortress, 1982); *Prayer, Personal and Liturgical* (Glazier, 1985); and *The Significance of Mary* (Thomas More, 1988).

ROBERT B. ENO, S.S. obtained his doctorate in Theology from the Institut Catholique of Paris in 1969 and has taught Patristics at the Catholic University of America since 1970. His publications include: *Teaching Authority in the Early Church* (Glazier, 1984); *The Rise of the Papacy*, forthcoming; and the first English translation of the recently discovered letters of St. Augustine.

GERARD H. ETTLINGER, S.J. earned a D. Phil. in Patristics from the Theology Faculty of Oxford University, England, in 1972. He has taught at the Pontifical Oriental Institute in Rome and at Fordham University and is currently a professor in the Theology Department of St. John's University, Jamaica, New York. His publications include: *Jean Chrysostome, à une jeune veuve, sur le mariage unique* (SC 138; Cerf, 1968); *Theodoret of Cyrus: Eranistes. A Critical Edition and Prolegomena* (Oxford, 1975); and *Jesus, Christ and Savior* (Glazier, 1987).

JOSEPH A. FITZMYER, S.J. is Professor Emeritus of Biblical Studies at the Catholic University of America and resides in the Jesuit Community at Georgetown University, Washington, D.C., along with Fr. Burghardt. He is the author of the recent book, *Paul and His Theology* (Prentice Hall, 1989) and one of the editors of the new *Jerome Biblical Commentary,* which is to appear shortly from Prentice Hall.

GERALD P. FOGARTY, S.J. received his Ph.D. in History from Yale University in 1969. Currently Professor of Religious Studies at the University of Virginia, he is the author of several books, the most recent of which is *American Catholic Biblical Scholarship: A History from the Early Republic to Vatican II* (Harper and Row, 1989).

DAVID G. HUNTER received his Ph.D. in Theology from the University of Notre Dame in 1986 and has taught Theology at the College of St. Thomas, St. Paul, Minnesota since 1984. He has published a book on John Chrysostom (Edwin Mellen, 1988) and articles in *Theological Studies,* the *Journal of Theological Studies,* and *Studia Patristica.*

CHARLES KANNENGIESSER, S.J. is the Catherine F. Huisking Professor of Theology at the University of Notre Dame. Currently President of the North American Patristic Society, his recent publications include: *Early Christian Spirituality* (Fortress, 1986); *Athanase d'Alexandrie évêque et écrivain* (Beauchesne, 1983); and "The Message of the Great Fathers" in *Christian Spirituality I* (Crossroad, 1985).

JOSEPH F. KELLY received his Ph.D. from Fordham University and is currently Professor of Early Christianity at John Carroll University. The author of more than forty articles on the history of exegesis, he has edited a volume in the *Corpus Christianorum* series and has written *Why is There a New Testament?* (Glazier, 1986).

EDWARD J. KILMARTIN, S.J., Professor of Liturgical Theology at the Pontifical Oriental Institute in Rome, is the author of numerous publications in the field of the history and theology of the liturgy. His most recent publication is *Christian Liturgy I. Theology* (Sheed and Ward, 1988).

JOSEPH T. LIENHARD, S.J. is Professor of Theology at Marquette University, Milwaukee, Wisconsin. He has published books on Paulinus of Nola and on ministry in the early church, and articles in such journals as *Theological Studies* and *Vigiliae Christianae.* He is preparing a translation of Origen's homilies on Luke, and completing a book on Marcellus of Ancyra and fourth-century theology.

FRANCIS X. MURPHY, C.SS.R. is Professor Emeritus of Patristic Moral Theology of the Academia Alfonsiana in Rome. The author of several books on early Christian history and ethics, his most recent book is *The Christian Way of Life* (Glazier, 1986). As Xavier Rynne he chronicled the Second Vatican Council for *The New Yorker*. For his seventy-fifth birthday, Shepherd Press is publishing his essays on *The Patristic Heritage*.